THE

BIBLE AND SCIENCE;

OR,

THE WORLD-PROBLEM.

By TAYLER LEWIS,

PROFESSOR OF GREEK, UNION COLLEGE.

Cun t fecit bona in tempore suo, et MUNDUM tradidit disputationi eorum, ut non inveniat homo quod operatus est Deus, ab initio usque ad finem.—*Ecclesiastes* iii, 11.

And there was a voice from the firmament that was over the heads of the living creatures.—*Ezekiel* i, 25.

SCHENECTADY:
G. Y. VAN DEBOGERT.

1856.

RIGGS, PRINTER, SCHENECTADY.

PREFACE.

Some apology is due for what may seem the miscellaneous character of the present volume, and especially the mingling of the controversial. Such apology is found in its history. There had grown upon the author's hands, Scriptural notes and other matter designed for an appendix to the third edition of the work entitled The Six Days of Creation. In the meantime, however, that work had been the subject of a number of extended reviews; no less than three by the editor of the Theological and Literary Journal, whilst the conductors of the Andover Bibliotheca Sacra have honored it by a whole year's notice, with a promise of continuance. The author's friends thought that he ought to make some reply. The Andover periodical, however, was closed to his defence, although his writings had been charged in it with "having a decidedly infidel tendency." A pamphlet, therefore, was thought of. This grew in size, and as it was found that the other matter would much exceed the original bounds assigned to it, it was thought best to combine both objects in the volume now presented to the public. Professor BARROWS' review in the Bibliotheca came out too late for notice. Some of his positions are already met, and we think successfully, in the Ninth chapter of the present volume. If the continuance he promises demands an answer, permission for that purpose may be asked in the columns of some of our religious newspapers, or of the editors of such monthly or quarterly periodical as may grant the privilege that has been denied where it was due.

The book is a protest against what the author regards as a most one-sided error of the times,—the false position of Physical Science, and its naturalizing effect upon the theology and religion of the day. In the zealous exposition of such an error, it would be no wonder if the work was found to be somewhat one-sided itself. The intelligent reader, however, will apply the corrective which the author could not well employ without swelling the size of the book, or unduly weakening the force of his argument by too much of an apologetic or explanatory tone. The volume is presented to the public with the conviction, that whatever may be thought of the mode of argument, it will be admitted to contain some timely and important truth.

CONTENTS.

CHAPTER I. *Page.*

INTRODUCTORY VIEW.

Question of the Creative Days—Its Pressing Importance—Science has its Bigotry as well as Theology—Two Classes of Scientific Men—The Keplers and the Galileos—Present Faith in the Bible, how different from the Old—Its true Internal Evidence as set forth by the Old Divines—The Bible Everything or Nothing—Undue Deference to Science—The real Naturalism—False and limited use of the word Science—Natural History—Extravagant Boasting—Natural Science, Causes of its Popularity—Easiness of Acquisition—General Smattering—Men love to be talked to Scientifically—Quackish Reasoning about Law and Nature—Spiritualism—Appeal to Utilities—The Bible Praised, but not Studied—Style of Preaching—The Bible not in the Heart of the Age—Literature and Politics—The Bible to be Interpreted, not Reconciled—The true Field of Revelation, All that it professes to teach............... 13

CHAPTER II.

Scriptural Interpretation in Connection with Science—Nine General Principles—Application to the Creative Record—The Difficulty of a Solar Day without a Sun as obvious to Moses as to Mr. Lord—If there is any such Difficulty it is Patent on the Face of the Record—It has not come from Science, but from False Interpretation—Interpretation, therefore, and not Science, must Remove it—Creation an Order of Appearances—Each Appearance a Morning—Succession, not Duration, the Radical Idea......................... 62

CHAPTER III.

Page.

THE WORD DAY, AND THE MYSTIC NUMBERS OF PROPHECY.

Various Senses of the Word Day—Summary of Principles concerned in its Interpretation—Eight Heads of Argument—The Prophetical Day—Analogous to the Creative Day—Numbers as used in Prophecy—Three kinds—Definite Numbers—Round Numbers—Perfect Numbers—The Word Day as applied to the Closing Dispensation of the World—Analogy with the Creative Account—Kedhem, or the Ante-time State..... 76

CHAPTER IV.

Kedhem, or the Ante-time State—Psalm lv, 19, "He that Inhabiteth Kedhem"—Sadducean Interpreters—Psalm lxviii, "The Heaven of Heavens of Old"—Spiritual in Distinction from a Cabalistical Sense—Space Sense—Messianic Character of the Psalm—Where is Kedhem?—The Rationalist—The Twenty-four Hour Interpreter—The Timeless State—The Question of the Eternity of Matter—The Absurdity involved in the very Inquiry..................... 120

CHAPTER V.

THE FOUR GREAT IDEAS OF THE MOSAIC ACCOUNT.

The Word—The Work—The Rest—The Day—These must be in Harmony with Each Other—The Old Arabian View—The Patriarchal View—Theory of Guyot—Of Mr. Lord—Of Pye Smith—The True Scriptural View is the one that has least Need of Science...... 142

CHAPTER VI.

SCIENCE AND THE BIBLE.

Spirit of the Scientific Patronage—Professor Dana's Apothegm—The Bible "the Boat, Science the Current"—The Natural in Creation—Claim of Prior Discovery—Claim of Science to have Proved the Supernatural—Science can not find the Supernatural—Must ever assume a Law for a Fact—Can not even find a God—An Atheist as good a Scientific Man as a Theist—Secret Wheels and Cogs in Nature—The Greater Durations—Science can not disprove Development—Can never refute the "Vestiges of Creation"—Bible alone can slay "The Vestiges."...................... 151

CHAPTER VII.

Page.

WE KNOW NOTHING OF ORIGIN EXCEPT FROM A DIVINE REVELATION.

The Vestiges of Creation—Who Killed the Monster?—Individual Generation as Mysterious as the Generic—Revelation itself the Highest Supernatural—Why should we be afraid of the Natural in Creation?—Animalculæ—Agassiz's Doctrine of Man—The Primus Homo—Science occupied with What is, and How it is—The Cosmical Movement—Science does not take it into Account—Hypothetical Discussion between the Vestigian and the Anti-vestigian—Nature's Gestation long, her Births sudden and complete—Doctrine of Types—No Meaning in the Language as used by some Scientific Men—The Atheism of "The Vestiges," in what it truly consists.......................... 184

CHAPTER VIII.

THE SIX DAYS AS FOUND BY SCIENCE.

The Writer in the Andover Bibliotheca—His Nebular Theory—The Reviewer finds no Difficulties—A hearty Faith is not so easily satisfied—The chief interest of the Mosaic Account—1st. Its Supernatural Character—2d. Its Hexameral Division—The true Greatness of the Mosaic Account—Greatness of Moses as compared with Aristotle or Bacon—Professor Dana's Seven Points—Of the First Three Geology knows nothing—Her Protests or Acceptances of no Value—Rests in Nature—The Scientific Scheme of Creation—As well Six Hundred Days as Six—The Reviewer's Boat driven by two Forces—The Word Beginning—Sudden leap from the Birth of the Light to the Growing of the Mosses—Immense Distances from which Light travels—Want of Chronological Harmony—Immense Hiatus in the Second Day—A Modest Note—Spectral Light of Geology—The Rakia or Firmament—Was it the Breaking up of the Nebular Rings?—Had Moses any such View, either as Fact or Conception?.......... 215

CHAPTER IX.

SCIENTIFIC SIX DAYS AT WAR WITH EXEGESIS.

The Word Bara—The Beginning—The Shemitic Mind—Words for Creation—The Hebrew—The New Testa-

Page.

ment Terms—The Philosophical Greek—The Arabic Words for Creation—Emotional Aim of the Bible—Did Moses think of an Absolute Principium?—Six Arguments: 1st. From the First Verse generally—2d. The Words Heaven and Earth; Do they denote Universality?—3d. The Earth the Locus of the First Energizing mentioned by Moses—4th. The Light after the Waters—5th. Heavens Built over the Earth—6th. The First Verse, if severed from the rest, must be Extra Dies—Parallelism of the Mosaic Account with the First of John—Patristic View of its 3d and 4th Verses. 268

CHAPTER X.

ANTIQUITY OF THE EARTH.

Geology claims the Sole Credit of the Idea—What may be fairly Conceded to her—One who is not a Geologist may Reason about Geology—The Geologist himself may be unfitted for Cosmical Questions—A little Science wakes up Thought in Thoughtful Minds—The Idea, once aroused, is seen everywhere—Antiquity of the Earth as seen in the most Common Phenomena—Nature, in general, Honest and Truthful—Geological Changes referred to in Job xiv—The Ancient Philosophy—The World-Problem—The Schoolmen and the Galileos—The "Students of Nature"—The Epicureans the Ancient Scientific Boasters—Natural Theology. 301

CHAPTER XI.

WHAT IS NATURE?

Can there be a True Nature?—The two Great Questions—How can there be Evil without God?—How can there be a Nature that is not God?—Can God make a Nature to go by itself?—Laws of Thinking higher than Laws of Nature—Deteriorations in Nature—Was there Death before Adam's Fall?—Nature as well as Spirit left to itself—In what Sense?—Motion by Impulse—The Axiom, "A Body once set in Motion will forever continue in Motion"—The Mystery of the Rolling Ball—Force—Is it an Entity?—Science finds Formulas—Philosophy Wonders—Faith Adores—Ideas, as well as Laws, in Nature. 336

CHAPTER I.

INTRODUCTORY VIEW.

Question of the Creative Days—Its Pressing Importance—Science has its Bigotry as well as Theology—Two Classes of Scientific Men—The Keplers and the Galileos—Present Faith in the Bible, how different from the old—Its true Internal Evidence as set forth by the Old Divines—The Bible everything or nothing—Undue Deference to Science—The real Naturalism—False and limited use of the word Science—Natural History—Extravagant Boasting—Natural Science, Causes of its Popularity—Easiness of Acquisition—General Smattering—Men love to be talked to Scientifically—Quackish Reasoning about Law and Nature—Spiritualism—Appeal to Utilities—The Bible Praised but not Studied—Style of Preaching—The Bible not in the heart of the Age—Literature and Politics—The Bible to be Interpreted, not Reconciled—The true Field of Revelation, all that it professes to teach.

THE following work, it will be seen, is closely related to another lately published, and entitled "The Six Days of Creation." It is very natural for an author to dwell on the importance of his subject; but in this case, certainly no earnestness of language could well be out of place. The question connected with the Mosaic account of the origin of the Earth and Man, has difficulties in itself; it has also been surrounded by others from without that are pressing more and more closely for a solution. A settlement of them is demanded, and this demand will not admit of much delay. The chasm of doubt is opening wider and wider. It must somehow be closed, and by materials, too, from the Scriptural side. The bridge must have its firmest abutment on that shore of the yawning abyss. A certain class of scientific men in scientific conventions, and a certain class of religionists in anniversary speeches, are much given to talking of "harmonies," but it has been in the main a harmony of one part, or at the utmost with a very slender accompaniment. It has, in other words, been made out almost wholly from the side of science. Now this may satisfy those who make it, for they have assumed the harmony in the beginning, honestly assumed it no doubt, whether it be from the strength or the easy pliancy of their faith, and, therefore, they can not appreciate the troubles of those who have no such scientific piety on the one hand, or professional religionism on the other, to give confidence to so easy an assumption. In other words, this reasoning will never satisfy the silent, yet ever inquiring, common mind. It ought to satisfy no mind; for when examined closely, it is found to be but a string of empty truisms which men would be ashamed to employ in other departments of reasoning. 'All truth is consistent with all other truth,'—'the Bible being true can not teach what is false;' 'two revelations from God (nature being assumed to be one of them in as proper a sense as the Scriptures) can not contradict each other,' etc., etc. Of how many lectures—and, we may also say, of how many sermons—do such verbal platitudes as these form the leading staple! It is time that this should cease, and that thinking men should address themselves earnestly to the difficulties of the question, whether they be intrinsic and real, or have been forced upon it by outward circumstances. Such truisms as the above may do for those who regard the matter as all settled on other grounds; but, we say again, they will never satisfy the thoughtful common mind. Nothing will do here but an honest interpretation of Scripture,—bold yet careful, impartial but not indifferent, free yet most hearty and sincere. The great question, the momentous question, involving nothing less than the degree of hearty credence to be given to the very first page in God's written revelation, this must be settled, *and settled from the Bible side*, or there comes in a flood of unbelief in all Scripture too fearful to contemplate. We say all Scripture; for there is really no other place after this, where any holding barrier can be erected. At any point lower down, the torrent comes rushing on with the accumulated force of all that has given way above. Creation gone—its place in the Scripture left a blank, or what is worse, a lying myth, who will give credence to the account of the flood in the demands of its historic exactness, or regard the succeeding events in any other than their loosest legendary aspect? The Patriarchs become dim mythological shadows; the God of the Patriarchs a θεὸς πατρώϊος, a patrial deity, to rank hereafter with Baal, or Thor, or Jupiter. Sinai can never wholly lose its grandeur, but it is the grandeur of a gloomy and terrible myth. Moses vanishes through the "Ivory Gate," and prophets follow him to the land of lying dreams. And so of Him of whom Moses and the Prophets wrote. The historical Jesus departs with the rest of the long ghostly procession. All is gone but the babble of the ideal Christ, and how long would that poor shadow linger in the rapidly deepening twilight that must follow the real setting sun. We wake from dreams, so called; but it is to a reality insupportable. We are suffocated with its appalling density. It is like a man who starts up from a vision, it may be a fearful one, (for all existence is such,) but only to find himself in a still more fearful horror of great and terrible darkness. Should the world ever come to this, then might we know what light there is in geology, or with what propriety it claims to be called a revelation. But we turn from the picture as one too awful to contemplate. Instead of dwelling on such an appalling view, it is sufficient, for our present argument, to present two general statements whose substantial truth every serious reader must at once perceive. 1st. There would be no belief in revelation worth the name, one generation after the common rejection of the absolute verity of the Mosaic account. 2d. There is no hearty faith in such account when it depends wholly or mainly upon scientific assumptions, or reconciliations so called, forced upon it from without. The Bible is to be *interpreted*, not *reconciled* with anything but itself. The very thought is almost equivalent to a rejection. We are even tempted to say that it is actually more insulting than frank, and it may be, sorrowing, unbelief.

We cannot overrate the importance of a right faith in this first chapter of Genesis. The difficulty, we repeat, whether regarded as foreign or intrinsic, was pressing hard, and must be met in some way, not by scientific reconciliations, but by fair and thorough exegesis. To do this, or anything towards it, might seem an ambitious attempt for a layman, but theologians were in a good measure standing aloof. Professional Biblical scholars were occupied with outside questions of style, of Scripture natural history, or the pertinency of certain words and texts to some exciting topics of the day, falling, in importance, immeasurably below the truthfulness of the creative history. The attempt, therefore, was made — we will not say the first, but the first to any considerable length and with a professed exclusion of outside scientific theories that might affect the fair hermeneutical result. It is not for us to speak of any merits of that work. No one is more sensible than the writer, of its many and serious defects. Still, it might be said, some views of interest were opened; some new ground was taken, in respect to which the author looked with anxiety to the examination of other Biblical scholars. He feared their adverse decision, not so much for his own, as for the great question's sake. Especially was this anxiety felt in respect to the reasoning about the great time-words that are so strangely used in the ancient Shemitic dialects, and the interpretations given to them. Here was the foundation of all the other argument. Here, it was thought, was found that peculiar feature in the ancient thinking which relieved all the other interpretations from the forced, or the mere possible, aspect. Here, if the view could be sustained, was that idea which the modern theology, and the modern conception of God's kingdom, had lost sight of, and which, if it could be revived and shown to have a true ground in the human thinking, and especially the earliest human thinking, would make to appear natural and easy what otherwise would have only a constrained, and therefore never satisfying, accommodation to pressing outside difficulties. Could the old idea of divided instead of blank eternities, (past and future,) or, in other words, the doctrine of olams and æons as taught in the book, be maintained, even so far as to entitle it to some share of serious consideration, then the indefinite creative day could be received with little difficulty as an interpretation not only possible, or speciously probable, but as most truly in harmony with the simplest and earliest conceptions of the earliest human minds. We say, then, for the great question's sake; for if any, whether scientific or religious, regard the doctrine of indefinite creative days as most indispensable for their cherished reconciliation, we see no other line of argument on which there is any fairer prospect, or indeed any prospect at all, of its being made out. Other views, such as those derived from the merely metaphorical sense of the word day, of which examples enough can be found, may furnish a possibility, a probability, nay, more, a captivating speciousness; but the mind does not rest in them, aside from such a conviction in respect to the ancient thought.

Whatever its demerits, the very attempt was entitled to respect and respectful criticism. And such it has received. The author would be ungrateful to complain of its reception by an approving press and an approving public. Still more encouraging are the private communications from readers, and that too of no low standing in our scholarly and literary world, professing gratitude for relief from serious and painful difficulty. Of five extended reviews, three have been warmly favorable, two bitterly hostile, agreeing in the spirit of the assault, though disagreeing in almost everything else. It has been the singular fortune of the book to be thus assailed at the same time, from two directly opposite quarters, and that, too, with an asperity of feeling beyond what usually arises from any mere literary or scientific antagonism. Another noteworthy circumstance is, that in two long and labored attacks there should not have been met a single one of those Biblical interpretations whose strength or weakness constitute the real merit or demerit of the argument. The Editor of the Literary and Theological Journal is so confident of having slain all the geologists, and so unshakably certain, moreover, that *day* means *day*, and can mean nothing else, except in prophecy, where it denotes exactly 365 days 5 hours and a half, that he probably thinks any matter of interpretation on the other side unworthy of serious notice. The question is with him too plain for argument. The Silliman Professor of Mineralogy and Geology in Yale College seems to ignore this whole department for another reason. Doubtless he could have shown himself at home in it had he chosen, but there was no need of it. It might have been of some value in the days of the old ignorance, when the best way of getting at the meaning of the Bible was thought to be the study of the Bible, but now science is the light of the age; "Science and the Bible" makes a very euphonic heading for an article in a Review, but the harmony itself must be made out from the former. In much of the current thinking of the day, the Bible holds a place very similar to that of the Japanese Mikado, or Spiritual Emperor, who has a court but no soldiers. It is to be held in great historical veneration, but science is the real monarch. To go to Scripture, therefore, to find the evidence of this concordat is superfluous work.

It has even been construed into disrespect for the higher authority. Of course the Bible must agree with science, that is, whatever certain scientific men say is science, although other scientific men deny both the science and the theology. "Must not all truth be consistent?" On the score of such profundities as these, the Professor would seem to resent the Biblical effort as making an unlawful entry into his jealously guarded domain. To have put the two authorities on a par might have been tolerated, though in the scientific parallelism science generally comes first; but that may be for the sake of euphony —"Science and the Bible" being rather more rythmical than "The Bible and Science." This, we say, might have been tolerated; but to represent science as vastly below revelation, not only in this thing and that thing, but in whatever the latter professes to teach us,—'to speak of the changing language of human science as altogether unfitted to convey the eternal verities of God's word—to maintain that its technics, and boasted formulas, may, in some remote latter day, sound obsolete and childish—to hint, that gravities may yet go the way of vortices and epicycles, that the Newtonian system may, in time, be regarded as but an advance on the Ptolemaic, and the present geology looked upon, in some future age, in very much the same light that we now regard the Aristotelian meteorology—to argue that the *permanent* and the *substantial* is to be sought in the Scriptures, while science can never get above the *transient* and the *phenomenal* without bringing in ideas from other regions that lie beyond its own true domain,—above all, to teach that whenever God utters his voice from "His own Holy Temple," all science, and all philosophy even, which is a higher thing than science, "should keep silence before Him"—this was resented as an indignity. Science was insulted, forsooth, and greatly wronged, although all that was said against her, or about her, was said in this relation, and fell far within the truth and spirit of the above statements.

In assuming such a championship of science, and such an imaginary wrong, Professor DANA well knew the spirit of the age in which, and for which he wrote, as well as the amount of moral courage required. It was an easy task, this writing a eulogy on Hercules. Was not science ridding the world of monsters? Had it not invented steam engines, and telegraphs, and daguerreotypes? Had it not, in the language of that Epicurean bard of old, who boasts so much like a modern lecturer, driven superstition from its haunts—that horrid monster—

> Quæ caput a cœli regionibus obtendebat
> Horribili super adspectu mortalibus instans;
> Humana ante oculos fede quom vita jaceret
> In terris, *obpressa gravi sub religione.*

Had it not delivered us from the fear of comets and falling stars, as say all the school books in their enumeration of scientific utilities? Had it not banished witchcraft from the earth, although of the modern spiritualism it hardly knew what to say,—this new power talking itself so scientifically, and having already drawn some of scientific note, both here and abroad, within its magic circle. But its greatest achievement was its patronage of the Scriptures, although here there has been no little division in its ranks,—not a few, who claim free thought, regarding this as a burden which science should not be required to carry.

Now we are not much afraid of being mistaken in the truth or spirit of these remarks. There are scientific men of loveliest piety, of most religious modesty. There are men of *religious science*, in distinction from a *scientific religionism*,—men, who, although they revere both names, would rather be called the followers of Kepler than of Galileo. There are writers, late writers, and those too whose works exhibit science of the highest order, whose references to the Bible, and quotations from the Bible, have some heart in them. To mention names might seem invidious.* But such men are among us, and they must know, and feel, that the representation given of the position of science in respect to the Bible is not only correct, but the only one consistent with even the lowest honor that can be conceded to a true revelation — a true voice from the invisible supernatural world. They must feel, too, that the truest honor of science arises to her from her recognizing and modestly taking this position. Such men must know and acknowledge that there has been, and is yet, an irreligious spirit manifested by not a few of highest scientific name, whilst, in other quarters, there is an assumption of patronage, which, though less hostile to the Bible, is hardly less odious. They can not think of denying such well-settled facts. With men like these the writer would deeply regret any difference of opinion — much more would he regret, if, in his own one-sided zeal, perhaps, for deeply-cherished views, he may have uttered a word, or thought, wounding to profes-

*There is one we can not help referring to. No one can read Lieutenant MAURY's Physical Geography of the Sea, without feeling that the Bible lies much nearer to his heart than any amount of physical knowledge.

sional pride, or derogatory to the honorable love of honorable and cherished pursuits.

But there is another scientific spirit to which we make neither concession nor apology. It is not so high nor so philosophical as the other, but it is more general, as it is more superficial in its general outside thinking, while it has accordingly more command of the ear and mind of the age. It is the pretentious, noisy, arrogant science. We say nothing of its merits or demerits in its own field; but it is thus justly characterized, because it claims to be itself the age, and asserts a superiority over all other departments, and all other forms of thought. Sometimes, and often, as every intelligent man knows, it is decidedly infidel, hostilely and contemptuously anti-biblical. It seeks no "reconciliation;" it cares nothing for "harmonies;" it rather spurns them both. At other times it graciously *accepts* the Scriptures as containing a collateral revelation, but one that must first be put in harmony with herself. Science — this kind of science — and whenever the word is used by us in a manner to call in question its arrogant claims, let it be so understood — this science assumes to reveal the higher and the older law, and when she speaks, what have Bible men to do but to pull up "their stakes" and "lengthen their cords," and follow on without venturing even to look into their travelling directory to see where they are going. There is, for example, Professor DANA'S highly eulogized friend AGASSIZ, whom in one place he would commend to the disparagement of the author of the book. We have all respect for him as a man of highest rank in his own department of science; but he is preparing for a new move; or rather, he has already made a new move; and in prompt correspondence with it, some in the theological world, yes in the evangelical part of it so called, are overhauling their creeds and dogmas, and apparently packing up for a start. This question of the unity of the human race, and their descent from one primus homo, differs widely from the geological question, important as that may be. The point presented is deeply vital, not only to the historical, but to the central faith. The difficulties raised respecting the manner and chronology of creation, may affect our belief most seriously, yet indirectly. Revelation might live, perhaps, though thus cruelly mutilated in the very fore-face. Even if compelled to surrender chapter after chapter, and book after book, the believing spirit would hold on to the last member that gave any evidence of historic vitality. It would cling to the last plank of the broken vessel. But this latter move of science touches the very core of Christianity; the assailed fact, or dogma, intertwines itself with truth that can no more be separated from it than the blood from the heart. And yet, even here, it is thought by some—yea, the opinion has been hazarded in the very schools of the Prophets—that we must not be rash in affirming confidently what the Bible does or does not teach, until we hear what science has to say. Let her make her move, and then it will be time enough to see whether the doctrines of the Fall, of the Primal Covenant, of the Federal Headship, of the Redemption, and even of the "Incarnate Mystery," (that wondrous thought that has heretofore kept its place in all views of the human ruin and recovery, and which even the freest Christianity has been reluctant wholly to part with,) may not possibly be so revised as to meet the case. The Church is advised to maintain, in the mean while, a philosophic calmness, though science should affirm us to be ten thousand instead of one, or take the unphilosophical, as well as seemingly anti-biblical, ground, that nature and species are mere terms of outward classification — that they are words of quantity grounded on the more or less of an ever undefinable resemblance, instead of the fact of an historic germ that can only be proved or disproved by revelation, and in which the present many historically meet at a point where they are actually as well as generically one. It is in this way, and from such examples, we account for the feeling that the Bible has little to do with any physical questions — that it has little to do with the origin either of the earth or man, and that, therefore, interpretation in respect to them, is so ignored, yea, treated as a positive disrespect to science, should it be maintained — as in such interpretation can not well be avoided — that when God speaks, all human knowledge, and human discovery, should take the lower place. It is this spirit which, as we shall attempt to show in its connection, is the real naturalism.

But it is in their temper, rather than in their positions, that these two reviews do most especially resemble each other. It is here that the religious and scientific bigotry can hardly be distinguished. There is, however, a difference. The first is bad enough, but it is, after all, more excusable than the second. The religious bigot thinks, at least, that he has a holy motive. He knows not himself, of course ; but the very ground and reason of his self-deception, make his zeal a higher thing, and a better thing, than the scientific bitterness that knows no such palliation. He is contending with the infidels,

3

not the well-known enemies of the common Christianity, but those whom he chooses to call "infidels in disguise," because they may question in any sense the infallibility of his own interpretations. He is a "defender of the faith," and every notion he has derived from his own traditions is a precious portion of that faith; and every man is, of course, an infidel who does not subscribe to it precisely as he expounds it, or who does not even anathematize errorists as he anathematizes them. He has, therefore, some plea to which the scientific bigotry can lay no claim. And yet, malevolent as this latter shows itself to be, degrading as it is to that science and literature which boast so much of refining our poor human nature, still is it strangely regarded by the world as the more respectable of the two. Its voice, in the present age at least, has the greater weight, and this is the reason why we bestow upon it the greater share of attention.

The religious bigot, after all, can not do much; at least now a days. He is fighting valiantly against the infidels, but the real infidels—and there are still some such—are not at all afraid of him. Indeed, they set great store by this faithful sentinel. Nothing delights them more than to hear his sharp cry ever ringing out, not against the real invaders, but the most honest and earnest defenders of revelation. Sometimes they will even laud him—we have known citable cases of this very thing—for his boldness, his frankness, his outspeaking, honest zeal. Rejecting, as they do, the whole idea of a supernatural revelation, yet, say they, if there is meaning to it at all, this honest man has got it. The First of Genesis is manifest fable, to be sure, but he clearly has the only sense, and that shows it to be a fable. Nothing can be plainer, they say, to any *man of sense*, than that all this talk about the Bible and the Church is of things *in nubibus*, and the lauded harmony of "science and religion" all a modern myth; but then, his nonsense is as good as their nonsense, and a great deal more honest. Anything, in short, to bring the Bible into disrepute, and with materials for this his infallibility most abundantly furnishes them.

But the scientific bigotry is more respectable — claims to be so at least — whether deservedly or not. It has, therefore, the more influence with another and wider class, and for a somewhat different reason. There are two causes for this wider influence. One is a diminution of a controlling and exclusive faith in the Scriptures,— exclusive, we mean, in all matters of which they profess to treat — the other the disproportionate space in the common mind, occupied by what is now called science. Our first proposition may seem a very bold one. Some would say it is utterly false and unjust. If there is any thing which peculiarly marks the age, they would contend, it is the direct contrary of what is implied in the assertion. First appearances, perhaps, might justify such an indignant protest. It is certainly an age famous for its laudation of the Bible, but still, we venture to say it, with a corresponding diminution of a living faith in it as the real Word of God, which is indeed to control our ethics, our politics, our literature, our philosophy, yea, our science too, if between it and that science, or any assumptions of that science, we discover a difference which no fair, honest, hearty effort of our minds will enable us to reconcile — a faith that in such a case would not ride over appearances, being little better than no faith at all. Yes, we laud the Scriptures; different classes of men seem to vie with each other in lauding the Scriptures. The Bible! is it not the religion of Protestants? Is it not the bulwark of our liberties? We eulogise it on the platform; we fight for it in our common schools; we make speeches about it on all occasions. But has it a corresponding influence, or anything like a corresponding influence, on the general mind of the age? This is the test. Otherwise our pompous eulogies are the very things to cast suspicion upon the strength and heartiness of the general faith. Take an age when there was no doubt of the power of the Bible and a Bible-taught theology,—when they controlled all movements, and entered into every department of thought. Such an age is not distinguished for its eulogies on the Word of God. There is something too hearty in its faith to allow of it, or make it necessary. All the writings of all the Ushers, of all the Hookers, of all the old divines of Holland, Scotland, England, and New-England, do not contain so much laudation of the Bible as one modern sermon, or one modern platform speech. But after all, what is its influence as a vital power entering deeply into the mind of the age? We say the mind of the age, for there are doubtless individuals, and very many of them, in whose souls the claim of a divine revelation, instead of being relaxed, has only taken a firmer hold. The rise of other powers, and their preponderance in the general thinking, has only driven them more closely and trustingly to the Word of God. There are men to whom it is their one book, their sole authority. There are those to whom, without the Bible, the universe is shrouded in darkness —to whom, without it, all science, and all philosophy, would give but a spectral light—to whom, without it, geology, boasting geology, would be but a lamp in the catacombs, a poor mummy light which we might faintly see, indeed, but could see nothing by it, read nothing by it, even of the greatest of physical truths, our origin, much less aught of the still deeper mysteries that gather round the questions of destiny and salvation. Such men are not much given to praising the Bible as the foundation of our liberties, or the great instrument of civilization. Their faith is not easy enough for that. They find in it too many difficulties. They see in it those great and terrible truths of salvation which throw into the shade all other estimates of its value as connected with even the highest aspects of life that are still but secularities. Neither do they claim any intellectual merit for their faith, even where they feel that they have as good a right to do so as any who challenge to themselves, and to their pursuits, a higher and more expansive range of thought. They can not, they dare not, disbelieve the Scriptures. The feeling has been sown deep in their infancy; it has grown with their nurture and their culture; it has connected itself, perhaps, with some peculiar experience having more of the Biblical element than is now usual, and thus, in all these ways confirmed itself, not as a blind superstition, but by leading to that hearty study of the Scriptures which furnishes their strongest evidence, and without which the Bible is never truly believed, either by an individual or an age. It becomes their "meditation by day and by night"—"sweeter than honey and the honey comb;" and thus, whether they have any great science or not, it "maketh them wiser than their enemies that be round about them."

Yet still we venture to say it, however rash it may seem in us, there is in much of this religious world, especially as exhibited in its more conventional and secular aspects, a poor diluted faith, a poor shivering faith that can not keep itself warm from the Scriptures, and so it runs to science and everything else. Its want of strength and earnestness is very much in proportion to the noise it makes about the Bible and the so-called "Harmony of Science and Revelation;" or "the two revelations," as it is fond of styling them. We have no doubt of its honesty, or its purity as far as it goes. This belief is genuine—it has a value in the preservation of the soul's health, and its ultimate salvation. It has a sincere regard for the Bible, but it is so immersed in secularity, and secularizing movements of reform—its Christianity is so much of this world, and allies itself with so many collateral influences from the world, that it has no time, and if it had time, has not heart enough to arouse, or strength enough to sustain, that whole-souled study of the Scriptures, that "meditation therein by day and by night," that consequent devoted love of the Book, which would teach them wondrous things out of it—thus making its bright internal evidence the most immoveable support of their faith. The deep study of the Scriptures is essential to any strong faith in them, and could men be induced heartily to engage in it, it might be recommended as the best of all cures for scepticism, or naturalism, whether of an individual or of an age. But here we are met by a difficulty which gives the proposition the appearance of a paradox. Without such faith there will be no such study. The truth is, that both are, at the same time, cause and effect. They must act and re-act upon each other. But without settling that difficulty, it is enough to present the fact, which few will deny, that the Bible, though generally and honestly believed, and with much interest manifested for its distribution, is not in the heart of the age, at least as it has been in the heart of former ages. It is not so much the one sole authority that it used to be, the one great superseding authority in all matters of which it speaks. It is not so much that the Scriptures have been rejected, as that other things have come into partnership with them, and, we may say, to some degree of superiority over them in the control of the common thinking — even the better and more serious common thinking — of the age.

We repeat, then, the paradox — the true remedy for this semi-scepticism which respects the Bible so much — which swears by the Bible while it serves other gods — whether it be the gods of politics, philanthrophy, or science, the god of social "ideas," or the "god of forces" — the true remedy for this is that devoted Biblical study of which we have spoken. Superficial reading, or mere formal reading, only breeds difficulties or indifference; instead of light it only reveals pitfalls and stumbling-blocks. A deeper study produces that evidence of which we read much in the old divines who lived just after the Reformation, but which is now seldom alluded to in modern books either of instruction or devotion. It is not the external evidence, commonly so called, or the historical proof of Christianity, valuable and indispensable as that is for all ages. It is not that other kind of evidence more usually named the internal, but which is as truly external as the first, whilst it has less of its conclusiveness. We mean by this, the supposed conformity of the

Scriptures to right reason, as it is called, or "the nature of things"—there being meant by this our own views of what *ought* to be true in theology, or ethics, or what we conceive to be true in science. This evidence, we say, is, in one sense, as much external to the Scriptures as the historical. In both cases it is a light we bring to the Bible, and not a light we derive from it. Hence, thus viewed, both are equally outward—that is, outward to the Bible. One is an outward historical knowledge, the other an outward knowledge of mind or matter which we call science and philosophy. This second kind of rationalism, though boasting a higher rank, is less conclusive than the first. The explanation is, that in the one case our reason is called to judge of what lies easily and plainly within its nearest sphere, such as the meaning of words, the laws of language, the fair principles of interpretation. In the other, we bring to the clearing of the Scriptures the very darkness they were intended to illuminate, or, if we take the road of science commonly so called, we enter upon a region whence nothing can be proved of the human, or the mundane destiny, because the unknown so immensely, so infinitely, we might almost say, exceeds the known. We may say, too, that in this attempted proof of the Bible by its conformity to what we call right reason and the nature of things, the very first principle of the purest reason is itself subverted. We measure the infinite by the finite. We make our thoughts the test of the Divine thoughts, our ways the test of the Divine ways; our natural science, or natural theology, as we call it, which is but the discovery of *links*, we revere as the very canons of that Divine wisdom which is known only in the revelation of *beginnings* or *ends*.

Such a proceeding to prove revelation is, moreover, in the very face of the revelation to be proved. It contradicts some of its sublimest utterances. "Your thoughts are not my thoughts, saith the Lord ;" "neither are your ways" (your ways of thinking and knowing as well as acting) "my ways." "For as the heavens are high above the earth" (the strongest hyperbole that language can employ) "so high are my ways above your ways, and my thoughts above your thoughts." This Scriptural language is evidently employed to denote things not only immensely apart in rank and magnitude, but also inconceivably differing in kind. Hence the value of that other internal evidence to which we barely alluded, but of which the old divines are full. The reader will not often meet with it in modern religious or theological works, but he will find it most prominently and most abundantly set forth in such writers as Owen, and Baxter, and Hooker, and Hall. He will meet with it in those men of ponderous learning and child-like piety, the old theologians of Holland who lived before Grotius and Grotianism had unspiritualized that noble Church; and we have no doubt that it might be found in the most religious of the Roman Catholic divines. It is that internal evidence that reveals itself to us by its own light; the light which the Scriptures themselves have kindled in the soul. It is what Hallyburton, in his reply to the rationalism of Locke, calls "the Divine glory beaming and burning in the Scriptures." It is the recognition of the majestic voice of God speaking to us therein, and in every part. It is not simply the intellectual assent to the logical consistency of its doctrines, however defectively or partially seen; it is not that "beautiful morality" which some infidels have been so fond of praising; it is not the loftiness of its oratory, or the sublimity of its poetry, but distinct from all these, and above all these, it is that *impress of Divine Authority* which comes from long, and devout, and loving communion with the sacred volume. It is that "satisfying light," evidencing itself to be true light by the fact that it enables us to see, not only itself, but other things by means of it, making reason more clear by revealing its limitations, and other knowledge more valuable by the discovery of its true yet inferior position. It is what one has called "the Divine majesty beaming in the Word." We would not trust our own language here, and so we adopt that of the venerable and learned men who so loved the Scriptures, and so lived in the Scriptures, we may say, that their mode of speaking about them sounds mystical, or hyperbolical, to our unbiblical age. They were not dreamers, nor enthusiasts, nor fanatics, but sound-minded men, noble scholars, logical interpreters, keen analyzers of their own psychological states. It was not only the Ushers, and the Cudworths, and the Owens who spake thus — though these might well be compared with the soberest scholars and theologians of our own age, — but the great Bacon, too, talks in the same style — the great Bacon whom so many sciolists so ignorantly worship. In the decline of his political and philosophical greatness it might have been, but it was after his mind had been brought into closest communion with the Scriptures, that he speaks of "*seeking* God in nature, but *finding* him only in his Word." It was a trait of the universal religious thinking. The writers to whom we have referred speak of it as a reality, a glorious reality, not confined to a few mystical dreamers, but belonging to the common faith of common Christians in that believing age.

This faith they regarded as supernatural; but whether supernatural, or having its seat in the natural faculties of the human soul, and in the natural exercise thereof, still was it ever the intimate companion of deep and hearty study of the Scriptures. It was only by intense meditation therein, that men's eyes were truly opened to discern the glorious light in the Word and thus to "discover wondrous things out of the Divine Law," and in no part more wondrous than in this earliest record of man and the world. To this hearty study of the Scriptures must the age return. There must be regained that single, honest, view of the absolute authority of the Bible in all matters of which it professes to treat or even speaks. No other faith is worthy of the name. A revelation, so received as coming from God, must be everything or nothing. It must be exclusive as well as conclusive. It can allow no concurrent, no collateral, authority. Nothing else that is styled a revelation, whether in nature or in history, can be put on a par with it, or, in any sense, placed in parallelism with it. Once admitted, as indeed the Divine supernatural voice, nothing else can even approach it,—nothing else that calls itself authority can hold up its face before it on its own field. Among all truths of reason so called, we can conceive of none more rational than this. And to this the Church and the age must return, or give up its loud talk about the Bible — the "Bible and Science" — the Bible and natural theology — the Bible and democracy — the Bible the palladium of our liberties — the foundation of our social, civil and religious rights. It may not be prudent to say it, but it is true, notwithstanding, and therefore, we will say it, that even before the Reformation, among divines of the Roman Church, and in the works of the schoolmen, written, as we are taught to believe, when the Scriptures lay buried and unknown, there was more of hearty faith in them than can now be discovered in the teachings of some who are the greatest praisers of the Bible. There is more appearance of devout reverence; there is a more spontaneous deference as to unquestionable authority; there is more of a loving resort to them as the ultimate decision, after philosophy has had her say, and science has delivered her message, whatever it might have been, for that or any other age of the world. If this living on the Scriptures, as, next to Christ, the soul's truest food, be the best test of faith in the Bible, then will an Anselm, an A Kempis, an Aquinas, yea, perhaps, unknown souls, not a few, from the cloister and the cell, rise up in judgment against the Bible eulogizers, and scientific harmonizers of the day. It may not be prudent to talk thus, but we are certain that there is truth, important truth, in what we say, and that the age should hear it. We appeal to serious men of all theological parties. Is the Scriptures in the heart of this age, as it has been in the heart of former ages? Is the evidence of this in the pulpit, in the press, in the theology, or the literature of the day? Does the mind, even the religious mind, go spontaneously to the Written Word? for this is the true test. In every difficulty does it first think of the Bible? In all the great questions of the day, as they are called, —the social, political, moral questions—those questions which all depend so much, for their truest solution, on right views of human destiny and its relation to the invisible worlds, and where the Bible must be supposed to give some light, if it give light at all — on all such questions, is it the first thought, what do the Scriptures fairly teach, or do they teach anything, either as precept or principle, to which all other reasoning can and must be made to conform? We talk much more about the Bible than ever the Puritans, or the Reformers did; is the common mind, the common religious mind, we mean, more familiar with it than it was in their day — familiar with it, not in the mere quotation of a few pet texts, which almost any party can get out of it, but in the spirit of the Bible, and its whole bearing upon the analogy of revealed truth? These questions might be carried into the higher departments. How is it with our professed Biblical study? Does it go into the very marrow of the Scriptures? We have got rid of some of the crudities of former preachers and interpreters, — we have read Old Mortality, and can talk bravely of the extravagance of the Kettle-drummles, and McBriars, and Mucklewraiths, though even this has more heart in it, and therefore, more truth than much that is conceived and written in the opposite style. But if there is an absence of their peculiar errors, there is also an absence, much to be lamented, of those rich views of divine truth, in its entire Biblical harmony, which the old English scholars, and the learned Leyden divines brought out of the ever-suggestive Word of God. Instead of that direct deduction of all high truth *from* the Bible which is now condemned as mystical, we have the most elaborate discussions *about* the Bible, and about the books of the Bible, and the natural history of the Bible. Instead of the "analogy of faith" which led men to regard each book as a part of a most perfect unity, such as it certainly must be if it is God's Word in any true sense, we have Lowthian criticisms on the varied human styles of its composers, all very true indeed, but very subordinate to the higher harmony which such a kind of criticism has ever a tendency to keep out of view. Such is the spirit of much modern Biblical criticism, rich as it is in its machinery of outward interpretation. It is fastidious of the impurities that belong to the bucket rather than the fountain; and, therefore, instead of drawing copiously and constantly from the deep wells of pure Scriptural thought, it is ever on the outside, at least in regard to essential, vital truth. In short, it is ever *about* the Bible, as though it were a curiosity to be examined, rather than the Book of the Lord given to us as a light shining in a dark place, and to which everything else in the mind of the believer should be so subordinate, that even if he does not derive his philosophy and his science from it, as a direct text-book, he is, at least, willing to say, and is forced to say, that he will have and can have no philosophy, and no science, that are in any sense really or seemingly at war with it.

We are far from saying that the modern reception of the Scriptures is not sincere and sound as far as it goes. Its greatest fault is, that it is not exclusive, as it ought to be if it would be anything. It takes the Scriptures as authority, as high authority, but not the all-controlling authority, on all matters of which they speak. Other Lords have come in and shared dominion with it. In our literature and our science there is a mixture of the "Jews' language" with "the speech of Ashdod." Especially has there been a dimming of that highest evidence of which Owen, and Hallyburton, and Pascal speak. The Lowthian spirit of interpretation sees it not, because it does not look for it. Along with this obscure perception of the true divine majesty and authority speaking directly in the Word, there is an increasing tendency to laud the Scriptures for those more secular teachings, or in those secular aspects of revealed truth, which are either greatly subordinate, or are forced upon it altogether. Hence there is so much mere talk about the Bible. Politicians magnify the Bible. Are they really going to the Bible, drawing nearer to the Bible, or is the Bible viewed as coming down to them? Literary men are sentimental about the Bible; social reformers cant about the Bible. The tendency sometimes manifests itself in an appearance which would be ludicrous were it not profane; the bully chief of the Empire Club breaks up a meeting of fanatics, as he calls them, because "they abuse the Holy Bible," and the vile makers of vile political platforms endorse the act, and the spirit of it, in their canting resolutions about our civil and religious liberties. This is not all hypocrisy; the lowered position of the Bible has made men *dread* it less, and so they "*respect*" it more. They seek to harmonize it with everything, and that general ignorance which comes from the want of earnest study, makes this, in most cases, a very easy and accommodating process. In short, the Bible is a favorite book of the age; it has a most convenient storehouse of texts and mottoes; it contains the articles of our faith, although we sometimes have to put them in a more philosophical and scientific form. It professes, indeed, to carry with it its own credentials, but as a general truth, men go abroad for its evidences.

Hence the undue weight attached to scientific and other foreign testimonies to Christianity. Science at the present day, in distinction from philosophy and theology, occupies a disproportioned, and therefore injurious space in the public mind. This is especially true of natural science, and still more so of that department strictly called *natural history*, and to which, in other times, as wise as our own in the philosophy of names as definitive of ideas, the term science, would hardly have been conceded at all. But whether that be correct or not, it is rather a singular fact in the history of human thinking, that these very branches have come to usurp the name to the exclusion of almost everything else. Let the word *science* be used, and how many, even among the educated who ought to know better, never think of Language, of Psychology, of Ethics, of Political Science, of Theology highest of all. Philology—it is the "study of words," and what are words compared with shells and minerals? Even the Pure Mathematics hereby finds a place except as an auxiliary to some of the usurping branches. Chemistry, too, is thrown in the back ground, while Conchology, Mineralogy, Icthyology, come trooping up, paper in hand, and demanding to be recognized not only as very respectable and very useful branches of knowledge, which they certainly are, but as science per se, in its highest and almost exclusive import. These are, indeed, beautiful pursuits. We do not wonder that they are ardently loved by those who have time to devote to them, and who have been drawn to their study by temperament and circumstances clearly indicating them as the paths of knowledge in which they could best connect their own happiness with the utilities, and not only the utilities, but the refinement of the age. One of the purest men, and clearest intellects, with whom the writer is acquainted, has devoted himself for many years to a thorough scientific hunt after that mischievous and evasive enemy, the wheat insect. He has traced him through three forms of generation, and discovered some curious facts of development* that ought to make Professor DANA less confident about his having slain the Vestiges of Creation. There is, doubtless, in many others engaged in similar pursuits the same earnest *amor scientiæ* so ennobling to our humanity in whatever form it may show itself, together with the same unwearied search of facts that may subserve the physical good. All honor to them; — but we appeal to such men themselves, or to the more serious and thinking among them, whether there has not been too much of an arrogant claiming, or at least employment, of the name science as peculiarly, if not exclusively applicable to these and kindred branches. Let any one examine the records of our annual scientific conventions. Three-fourths of their proceedings relate to natural history properly so called. Of the remaining fourth, astronomy has a fair share; mathematics pure brings out its paper now and then, whilst all else beyond this physical region, is as much ignored as though it had no claim whatever to the dignity of a science, or the consideration of scientific men. And so too of the latter phrase — a man of science; — let it be mentioned, and at once some physical ology, or some branch of natural history, suggests itself

*We refer here, not to development from inanimate matter, but to some curious facts of what may be called double generation—the immediate offspring so unlike the parents, that they would be regarded as a new species if the fact of origin was unknown.

to the common mind. It thinks immediately of shells, and mosses,—at the highest of gases, fossils, or telescopes. Legal science, political science, ethical science, Biblical science, hermeneutical science!—the terms indeed are recognized, but they are regarded as being used by way of accommodation rather than by intrinsic right. Now this utter distortion of names and ideas is a mark of a one-sided, if we may not call it superficial, age. It is the language of a generation, and of a thinking, immersed in the physical; and we protest against it. It gives an undue advantage. In an age when men read and talk far more than they think, it clothes certain opinions of a certain class with an authority which does not belong to them. There is a sufficient instance of this in the very example that has called out these remarks. Why should the dictum of a geologist be deferred to on a question of the interpretation of Scripture? There is no reason for it; there is every reason against it; and yet it carries weight, and carries along with it too the timid religionist, because it comes forth under this high-sounding name of science, so unjustly and even absurdly usurped for a department of knowledge extremely limited in extent, and very far from being the highest in idea or in aim—in intellectual difficulty, in intellectual rank, or even in utility when judged by the highest and truest standard.

In reply to what is here said about the great disproportion of such subjects in scientific conventions, it might, perhaps, be alleged that there is a reason for it, without its being attributed to any such usurpation or exclusiveness. The great majority of the papers read are on natural history, or, at the widest, what is called physical science, because these furnish the topics that are the more directly popular, or acceptable to the common thinking. There is some truth in such apology — but is it for the glory of this kind of science that it should be so? Does it form an honorable ground for its extravagant boasting? Physical science, especially in the departments to which we have chiefly alluded, is popular for several reasons. In the *first* place, it is more easy of acquisition. To be thorough and eminent in any one of these does indeed require a life devoted to it, as to any other pursuit in which decided excellence is the aim. But their general acquisition, to a respectable extent, lies within the power of almost any mind of ordinary intelligence and ordinary opportunities. We do not at all wish to underrate them, although the immense boasting they have made, or that has been made for them, fairly justifies any attempt to reduce them to their true place in the wide map of human knowledge. Take the one which may be said to have the least science, strictly, of them all — that is, is most built on outward classification instead of inward organic life running up into that universality of law and idea whose tendency is to connect all knowledge that partakes of it into one catholic thinking. Take Conchology, for example; even here we concede that to be a good conchologist requires a peculiar habit, a peculiar talent, and a peculiar and patient observation that all do not possess. An enthusiastic devotion to it is very honorable to a man, if it be accompanied by an appropriate modesty; but it is very far from requiring the highest order of mind, and it becomes very foolish when, on the score of its being so peculiarly and exclusively science, it challenges for its devotees a deference in other matters, and in widely different if not altogether higher departments of knowledge. He who makes himself thorough in this department of science, occupies a high position, and ought to occupy a high position, among useful and intelligent and cultivated men; and yet it is true that almost any one who has any inclination for the study, and time for it from other pursuits, may make himself very respectably scientific here with little effort, and in a very short time. The same is true of Geology, the most vaunting of them all. It calls out the same and no greater faculty of observation, no greater powers of thinking, though connected with more important and interesting results. It has, however, one peculiar "utility" that the others do not possess. To many minds—we do not fear to say what is so fully borne out by facts—to many minds, it has a charm from the supposed fact of its furnishing a ground of objection—whether true or false—to the credibility of the Scriptures. It is this which gives it a large share of its importance, and none better know the fact than those of its religious, Bible-loving students who most sincerely wish to counteract its influence. We are conscious of telling truth here, and therefore shrink not from its assertion. It is the general spirit more than any facts of geological research, that is hostile to the Scriptures. It is the general spirit as manifested in two ways, the bold and sneering opposition of many Geologists abroad, the apparently friendly but hardly less mischievous asssumption of its being a sort of collateral and even higher revelation, that is made by others under orthodox influences in our own land. Good men and Christians, who are, at the same time, very "scientific men," are trying hard to counteract this; but the dishonorable popularity which the study has derived from its being supposed to minister to this anti-biblical spirit, can never be seriously affected from the scientific side. Geology—serious Geology we mean—can never be relieved from it, until thorough, honest, reliable interpretation takes the place, and the authority, of one-sided scientific "harmonies of nature and revelation." For the reasons we have given, Geology is popular; it is a favorite science of the day, but it really demands no greater powers of mind for its observations or conclusions than other branches of the same scientific genus. It has a much grander sound, indeed, to talk about boulders and glaciers, and yet these may be actually coarser and less artistic works of nature than ferns and mosses. Geology is diligently engaged in examining the epidermis of the earth, it is making curious discoveries among its dorsal fins, and some are most diligently hunting there for human bones, but it may require no more intellectual power to do this, than to classify plants, or dissect an animal. It deals too, or assumes to deal, with immense times deriving interest from other associations, but having, in themselves, no more intellectual value, and less intellectual interest than the question of the change and periods in the germination of the seed, or the growth of the fœtus. The pride of Geology in this aspect, is as absurd as it would be to regard the mere anatomy of the mastodon as a matter of more scientific importance than the careful observation of the insect in its wonderful transitions from the egg to the grub, and from the grub to the winged state.

These sciences are easy. They are more easily acquired, and this gives them another advantage. In consequence of such facility, they are, in the second place, more generally diffused than other and more difficult studies; or, rather, there is a more common diffusion to a certain extent. There is a more general smattering; and this contributes more to their popularity than even a deeper and more difficult knowledge. They are the popular studies of the day, pursued in our schools and academies to the neglect of the more solid, and, in the end, more truly useful branches of knowledge. There is every where a little Physiology, a little Mineralogy, a little Geology, etc. Of course, there is obtained, in general, but a smattering in each; but this is enough to fill the common mind with a wondrous conceit of science. It is a scientific age, it is often said; the term being ever used in reference to physical science as the only thing known to be entitled to the name. This gives a great advantage to the common lecturer. Audiences love to be talked to scientifically. It gives them a very scientific opinion of themselves. Each hearer fancies himself a Galileo, a defender of knowledge and progress against bigoted theologians and persecuting priests. The lecturer, though he may be himself a thoroughly scientific man, and one who truly loves science in its higher aspects, yet adapts himself to this state of things. Instead of the rigid demonstration he would employ, if he really meant or hoped to instruct his audience, he dwells on the lower practical business aspects, or, if he would seem to rise into something higher, it is what may be called the thaumaturgical presentation of science that has the greatest charm for the hearer, and the greatest temptation for the speaker. We mean by this those curious facts which are mainly calculated to astonish* men, though having no more, and often even less connection with fundamental scientific truth than others which the lecturer or the book-maker neglects, because they are less adapted to his purpose of immediate excitement, and hence immediate applause. A rigid exhibition of the mathematical modes of determining the distances of the planets would be dry and wearisome. To most audiences, moreover, notwithstanding the boast of its being a scientific age, it would be unintelligible. But to make a grand display of decimals, to talk of millions and billions, and distances which the cannon ball could not traverse in a thousand years, and rows of figures reaching round the earth, this gives them a wondrous view of the science, and of the still more wondrous human mind that can make such computations, and entertain such far-reaching *ideas*. Thorough and patient instruction in the doctrine of transits and parallaxes, with the necessary demonstrations and diagrams, would drive the wearied audience from their seats; but let them be told, in thaumaturgic style, of the wondrous swiftness of light, and how a luminous stream two hundred thousand miles long enters the eye every time a man winks, and there is immediately a hail-stone chorus of applause. The lecturer has hit the mark. The audience came to be amused, and he has adapted himself to their wishes, and to the degree of science which is just sufficient to call out such a feeling. The man of true

*It is *astonishment*, not the philosophic *wonder*, which is very different. One belongs to the imagination or mere sense-conception, the other to the idealizing mind. The one has its exciting cause in merely curious facts presenting an odd or strange picture; the other is aroused to those mysteries of nature and prime causality of which the highest science, as well as the humblest facts, is merely suggestive.

science, we say, often does this. He is compelled to do this or lose the reputation of a popular lecturer. But the quack, too, takes advantage of it. He knows the general tendency to talk about science; and how fond audiences are of being addressed scientifically, and how prone they are to take a certain stereotyped, story-telling language of science as rigid science itself. Hence, under a babble about "laws," and "natural causes," and "developments," and the "organic and inorganic," etc., almost any kind of foolery passes current. All these adopt the same lingo, whether it is the man who wishes to recommend some quack medicine, or the lecturer on Biology, or Phrenology, or that miserable concoction of inane delusion, childish reasoning, and wicked imposture, that goes under the name of modern spiritualism. The chief cause of the success of this species of quackery is its continual assumption of a sort of scientific gabble. It is ever talking about laws, and fluids, and forces, and electricity, and magnetism, and there is just enough everywhere of a certain kind and certain depth of science to give it its present pretension and its present popularity. There have been ages of far less natural knowledge, when this thing would have been spurned with contempt. Delusions taking the form of religious superstitions, and claiming connection with the supernatural, might awe the soul; but the days of witchcraft, and of the belief in a satanic influence had too much philosophy, and too much love for the Scriptures, to entertain the least respect for such a satanic naturalism or naturalizing spiritualism as this.

There is, in the third place, the continual appeal to utilities, which is another great element in the popularity of this kind of knowledge. One finds it so much more of a facile task to persuade men of its immediate practical bearings. This is so easy that even the devoted student of natural science, who knows that he pursues it from that pure love of theoretical truth which is one of the highest traits of our nature — the man, in fact, who would give his days and nights to his laboratory whether any utilitarian inventions came from it or not — even he is tempted to take what he knows to be the lower motive — the motive by which he is conscious that he himself is least influenced — and hold it forth as the main thing in all his appeals to the public for educational encouragement in his favorite pursuit. Hence this becomes so prominent a theme in introductions to text books, and in the common notices of scientific progress. Chemistry is of vast importance in the practical arts. It is a great aid in the manufacturing of paints and soap, it furnishes us tests whereby to distinguish poisons, and quack medicines; as though these ludicrous impositions that science may multiply, but which it will take something more than science ever to drive from the world, were the only kind of quackeries from which we have now-a-days anything to apprehend. So Geology discovers coal mines, and Astronomy is a great aid in navigation, and Navigation is essential to commerce, etc., etc. Thus science, natural science, becomes popular by having ignored and kept out of view its own highest effect and aim. In like manner, Colleges are sometimes praised, not for the minds they have produced, not for having elevated and spiritualized the tone of thinking in their age or neighborhood, but for the agricultural improvements and mechanical inventions which, in some far-fetched way, are ascribed to their influence. And then there is the everlasting sing-song of the steam engine, the daguerreotype, and the magnetic telegraph, as though the rapid transmission of a thought were of vastly more importance than the quality of the thought transmitted, or the age was to be lauded for the improvement of the one, whatever deterioration might take place in the rank and true value of the other.

All these causes have given natural science a space in the public mind which is altogether disproportioned to its real worth; and in the midst of many acknowledged utilities we are suffering also serious evils in consequence of it. The cause of true education is hurt. The profounder, and, in the end, the far more useful studies lie too much out of the common track to be so easily appreciated. It is far more difficult to make the public feel their real merits. The higher intelligence sees, or ought to see this, but in this class, too, there are popularity hunters, and instead of sustaining by extra aid those really most useful branches whose utility, however real, lies remote from the first and most obvious thinking, they are for putting all things on the same democratic level, and making the test of value in any spiritual, as well as in any material, thing, the immediate public patronage as coming from the immediate public demand.

Outside causes have contributed to the same unfair preponderance. All the circumstances and wants of the age tend to magnify physical knowledge, or "science" so called. Philosophy has completed one of its cycles, and is now occupied more with its past history than with any quickening view, whether new or old, of the universal problem. There is our thin rationalizing theology, all reasoned out of nature, or the nature of things, as it is called, rather than the Scriptures; there is our utilitarian ethics, our shallow radical politics. "Science," as it is called, is not only more easy, but more really beautiful and worthy of loving study than some of these in the aspects in which they are now presented, and we do not wonder that men are rushing after it. Hence, for our age, science, natural science, has acquired a place and a space that do not belong to it; it demands a deference from all other departments of thought, which is not due either to its dignity, or its true utility. In the language of prophecy, "it has become the horn having a man's voice speaking great things," and the world, even the religious world, is wondering after it. Here we find the secret of that pitiful attitude which is not unfrequently witnessed among religious men — that pitiful attitude that would beg an affidavit of the truth and value of our Christianity from some leading politician, or of that poor faith that exhibits so wondrous a delight at a compliment paid to the Bible in a scientific convention, or reserves its cautious decision on the most important interpretations, and the most important doctrines of the Bible, until science — this kind of science — has spoken.

But we protest against it. The Scripture is to be interpreted from itself, and by this we mean, not only its own direct utterances, but all things that by fair hermeneutical laws stand connected, historically and psychologically, with the conceptions of those who were made the medium of such revelation, and with the language which they were directed or permitted to employ as the direct out-birth or growth of such conceptions. In a late admirable sermon before one of our ecclesiastical

Assemblies, a distinction is made, in this respect, which has the appearance of being not only fair for the Scriptures, but philosophically sound. Still, with all our respect for the pious and learned author, we can not accede wholly to his position. When carefully examined, it seems to us to surrender the main ground of the Bible authority and put it too much under the patronage of science. " Where the subject belongs more properly to revelation," to use his own language, " we are to be governed by the laws of interpretation, and Scripture thus interpreted is paramount. Where it belongs more properly to science then her decision is to be deferred to." It seems fair and rational; but the very illustrations immediately brought forward show, we think, the fallacy of the distinction. The creation of man as one primus homo, the author would regard as belonging to the first class; the question of creation, or of the indefinite creative period, he concedes to the second.* In the one, accordingly, science, whatever she may seem to discover, must yield to exegesis; in the other, exegesis yields to, or rather, is to be made out by the decisions of science. Hence, he says " the question whether the word day (yom) in the First of Genesis signifies a period of twenty-four hours, or a longer period, may be safely left to be determined by the investigations of Geology." We can not admit the ground of the distinction. The attempt to make it only gives rise to a still more difficult question than either,—that is, if it is to be settled by our philosophical reason without appealing to Scripture itself. It is this. What questions " belong more properly to revelation" ? Can anything decide this but revelation itself properly interpreted ? Can any one tell us what God ought to teach us, or may properly teach us, except God himself? "Who hath been his counsellor" in this respect? The question keeps coming up — What was the Bible intended to teach us? *Just what it does teach us*, is the only answer consistent either with reason or a proper deference to what we believe to be a divine authority. It alone can define its own province. To concede this to anything outward is to abandon the whole ground. If the interpretation of YOM is to be taken from philological science (including in the term all of history, of archæology and of psychology that belongs to it,) and given to Geology, why should not the word ADAM, in like manner, be surrendered to Physiology, or anything else that may put forth its great pretensions under such a name? If one is to be given up to Professor DANA, why should not the other, in like manner, be yielded to Professor AGASSIZ, who maintains, or must maintain, if he pretends to interpret Scripture at all, that the word ADAM must be taken generally, or generically, to denote *humanity** instead of one single man. This he says it must mean to be consistent with certain facts he has discovered, or thinks he has discovered. Now we do not think much of his facts; but his reasoning would be as good as that of Professor DANA'S, and the concession to him equally rational. If, as interpreters, we agree with either, or disagree with both, it can only fairly be upon the ground that such opinion is really consistent with the words and context of Scripture, or that there is something on the face of the language which excludes one interpretation

*And that, too, not as *one in many*, grounded on one-ness of law and idea developed from a once actual unity, but as a *many in one class*, grounded on resemblance and held together by arbitrary *definition*.

of science (if we may call any decision of science an interpretation) and demands the acceptance of the other, either as directly made out, or simply because there are greater hermeneutical difficulties in rejecting it. Thus, for example, we fairly and safely believe in the *one primus homo*, and in the *indefinite periods*, on the same hermeneutical grounds. The word ADAM *may* have a generic sense, as the word YOM may have either an unmeasured or a twenty-four-hour sense. We believe, however, that ADAM means a single man, because there are insuperable hermeneutical difficulties connected with the other view — difficulties arising from the immediate context and from other parts of the Bible. So we believe that YOM in Genesis I, was meant to be indefinite, or at least, could not have been intended for a solar period of twenty-four hours, *because* such view can not be *exegetically* reconciled with the account of the first ante-solar days — *because* it creates a difficulty that must have been as patent to the first writer as any science can now make it,— and *because* the other interpretation best harmonizes with other parts of the Bible and the soundest ideas we can form of the ancient thinking. On such grounds,—all hermeneutical in distinction from geological,—we base our decision. If science agrees with it, so much the better for science. The interpreter may admit that some of her discoveries, or her loud talking about them, have aroused him to a more full examination of the matter. But this is all that can be rationally conceded in the case. To make natural science itself the interpreter of Scripture is as great a solecism in language as it is an absurdity in idea. The highly respected authority we have quoted would certainly not carry it thus far. If he means that one of these positions is more important than the other, and that on the less vital question we may concede more to science, we should not differ much from him. But this can not affect the principles or true idea of interpretation. The greater or less importance of the truth, if it is truth, which God has condescended to teach us, can make no difference as to the mode by which it is deduced, or not deduced from the Scriptural language. Whatever can not be made out, and fairly made out, from the Scriptures, is not taught in the Scriptures—is not a doctrine or dogma of the Scriptures We can not well conceive of any proposition more rational or more directly applicable to our present subject.

It is further urged that it was "from want of attention to this distinction, there arose the persecution of Galileo," and the controversy in respect to Joshua x, 13. We would most respectfully venture to call in question both these views. There is good reason to believe that the Italian shared the free-thinking spirit, at that time prevalent, with other savans of his age and nation. He was as fond of controversy as the priests, and provoked it by a display of his science in that very way that would look most like a collision with the Scriptures. It was the scientific narrowness against the hierarchal narrowness—with this difference, that the priests, mistaken as they may have been, both in scientific fact and sound interpretation, were contending for truths, and consequences as involved therein, with which all the science of Galileo, and of all the savans of his day, or of all succeeding days, bore no comparison, either of value in itself, or of interest to man. That there was something wrong in the spirit of this oft-quoted witness, is made evident from the case of Copernicus, who published freely the same views in Astronomy, as also other men of his day, without calling out any persecution, or, in fact, the least opposition from the Church. The error of the enemies of Galileo was an error, not of science, but of interpretation. It was that common fallacy of confounding language descriptive of a fact, as represented by a phenomenon, with the more or less remote causality of that phenomenon. There are hundreds of passages of Scripture where the same blunder might be made as well as here. That there was a supernatural prolongation of the day is the phenomenal fact. The "sun did not go down" at the usual time, but continued in the heavens. This is all that the language of Scripture is responsible for. The appearance might be identical with the causality, or it might not. There might be a near or a remote connection. There might be in this causality but one wheel, and that the actual motion of the sun around the earth;—there might be in it wheels so many that even the best modern science has not begun to count them. As long as no difference between the phenomenon and the causality was known, or even suspected, it made no difference as to the interpretation. The actual reality of the miracle was as sure, and as great, on one view as on another; but to have made the language responsible for any causality that might exist, or be supposed or suspected to exist, would have been as much a violation of sound hermeneutical principle before the scientific discovery as after. And so all the best minds in the Roman and Protestant Churches at once perceived it. The case has been kept up by a certain class of scientific writers, who for some reasons find it too valuable to let drop. For centuries it has given no trouble to any devout man of ordinary intelligence, and yet the stale story is repeated ad nauseam. We can hardly hear a lecture without it; as though, at this day, men of science were actual martyrs, or professed it at the peril of their lives. In view of the exceeding staleness of the story, and the infidel hostility it often so unmistakably manifests, we might almost be led to regard the priestly intolerance as certainly a more respectable, though equally unjustifiable, exhibition of human nature. It may seem that we are dealing in paradoxes, and yet there are good grounds for saying, that the governing principle of the Italian priests was in substance, if not in form, very much like that of some modern men of science. The appearances are different; the spirit and end are the same. The reasoning, too, possesses some striking points of resemblance. The interpretation of the Bible made by the priests was to them a finality; just as some now hold in respect to the language of science. The Scriptural language denoted only the phenomenal fact according to the then knowledge, or rather, want of knowledge, of the causality; but those "literal interpreters" held it responsible for the ultimate causality itself as irrevocably determined by that knowledge. Now, just in the same manner, and with the same bigoted spirit, too, talk some of our modern men of science. They have groped their way along to a few more interior links of this immense chain; they have got a few inches beneath the surface of things, and, therefore, they resent the bare suspicion that gravities may yet be found imperfect, as vortices have been, or that the present language of science may ever become obsolete, or be laid aside as grounded on conceptions found to be inadequate and therefore delusive. For the language of Scripture we need never fear this; since it is built on those first phenomena that are the same for all ages, for all eyes, and therefore can never vary whilst human eyes and minds remain the same.*

* We do not attach much importance to the particular Hebrew verb used Joshua x, 13. It may be said, however, that the word דמם or דום, has nothing to do with the idea of motion. It implies neither motion nor stoppage, but simply a *remaining of things* as they are, or were, at any one moment of time. Such is the radical idea of the root in the Arabic, although in the Bible the most common thought connected with the word is that of silence, quietness, or repose. This radical idea appears most expressively, as well as beautifully, in an Arabic formula which has every appearance of great antiquity. They say, (using this verb,) "the sun *stands still* in the summit of heaven." Or, as it is better given in the Latin, *substitit sol in culmine cæli*. It is their phrase for what we would call *high noon*, when the sun seems to be almost motionless, and the hours move exceedingly slow. The Greeks have the same etymological image in their phrase σταθερὸν ἦμαρ, which is also applied to the noon, or the time when the sun seems to stand still. The reader will find a very clear explanation of this language as given by the scholiast Hermias on the Phædrus, p. 342, and quoted by Ruhnkenius in his Notes to the Lexicon of Timaeus. The contrast is beautifully presented between the seemingly motionless position of the sun at noon, and the comparative haste with which he rises and sets: at which latter time, especially, the rapid lengthening of the shadows furnishes the deepest contrast to their apparent meridian immovability. We dwell on this to show how purely phenomenal the word is, and how little it has to do with any matter of fact, or scientific, belief about the cause of the appearance, whether as existing in the earth, or sun, or both. The latter would be the answer of the highest philosophy; for all motion, or change in the relations of two bodies, is ever relative, as long as we bring in no third thing in respect to which one of them may seem to be immovable. In this case the language is not only phenomenal, but, in some sense, *subjective*. It is not only the appearance as presented to the *sense* alone, but that sensation, or rather perception, as affected by other thoughts and other associations of the mind. So might we treat the appearance recorded in Joshua, as a subjective slow moving of time, if all the other aspects of the account did not irresistibly force to the belief of an outward miracle in nature and natural causality.

The Bible must be interpreted by itself and of itself. We present it as the pervading thought of this introductory excursus on the spirit and position of science. It will be the leading idea never lost sight of in all the remarks that follow. The creative account must be interpreted from Scripture alone; and, when so interpreted, it will yield us a satisfactory resting place in certain great out-line ideas independent of science, but which she may fill up, if she will do it modestly and reverently, as she pleases;—SIX GREAT DIVINE WORKS, having respect not to the universe, or universal cosmos, but to our earth—each of these commencing with the going forth of a supernatural Word, and the energising of a supernatural Spirit,—and all followed by an ineffable divine REPOSE which still continues. Or, to state it another way—SIX GREAT DIVINE WORKS in SIX GREAT DIVINE DAYS, or periods—these periods incommensurable, that is, outside of any present cosmical measurements that might be used to determine either their brevity or their length—called *days*, not metaphorically, but because they are true days in their cyclical law—called also, and by the same authority, TOLEDOTHS, or GENERATIONS, because they were real *births* and *growths* through which God conducted this world from its chaotic infancy up to the crowning work in the creation of humanity, and the covenant made with the primus homo or head of the race.

We must have a fair interpretation that may stand, let Geology go where she will; and no one knows where that may be. She is now getting into no little confusion and speaks uncertainly. The time may possibly come, when she may give up her pleiocene, and eocene, her millions and billions of ages. She may discover or get some hint that there have been quicker powers in nature than had been dreamed of,—that there are reserve laws that operated of old, and that may operate again when the new period of travail comes after the long and silent gestation—laws and forces that may bring out, in very short times, series and generations that under other influences would seem to require an immensely longer duration. In such case, those in the Church who have had the most to say of "harmonies" might be disposed, perhaps, to retreat with her; and yet fair interpretation would remain unaffected amid all the changes of the science, or of its religious or scientific followers. Such fair interpretion would even then, as now, content itself by saying,—we have no right to set definite bounds either of *hours* or *ages* to what God has left indefinite—we have no right to measure what is left incommensurable by any cosmical standards which were themselves uncreated, and could not, therefore, have been measurers of the creative works.

Yes, the Bible must interpret itself. We must believe—if we believe at all—that it was meant to teach just what it does teach us. Thus, too, our highest and deepest ground of faith must be in the devoted study of the Book itself. Here must be our anchor. All evidences derived from science, let her be ever so favorably disposed, will fail us, and will fail the age, unless we hear that voice of authority speaking in the Scripture and to which the old divines so frequently refer. We have said that the thought was comparatively rare in modern times. It is, therefore, with no ordinary pleasure that we cite the testimony of one of our profoundest thinkers. The same idea is presented in a late Address of M. Guizot, at a late meeting of the Protestant Bible Society of France.

In distinction from all external testimonies, whether historical, philosophical, or scientific, he insists upon this "Divine Presence in the Scriptures," as the deep, soul-felt ground of their authority. "The examination of the Scriptures," says this pious statesman, "reveals difficulties, but these are only occasioned by human ignorance and human infirmity. Above them all appears the Divine character of the Sacred Books, the Divine Breath which fills and animates them. The movement may be sometimes obscure, but God is ever there. In every part is he to be seen, heard, felt. Through all difficulties, and through all obscurities, there is the constant view of God's presence, the constant sound of his voice." He makes no distinction between the New Testament and the Old. The Divine Presence is everywhere—no less majestic in some of the oldest than in the later portions of the same inseparable revelation. This noble testimony is no mere rationalizing, either after the manner of Locke or that of Cousin. Each would be equally external here. The idea of M. Guizot is the same with that of Owen and Hallyburton, and presented in nearly the same style of language. In his political retirement he has been a devout student of the Scriptures. Here is the ground of his faith. The same faith can only become general when the age gets tired of talking about "nature as a divine revelation," and in its exhaustion and its weariness sits down to the Bible to learn *how little we know*—how little all things else can teach us of the human origin, the human destiny, the true human history—in short, those higher truths of nature as well as of morals, aside from which philosophy is as sounding brass, and science but a tinkling cymbal.

CHAPTER II.

Scriptural Interpretation in Connection with Science—Nine General Principles—Application to the Creative Record—The Difficulty of a Solar Day without a Sun as obvious to Moses as to Mr. Lord—If there is any such Difficulty it is Patent on the Face of the Record—It has not come from Science, but from False Interpretation—Interpretation, therefore, and not Science, must Remove it—CREATION *an* ORDER OF APPEARANCES—*Each Appearance a Morning—Succession, not Duration, the Radical Idea.*

THE argument for the creative days has been already so fully treated that we would not weary our readers with even the appearance of repetition in respect to any matters of detail, or particular interpretation. There is, however, a synoptical view of the whole ground, that presents itself under somewhat new aspects, and which we would desire to give in a more condensed, and as we think, more convincing form.

The interpretation of the Bible must, of course, require more care than that of any other book. The principles of such interpretation must be high and broad just in proportion as we regard the author of the Scripture as divine. Yet still they lie within the fair range of the human intelligence; they must be the rules of reason and common sense properly elevated by a feeling of the sacred work in which the mind is engaged. We will proceed to state a few of those we cannot help deeming the most important.

1st. The record should be interpreted from itself. In doing this, single words should be defined by their use in other parts of the Bible, and especially as they lie in nearest connection with the passage explained.

2d. The difficulties acknowledged should be such as exist in the record itself—on the face of it. They must have been difficulties obvious to the writer and the men of his day for whom he wrote, and, therefore, inherent in the very nature of the descriptive narration. It follows from this, of course, that the solutions must be such as are furnished by the record; in other words, they must be such as might have been accepted by the writer and the men of his day.

3d. Whether the language is extraordinary or not, must be determined from the extraordinary nature of the facts recorded, and the known difficulty of setting them forth in any other way. This will not change the *radical conception** of a term; otherwise the language becomes entirely arbitrary and cabalistical; but it determines whether it is to be taken in a limited or an enlarged sense, and whether we have any right, a priori, to expect any such expansion of the word and the thought.

4th. If the idea of the ineffable and the anomalous is forced upon us in some parts, we may lawfully carry it

*As this term is frequently used by us, and is greatly liable to be misunderstood, we will define it, once for all, as that image which is most prominent, and most permanent, in the pictorial representation the mind is compelled to make of the idea, or thing thought. Thus, in the word and idea *day*, *period*, περίοδος, revolution, cyclity, ever remain, though other features, such as any particular duration, or modes of marking it, may conceptually vary to any extent.

into others in close connection with it. For example—if, in the creative account, we are compelled to admit that the Word, the Spirit, the Work, the Rest, are extraordinary or ineffable ideas, not to be measured by ordinary conceptions, we carry out the spirit of the interpretation when we apply the same rule of conceiving to the *times*. If God's *work* is not like our work, if his *rest* is not like our rest, then his *day* of working and his day of resting are not like our day. They must be in harmony with the other ideas, unless instantaneousness or suddenness is meant to be a chief feature of the account; of which there is no evidence, or rather there is the evidence of the contrary, on the face of the Mosaic narrative. We can not imagine anything more fair or rational than this.

5th. The individual or peculiar conception of the writer is not to be disregarded. Otherwise we make him a mere outward amanuensis; we have nothing to fix the idea or ultimate fact which his conception represents; we have nothing to determine it to one thing more than another; and thus, under pretence of magnifying revelation, we take from it all possibility of any definite interpretation that shall be catholic for all sane minds.

6th. The conception of the writer once ascertained is authority for the *fact* he would narrate, or the *thing* he would describe, as separate from all other facts or things; but it is not authority for the science of that fact or thing. Thus the language of Moses, in the account of the second day, shows that there lay in his mind the phenomena of the sky or atmosphere. He meant to narrate the making of this in the order of the terrestrial creation. The *fact* binds us, however erroneous may have been the attending *conception*. When we extend the language here to the nebular rings of science (whether real or imaginary) we travel out of the *fact*, as well as the *conception*. The consequence is that instead of a catholic interpretation, we have one that comes and goes with the varying mind, and varying imagination, and varying science of every age and of every special interpreter. Hence follows rule

7th. All science must be excluded, as well as all deductions from any science, which we are sure was unknown to the writer. Otherwise God did not make use of the mind of the writer, or the linguistic conceptions of the writer, but only his articulating organs or letter-tracing hand. Hence it follows, that the Bible contains no discoveries in science, properly so called, nor any revelation of facts which science is able to discover, but only of those great physical truths of origin which, in their very nature, lie beyond the field of all science — in themselves unknown alike to all — and which may be as easily announced to the common as to the most scientific mind.* Hence,

* We have elsewhere remarked upon this as drawing a distinctive line between the Bible and everything else assuming to be a revelation. It wholly avoids committing itself to any scientific or philosophical speculation, or to the language peculiar to such speculation. This is not from caution, but because the Bible thoughts are, in themselves, essentially above any theories or discoveries in science. In the sacred books of the eastern religions, the tendency to philosophise is plainly discernible. They contain pantheistic ideas which are evidently *after thoughts* of philosophising minds, such as the Egyptian priests or Indian Brahmins, striving to escape from common notions, and seeking to employ a vehicle somewhat different from the common speech. Extravagant and mythical as they are, they betray their human origin by their very attempts to get above humanity. Although there is no pantheism in the Koran, yet no one can study it carefully without seeing that Mohammed, ever and anon, has some crude scientific notion that warps his language. He talks of the earth, not phenomenally, as the Bible does, but in such a way as to give some of his extrav-

8th. That interpretation labors the most, which, in clearing up supposed difficulties in language, or narration, has to seek the most aid from the inferences of a science now known, but then unknown. Thus, Mr. LORD's theory is false, because he can not make a solar day of the first period, or give any consistent work to the fourth period, without bringing in rotating hemispheres, and varying inclinations of ecliptic axes, that, whether true or false scientifically, were utterly unknown to Moses either as facts or conceptions, and could, therefore, have been of no aid to him in solving a difficulty which, if it exists at all, lies now, and must have lain then, upon the face of the account.

agant Arabian traditions respecting the earth's form and place the appearance of cherished scientific hypothesis which he would put forth for its own sake. Sometimes, too, he gets hold of a psychological conceit, the display of which evidently forms a prominent design in the passage where it appears. Thus, the dependence of the time-conception on the conscious succession of thought had not escaped the musings of these sons of the desert. It is alluded to in Oriental tales, such as the striking story of the Magical Water to which Addison alludes in the Spectator. Now Mohammed evidently has this in view in his account of the Miraculous Sleepers in *Sura* XVIIIth of the Koran, entitled *The Cave*. On waking from their long unconscious state, they were asked for their estimate of the time that had elapsed; and Mohammed says that it was for the very purpose of testing them in this respect. It is evident that the philosophical interest, and the philosophical notion crude as it is in his mind, are predominant. How very different our own Holy Scripture. Time is nothing to the *un-thinking* it is *all-present*, without length or shortness, to the *All-Thinking*. And this idea is given us in the Bible, but not as a psychological truth or as having a philosophical value. All is subservient to a higher purpose, the ineffable glory of God. "A thousand years in thy sight are but as yesterday, when it is past, and as a watch in the night." Anything which should have looked like the set language of any philosophy, with any design, however faintly appearing, of making this philosophic interest predominant, would have impaired the thought, or rather the emotion of the thought, which is the vital thing; and so there is a resort to the impassioned poetical speech of the higher spiritual region.

9th. Therefore—The only office of science in respect to Biblical interpretation is to stimulate enquiry, and then chiefly as to the fact whether some plain statement of the record may not have been disguised or obscured by having had forced upon it changed conceptions arising from modern scientific discoveries. When it has thus aroused the mind to examine whether certain modern prejudices in regard to Bible language may not be false, it should never be allowed to force upon the Scriptures any mere possible interpretation to make the sense accord with any real or supposed state of scientific facts.

Let these rules be kept strictly in mind and we have a guide to a trust-worthy interpretation of the First of Genesis, carrying us safely between the ever-shifting demands of science, and the insane bigotry that would shut us up to one of the most narrow of modern conceptions. We get, as one might a priori expect, the extraordinary, the boundless, the sublime, without committing ourselves to nebulæ, or the uncertainties of ever-lengthening telescopes, on the one hand, or the narrowest anthropomorphism on the other.

The whole of the creative narrative in Genesis is sublimely pictorial; since in this way alone could it be sublimely truthful. Any other method of bringing it down to us would have involved more error and less reality. But as we have it, nothing could be more splendid for the imagination, and, at the same time, more satisfying to that philosophic intellect which regards all nature as but *appearances* of things unseen, and all science as but an arranging and classifying aid in the study of such appearances—following, indeed, its conclusions to a great distance, yet never really penetrating into that invisible world which lies back of them all.

The Mosaic Creation was an order and succession of appearances.

"In the beginning God made the Heavens and the Earth." What appearances are here intended? What beginning? What Heavens? What Earth? The language following explains this brief language of the Title or Caption. The writer, in what is said afterwards, commences with the Earth, although in the title itself it has the second place. The reason of this is plain. In the caption, where chronological order is unnecessary, or postponed to the order of ideas, the most striking object in the picture, or conception, is put first. On the other hand, in the narration itself, the time series rules. The creation of the *earth* is first set forth because it actually is first in time,—the heaven is built upon it, that is, the *sky* or atmospherical heavens, which is all that Moses had in mind, or was inspired to have in mind. This creation of the earth consists primarily in the change wrought upon that dark state where creation, the Mosaic creation, begins. It is brought forth into light and visibility. *It is made to appear.* The Spirit goes forth brooding on the waters, and this was the beginning recorded by Moses. There is a much more ancient beginning mentioned, John i, 1. That was from eternity. There may have been, *in time*, many other inceptive epochs in the great spiritual and material works of God. But this beginning, of which Moses informs us, was in the evening. With the Spirit comes the Word, and, straitway, there is an *appearance.* Light appears, and this was the morning. Those mighty beings called "Morning Stars," the yet unfallen Luciferi, "sing aloud, and the sons of God shout for joy." This was the morning. How can we think of a common morning here, or keep out those ideas of the extraordinary, of the ineffable, which, if once admitted, must give character to the whole subsequent account. God called this morning day. It is his own definition of the term. He does not define it by subsequent ideas, but by phenomena already mentioned. In thus naming there is no reference to duration, or to any measurement of times, but to division and contrast. It was the *morning* as compared with the old *night* of chaos, the new *appearance* as compared with the old invisibility. It could not have been a solar day; for as yet no sun, no moon had *appeared* in the heavens, although there was, somehow, a glorious light upon this infant world. Whether existing or not, these sky lamps were yet among the things unseen. Even the heavens, in which they were to have their optical manifestation, had not yet *appeared*. There was no sky, no *rakia*, or firmament, above. This certainly is safe interpretation. We cling close to Moses here. There was no visible sun to measure time, but still there was a day, a period characterized by most remarkable powers and manifestations. There was the Brooding Spirit, the Commanding Word; there was the terrific darkness on the waters, and the creative light that shone, not *from* a sun, but *out* of the darkness (ἐκ σκότους) as Paul says, in his significant comparison, 2 Cor. iv, 6; and thus "there was an evening, and there was a morning, one day." Who shall think of twenty-four hours here? We repeat it—because the more we meditate upon this strange language, the more strange it seems that any one should have ever had such a narrow conception whether in ancient or modern times.

Again goes forth the Word. The Firmament *appears* —the expanse above with its sailing waters—the old glorious, and yet still glorious sky. "And God called it Heavens." He has interpreted the language for himself. It is the same heavens mentioned in the first brief titular verse. Here we have a more particular account of its creation, or *building*, (κτίσις) in the work of the second day. This was the *making* of the heavens. Were they optical in some way? Were they lit up by an aurora, such as we have seen revealing the vaulted sky in a moonless night? We know not. Imagination may be soberly indulged, but all scientific hypotheses, as such, are worthless and contemptible. Was it so named in reference to the after appearance, when it reflected the light of the celestial lamps? Such a view may be indulged; but it is all conjecture. We cling close to Moses when we say there was a sky, a heavens, although no sun, no moon, no stars had as yet *appeared* therein. These were as yet invisible, and, in this sense, as non-existent to our earth as the satellites of Jupiter before the days of Galileo, or many of the nebular clouds before the making of Lord Rosse's telescope. But there was now a sky;—and here comes the same language, may we not say the same self-interpreting language, telling us, in unmistakable terms, what these strange mornings and evenings really are. Let the reader mark the constant order. There is a *division*, and then an *appearance*. As first the waters appeared when the light shone on them, or out of them, so now a sky *appears*, although no sun nor moon as yet appear in it. What prevented their being seen we know not. We have only to interpret, and to bring our imaginations into harmony with such interpretation; but Moses says that they were not appointed to their office, until the fourth day. Until this time — to use the paraphrase of the Son of Sirac — "they did not stand in their watches, giving light in the high places of the Lord." But here is a new division and a new appearance, and immediately is it said, there is a new morning, and a second day. What can be plainer, if a man will but throw away science, all narrow modern conceptions, and bring himself into the power and spirit of the language? *Each appearance is a morning*, so named from the fact of appearance, without any reference to duration or any present divisions of time. The language interprets itself. Each *appearance* is a *morning*. The appearance of the light was the first morning. The appearance of the sky was the second morning. The appearance of the earth rising out of the waters was the third morning. The *appearance* of the heavenly bodies, sun, moon and stars, in the sky or firmament where they had not appeared before, — this was the fourth most glorious morning. Each has its corresponding divisions so arranged in consecutive and ascending order as to make the conclusion irresistible, to a sober thinking man, that such first naming of the *day*, *night*, and *morning* is the clue, and was meant to be the clue, to all the rest. Divisions — contrasts — and contrasted successions, are the prominent ideas. Duration comes in not at all, unless we force it upon Moses. They were unmeasured days. We say this on the soberest principle, because there was no sun to measure them, and because we are expressly told when solar-measured days began, as if to mark the difference in a way that could not be mistaken. These divisions, moreover, were supernatural. God made them, as Augustine says, to distinguish them from the natural or the sun-made intervals of time which now exist.

The difficulty of a solar day without a sun must have been as obvious to Moses (had such been his view) as to us. It is not at all a difficulty made by science. The fact, therefore, that the writer does not attempt to solve it, or explain it, not even recognizing it, shows that he could not have regarded them as solar or common days. He had good reason to think that his readers would be so impressed with the feeling of the marvellous, the extraordinary, pervading the whole style and structure of the narration, that they would not need an explanation.

And here we may refer to our third rule, which those who can only see real or apparent salient points, might be ready to cite against us. 'The language must be defined by that which lies nearest to it, unless there is something in the face of the account that positively forbids.' We applied it to the word heavens, when we said it must have the same meaning in the third verse as in the first. The objection has been taken—why should not the word day have the same meaning in the second verse, as when used below of undoubted solar days? We might reply, in the first place, that it has the same meaning if, when we speak of a word's meaning, we look only to the essential idea. The nine-hour day of Jupiter, the twenty-four hour day of the earth, the six months' day of the pole, the millenial day of some of the immense astronomical cycles, or, in fact, any temporal period of a cyclical self-measuring character — all these are alike days in the essential idea, and the application of the term to one of them is no more metaphorical or secondary than it is to another. But if such answer is not satisfactory, we have one that is conclusive; and that is, that aside from any difficulties of science, the very record on the fair face of it forbids the inference from which the objection is supposed to derive its force. In the use of the word heaven no intimation is given of a different meaning, or we may rather say, a more or less extended application of the same idea.* The heaven made and mentioned in the third verse is the heaven mentioned in the second — the same in phenomenal conception, the same, we think, in supposed extent. But the day mentioned in the first and third verse, though truly, and not merely metaphorically, a day, or self-measuring period of time, was not, in extent at least, and other diurnal incidents, the day mentioned in a part of the fourth verse where the dividing office of the sun is first set forth. For this transition, there are certain irresistible evidences lying on the very face of the account. We repeat them because it is strange they should have been so over-

* The word heavens presents, in other aspects, a complete parallel. It carries the same essential idea, whether we apply it to the atmospherical heavens or the astronomical, although one is inconceivably more remote than the other, and in itself may present any number of gradations of the same conception. We find this latter, or astronomical sense, coming into the subsequent Hebrew writings, where they speak of the *heaven above the heavens*, 'or *heaven of heavens* (as though we should say day of days); but whether in the nearer or the larger view, it was the same radical conception, satisfied by the same term, and allowing of an immediate transition from one to the other, without surprize or any seeming need of explanation. Just so, in this very record, we have an undoubted transition in the use of the word day in the beginning of Chapter II, where it is applied to all the creative generations taken as one cycle.

looked in modern times, although they arrested the attention of older commentators. These latter mentioned days are expressly described as *sun-divided*—the first were *God-divided.* The one class lay within the natural ongoings of a system set in order, the other belonged to the supernatural originations. The one was connected with and measured by cosmical relations from without, the other had its measurement only from the work or law of working within; the one class were solar days keeping times for the inhabitants that should be on the earth, or for the internal economical arrangements of the earth itself; the other were *æonic* or olamic days measuring the earth's relations to the universal ongoings of time, or the great worlds or ages before and after. The proof of our assertion is, that there was no sun in the sky to divide them—the very manifestation of the sun is one of their works. It being certain, therefore, that they were not common or solar days in the more important idea (important we mean for a solar day) of being measured by the sun, we have no warrant at all for forcing in the narrow and far less essential idea of that exact duration which such a mode of measurement now gives, and on which such duration is entirely dependent. But this we have elsewhere discussed at length, and to it the reader is referred. It is an argument that Mr. LORD has made no attempt at answering, although it was put directly in his way. Why should the exact duration be insisted on when other and more essential elements of the idea of a common or solar day are necessarily excluded? The question is not answered. We do not think it can be answered.

But to resume our sketch. In the same manner might we go through the other great days. They present a continual succession of *appearances* or *mornings*. We had spoken of the glorious fourth day, when the Meorim or Great Lights (lighters, luminaries) are hung out in the heavens. Again goes forth the Omnific Word. There is a new *appearance*, a new life;—and this is the fifth morning. Again—an appearance still more remarkable—a higher life, and lo! a sixth new morning. And here the hitherto uninterrupted mention of the mornings and evenings ceases. The calendar closes, or rather this remarkable feature of it, before the creative history is fully completed. A seventh great day is mentioned, but not a seventh morning. It is the beginning of God's ineffable repose, whose glorious morn is not yet fully ushered in. Nature yet sleeps. It is the Sabbath eve of the world. What its full morning will be, can only be learnt, as far as it can be learned at all, from the prophetic Scriptures which are but the *complement of the creative history*. Science will never discover or define it.

There is no forced interpretation here; that is, it is not made by pressure from without. Everything we have said is in harmony with the spirit of the record and the grand ideas it most naturally suggests. Everything comes into place and proportion, if we will only take the right stand point—if we will only divest ourselves alike of our modern science, and our modern bigotry, whilst we interpret the first supernatural voice of God to our world, in a manner consistent with its enchanting simplicity, and on a scale commensurate with its ineffable grandeur.

CHAPTER III.

THE WORD DAY, AND THE MYSTIC NUMBERS OF PROPHECY.

Various Senses of the Word Day—Summary of Principles concerned in its Interpretation—Eight Heads of Argument —The Prophetical Day—Analogous to the Creative Day —Numbers as used in Prophecy—Three kinds—Definite Numbers—Round Numbers—Perfect Numbers—The Word Day as applied to the Closing Dispensation of the World—Analogy with the Creative Account—Kedhem, or the Ante-time State.

NEXT to the general principles of interpretation would come the more particular arguments applicable to words of time, and especially the leading word *day*. In respect to this whole class of terms, there is an important and interesting enquiry. Have we good reason for thinking that there is a wide difference between the most ancient and the most modern mode of conception connected with them? Hence the great question which is the hinge of the whole discussion, and which we would state clearly, yet in a manner wholly independent of science, or of any scientific deductions. Was the creative day just twenty-four hours in length, or was it indefinitely longer, and yet a real day, not metaphorically, but strictly and truly a day, in its essential, cyclical, self-measuring idea, though undefined in the merely incidental feature of its duration, whether relatively long or short—that is, in comparison with any times out of itself. Whether such a view would satisfy any real or fancied difficulties of science, was not the enquiry. It was hoped it might do something towards such a result. Scientific men differ about it. Some of highest note think it would furnish a fair ground for a harmony; others would still reject the idea of reconciliation on this or any other ground. It would be absurd in the writer to say he felt no interest in the fact of such agreement; but he certainly can say that he would not allow it to affect the principles or method of the Biblical enquiry. What is the fair interpretation of the word *day*, as it stands in a certain very ancient Record dealing in very extraordinary ideas, and expressed in very remarkable language? This enquiry pervades the book which has been charged with naturalism; everything is subservient to such an issue. All seemingly divergent discussions grow out of it, return to it, and terminate in it. The arguments, or heads of arguments, in support of it, may be thus briefly re-stated, and presented in one view to the reader. There is,

I. The metaphorical sense. This, although the first, does in fact furnish the least reliable argument. It has been the one usually and mainly employed in favor of the general idea of long periods, and yet it is one on which alone we would not dare to rest the great question. It gives a *possible* interpretation, barely reaching to a probability, perhaps, but nothing beyond it. We want something more than metaphors for a foundation here. We make the distinction because this metaphorical sense has been confounded with something widely different and entitled to far more consideration. This is,

II. The cyclical idea, or the evidence for the cyclical meaning of the word day. A metaphor, as the etymology implies, is a change, a transfer of a word from one department of ideas, and that its native department, to another. The essential notion is exchanged for a resemblance or analogy more or less fanciful or real. In the essential idea of the word day, the chronological, or the thought of an absolute time complete in itself, yet standing in some relation to other absolute time, or times, is an inseparable element. The metaphorical use, on the other hand, *transfers* the word to the expression of a mere *state* of being having strictly nothing chronological, that is, no real connection with absolute time or any like recurring periods before and after. Thus the "day of joy," the "day of adversity," the "day of prosperity," etc. These are all metaphorical. They denote no real time — they are subjective mainly, and belong not to the absolute chronology of the earth, or the universe. Now take another class of expressions — the "days of creation," the "day when God made the heavens and the earth," including all the subdivisions (Gen. II), the "days of prophecy," the "latter day," the "day of Christ's reign," the "last day," the "day of Judgment," the ἡμέρα αἰῶνος of St. Peter, (2 Pet. iii, 18) — these, it must be felt at once, have a very different character. They are chronological,— completed by an inner cyclical law of their own, or by the divine supernatural divisions, yet connected in the great chronology with similar periods going before and following after them. To a superficial view, this may seem a metaphorical sense, but it is widely and essentially diverse.

III. The mention of the morning and evening, and the peculiar order in which they are repeated as indicative of something remarkable in the day requiring such emphatic repetition, and as explanatory of the name from the fact of two such contrasted states of one period—whatever those states might be.

IV. The absence of the sun until the 4th period, and the consequent impossibility and unimaginability of those more common characteristics that mark the common solar day.

V. The employment of words of *generation*, or terms carrying in their roots the ideas of *growth* and birth, that is of nature—like the Hebrew תולדות—and the using these for the ages, growths, successions, or *days* of the earth.

VI. The remarkable language that is held respecting the earth's first productions in the third and fiftth days,—language implying growths, natural causalities, (though divinely quickened,) and hence driving us to the idea of successions, and consequent durations exceeding one revolution of the sun.

VII. Argument from the Sabbath—the divine Sabbath as a continued and present repose from creation.

VIII. The ground of the whole discussion as sought in the old idea of the olams or time-worlds, or *ages*, so strangely used in both the old and later Scriptures for the very *worlds* themselves.

Such is the outline of the argument and its pervading aim. It may be said of it here that all that looks like naturalism (and the careful reader must see that it is only in appearance or from a perversion of language) grows out of closely following the record, in the remarkable language applied to the vegetable and animal growths —"Let the earth bring forth—Let the waters bring forth." If it is naturalism at all, it is the bold naturalism of Scripture, such as a poetical myth-maker, or a sentimental religionist, or even a science that takes special pains to be pious, would never have ventured upon. If it is naturalism at all, it is a naturalism grounded on close interpretation of the only record, and ready to be abandoned at once whenever that interpretation is shown exegetically to be false. We do not wish to be wiser than what is written, or, through fear of an odious name, to shun the acknowledgment of what seems to be really revealed as God's chosen manner of working. The hypothetical reasonings, which have been so unfairly distorted, and even called "the prominent positions" of the writer, every candid reader must see are simply statements (with answers to them) of objections that might be made on other points, if such were the true interpretations in those that are directly treated.

This argument in its broad outline—we say it freely and fearlessly—has not been met. The book has been the subject of two hostile reviews, one assuming the special guardianship of the Bible, the other the no less zealous championship of science. Of both, however, it may be truly said that they have not affected, and hardly touched, a point on which the true merit or demerit of the work might be said to depend. The editor of the Literary and Theological Journal keeps up a standing cry of infidelity, danger to the Scriptures, undermining the faith, Platonism, etc. He sees a total wreck of all belief in revelation, if this twenty-four hour idea is in the least called in question. How the faith and integrity of

Scripture is so vitally connected with this particular interpretation he does not pretend to say. Why there might not be a long day in creation as well as in prophecy, in the archæology, as well as in the eschatology of Scripture, is nowhere shown, or why the large scale of the word and the idea is not as rational and as natural in the one case as in the other. The interpretations are not even examined to any extent worth noticing. Words, idioms, texts, in the analysis of which great pains have been taken, whether to any purpose or not, have not even been noticed. The startling difficulties which on the twenty-four hypothesis lie on the very face of the account, are hardly alluded to as difficulties at all; except it be to bring in a great number of purely gratuitous scientific guesses—the strongest evidence that this easy literal theory, as it styles itself, is, of all others, the most difficult and unsound.

In addition to this general outline view of the word day, in its varied, hermeneutical uses, there may be properly presented here a few remarks on Mr. LORD's employment of the same word, and his inconsistency in so freely applying to prophecy what he denies in any sense to creation. This belonged more strictly to the second division of our summary, or that grounded on the distinction between the metaphorical and cyclical meaning. As it would, however, have interrupted the order of outline, we have reserved it for this part of the chapter. The fact to which attention is specially called is, that, Mr. LORD, and others of the same school, are compelled to bring in the aid of this cyclical idea in the interpretation of the prophetical Scriptures. What he will not listen to for a moment when predicated of the beginning, or *first times* of the earth, he takes for his fundamental thought in all that relates to the closing days of the mundane history — or, to speak a little more pointedly and pertinently,— what he regards as most infidel and dangerous in archæology, is most Biblical, most evangelical, and most pious, in eschatology. He never thinks of limiting the Day of Judgment as revealed in Mathew and Revelations (if both passages mean the same) to a period of twenty-four hours; in fact his reasoning is altogether inconsistent with any such idea; and yet it is most emphatically called in the Gospels the Last Day — or the Latter Day. So also of the day of prophecy in general. He is compelled to regard this as something different from the common solar diurnal measurement. The style of speech, the hue of thought, the elevation of idea, the accompanying emotion, which are all connected with the glowing, aweing, mystical and mysterious language of prophecy, will not permit. He is forced to take up his position in a wider and freer space. We are in the midst of the extraordinary, and ordinary words naturally and easily take on extraordinary meanings — that is, meanings not radically different, but on a larger scale. We have that feeling of vastness which so much more freely arises in the contemplation of the unknown, unmeasured future, or the remote unmeasured past, than in the survey of the well mapped historic present, as we may style the region that lies divided and subdivided in the current astronomical chronology. This is the real ground for expanding, both in emotion and idea, the time words of prophecy. Mr. Lord feels it like other commentators, but when hunting for reasons in favor of such a mode of interpretation, he returns right back to his old narrowness. He would sustain this extra-twenty-four hour view of the word day from a few passages of Scripture which have with it merely an incidental association of thought, such as Ezek. iv, 4, 6, Daniel viii, 14; but these when examined are found to be far from sufficient in themselves to furnish a trusty ground for so important a principle of interpretation. Mr. LORD is not content with it. His next thought is a glimpse of the truth in the innate cyclical or periodical idea of the word day. The essence of it is revolution. But the year also is revolution. Therefore a day may stand for a year. We will give his own language (Lord on the Apocalypse, p. 252): "A day during which the earth revolves upon its axis has a *resemblance* which fits it to be a *symbol of the period of its revolution* round the sun." Although there seems to have been chiefly in his mind the mere outward *resemblance*, yet still he recognizes, although very inadequately, the cyclical *idea*. Instead, however, of making *day*, thus viewed, the representative of cyclical period in general, he treats it as the arbitrary symbol of another period, simply because that second period is a multiple, or pretty nearly a multiple, of the first. It is just as though, in space, he should make a circle of one foot radius, the symbol of one that had a rod or a mile radius.

"In like manner," he continues, "a month, during which the moon revolves upon its axis, has a *resemblance* which fits it to be a symbol of the period of its revolution round the sun. The forty-two months are therefore by the same law (the law of mere quantitative resemblance!) twelve hundred and sixty years, and solar years *doubtless*; as, though the monthly division was drawn from the revolution, yet it was reckoned of thirty as well as of twenty-nine days, and the year itself was determined by the revolution of the earth round the sun."

But the greatest difficulty found by Mr. LORD,—as

appears from his effort to remove it,—arises from the fact that the solar day cycle, in its absolute duration, is not any aliquot part of the *annus*, and therefore, on the principle of divisibility alone, can no more symbolize it than the side can symbolize the diameter of the square. The two quantities (viewed simply as quantities, or aside from their common cyclical idea) are incommensurable; —in other words, no number of our present days, carried to any conceivable height short of infinite, can ever make any exact number of our present years. Extend the ratio ever so far and there are fractions still. The year we know is not 365 days, but 365 days, 5 hours, 54 minutes, so many seconds, so many thirds, etc., etc., etc. Here, therefore, he is compelled to break his own symbolic law (which he has a perfect right to do since it is a law of his own making,) or introduce a looseness that renders it worthless. But let us hear his own statement of the difficulty:

"It may be thought an obstacle to this construction that, as the period of a lunar revolution is not thirty days, forty two lunar months are not equal to twelve hundred and sixty days. But neither are twelve hundred and sixty days equal to the number in three and a half years, nor the number in forty-two months, of thirty days each, equal to the number in three years and a half; the astronomical year consisting of 365 days and a fraction in place of 360, at which it was reckoned by the Jews and other eastern nations, yet three hundred and sixty days were taken as the period of revolution of the seasons, or the year, although they were known not to be the true period, and thirty days were taken also as the period of a lunar revolution, or a month, although they were, in like manner, known not to be the true period."

Now what a calculation is this? Especially when we bear in mind, that it is a leading idea of this writer, that these numbers were given to enable us to fix satisfactorily the prophetic times and seasons as they actually occur in history, (whether of the past, the present, or the future,) to determine accurately their beginnings, continuance, and ending. This he regards as an important and chief design of the prophetical writings. It is a maxim of law, *de minimis non curat lex;* but this will not do in prophecy, if the fixing of times is its chief, or one of its chief objects. But it is not a question *de minimis.* The throwing away five days and a half in each year would make quite a difference in the beginning and ending of any period he might choose to estimate. It would leave these important dates — important if it is the design of prophecy to have them fixed — a generation or two in utter uncertainty. In a millenium of 365,000 years, which is Mr. Lord's computation, it would make a difference of 5,000 years. If we take into the estimate merely the fraction of a day, 5 hours, 54 minutes, etc., then, instead of 365,000, it would be 365,296 years, with odd months, days and hours still remaining. There is the same difficulty, only arithmetically more perplexing, attending the computation of months as intermediate between the day symbol and the year. Mr. Lord is compelled to throw off all the fractions, and this on no other authority than his own artificial law. How does he know but that there may be mysteries in these fractions, or that they may not symbolize occult times, and occult events, which may have an important bearing on the great result. They may represent secret nooks or niches in history, either of the past or future, that, instead of deserving to be thrown away, in this manner, may demand his deepest symbolical research. If he has a right to reject these, another commentator has a right to take them into the account, and rectify his computation accordingly. Such consequences would seem to come directly from the rule or principle adopted, of making one measure of time or space a symbol of another, not from the general cyclical idea, but chiefly on the ground that in arbitrary quantity one is a multiple, or nearly a multiple, of another. We would treat this subject with all reverence. Every interpretation of Scripture brought out by any serious mind is entitled to our respect. But we can not help distrusting a method which would thus make important periods, or rather important ideas, in prophecy thus to depend on the varying calculations coming from adopting this or that canon by which scientific or unscientific ages and nations have regulated their ever ill-regulated calendar. If the day may symbolically represent a little less or a little more than the year's revolution, (to say nothing of the fact that both the daily and the yearly revolution may in some remote periods be astronomically very different from what they now are,) then it may represent whatever the fancy of the interpreter may connect with such arbitrary measurements.* Instead of treating the prophetic arithmetic in this conven-

* It need only to be remarked that this is said wholly of the actual fulfilment. Such fulfilment will, of course, be exactly true on some principle in nature, or in numbers, or in natural and historical causes, that will allow of no uncertainty. But in the manner of representing it, whether symbolically, or by any other kind of language, words, and the attending conceptions partake of all the imperfections belonging to every kind of human media. The sacred writer may use 30 days for a month, and 360 days for a year,—we think he does so,—but it is not easy to bring ourselves to believe, that if the millenial aeon is to be exactly 365,000 years, it will not be that number of years in their natural, perfect estimate, but, in fact, 364,704 such years, in order to correspond to an imperfect mode of reckoning employed so far off in the infancy of our world. In other words, the prophetic fulfilment can not share the imperfection of the symbol (for that imperfection is a *changing quantity*) and, therefore, on this principle, the interpreter is bound to apply his science to verify the result. We say, *on this principle*, for the very fact that such scientific estimates must be applied, shows that the multiple principle itself, as thus employed, must be fundamentally wrong.

ient fashion, the safest, although perhaps not the easiest, way, would be to keep in the fractions. Some of the Millerite calculations had to be altered and re-altered on this principle. At times the error was supposed to arise from the fractions being put on, and again from their being left off. Peace to those deluded men. We would not join even the religious world in scoffing at them. There is something more sublime in their error than in many of the world's most lauded truths. They had a great principle of faith to which we who so often repeat in our creeds that "Christ shall come to judge the quick and the dead at the last day," have become too indifferent, if we may not say too sceptical. But they erred as to times. They carried out too faithfully that same idea of multiples to which Mr. LORD tries in vain to adhere, and in which attempt, both he and they go contrary to the Scriptural declaration that it is not for men "to know the times and seasons which the Father hath put in his own power." It is not on the ground of equal quantitative ratios, exact fractions, or aliquot parts, but as representative directly, and not metaphorically, of the cyclical idea, that the word day seems to be used in the language both of creation and prophecy. In both cases great outlines, orders, successions, contrasts, and relative proportions of events, are shadowed forth, rather than exact durations, whether of hours or of years, or any current dates in the anno domini astronomical calendar, whether regulated by the Cæsar, the Parliament, or the Pope.

Mr. LORD starts with something of this cyclical idea, but spoils it in carrying it out. A little thought would show us that the day in prophecy is not to be bound down by any such nice calculations, any more than terms of space used in a precisely similar manner. A furlong in the Holy City might just as well be made a symbol of a mile, or of a league, or of a geographical degree, and with even more ease, for these measures are exact multiples and divisors of each other. We might just as well attempt, in this way, to give the dimensions of the New Jerusalem as its chronology,—its territorial extent in space, as well as the months and years and millenia of God's kingdom in time. The Apostolical Seer has presented to us a glorious picture of the Civitas Dei—its twelve pearly gates, its harmonious geometrical dimensions, its river of water of life, its trees and fruits, its "gardens and its pleasant walks,"

> Its bulwarks of salvation strong,
> And streets of shining gold.

Now, in utter contempt of all this spiritual beauty, one might as well attempt to bring it into feet and barleycorns, or to determine its latitude and longitude on the celestial sphere, as apply any analogous computation of current years or centuries to the ages that precede it, or that measure its continuance.

There are in Scripture two very distinguishable methods of employing numbers in their relations to time and space. Both of them are found in the prophetical writings. These are, 1st, definite numbers, or those that *appear to be such*, and, 2d, what may be called full and perfect numbers, or, as we sometimes style them, round numbers. The first class would *seem* to be used for no other purpose than the mere designation of quantity, or to mark definitely some actual number, extent, or magnitude, in that of which they are predicated. In the use of the second, precise quantity, if it be meant at all, is more easily seen to be a subordinate idea. The structure or peculiar law of such numbers shows that some other thought connected with them is predominant. This may be fullness, roundness in the sense of harmonious complement of parts, or, if it be quantity at all, it is quantity in its more general and comparative aspects of greatness or brevity rather than precise numerical extent. Such numbers as the 1260 days of Revelations, and the 1260 and 1290 of Daniel, would seem to have their place in the first class. As belonging to the second, there would easily suggest themselves "the twice ten thousand chariots of God," in the LXVIIIth Psalm; the "ten thousand times ten thousand" of the celestial armies mentioned by Daniel; some of the estimates in Ezekiel's Vision, such as the successive thousand cubits of the mysterious river that came forth from the temple, the 144,000 whom John saw standing on Mount Zion, the cubical dimensions of the New Jerusalem, the numbers 3, 7 and 12, as variously used in the Bible, and especially the 1,000 years or millenium of the Apocalypse.

It is the first kind of numbers as used by Daniel and John, or as they *seem to be used* by them, that has formed the favorite study of a certain class of commentators. The great yet ever unsuccessful effort has been to get the 1260 days into current anno domini years, with a fixed beginning and end corresponding to some known events in history. This has been on the principle of a day for a year regarded as sanctioned by such passages as Ezekiel iv, 4-6; or on the more satisfactory ground, which Mr. LORD partly assumes, of the common cyclical idea, whereby one may be taken as the representative of the other. It is, however, a very fair question, whether these numbers are really intended for definite representatives, or do not, in fact, and notwithstanding their appearance of precision, belong to the second class. That they can be reduced to it, we think can be made to appear from the following considerations. The careful reader can not overlook the fact that, in both the prophetic parts of the Bible referred to, these apparently so definite numbers occur in unmistakable connection with another expression of the opposite character, but evidently intended to denote the same time, times, or periods, whatever they may be. Ever accompanying the 1260 days, both in Daniel and John, are the "time, times, and the dividing of a time" of the one, and the "time, times, and half a time," of the other*—or, if we employ the dual, as it is clearly implied in the plural form of the Hebrew word, it would be, "a time, two times, a dividing of a time." Now the one of these, or the 1260 days, has a strong appearance of arithmetical precision; the principal feature of the other is its mystic indefiniteness,—and yet there can be no doubt that they refer to the same periods, and include the same class of events. The question, therefore, fairly arises—which of these presents the fundamental conception, and is therefore to control in the interpretation of the other. We have no hesitation in answering, the latter. The indefinite is the ground, and the apparently definite is derived from it. Aside from

*Daniel, xii, 7, vii, 25, Apoc. xii, 14. "And he sware by Him who liveth for ever that in a time, times, and division of a time, and when there shall be finished the scattering of the Holy People, all these things shall be completed." Vulgate—*in tempus*, tempora, et dimidium temporis.—LXX—καιρὸν, καιροὺς, ἥμισυ καιροῦ.

such a view being more in accordance with the general style of prophecy, which is emphatic in respect to courses of events and ideas, whilst it is designedly enigmatical in respect to precise times and seasons, being truly a revelation of the one whilst it is in general an obvelation of the other—aside from this, we say, there is a stronger reason, and one which seems to us to be conclusive. Unless we regard the "time, times, and dividing of time," as the fundamental conception, we can find no significance in these larger divisions. That is, on the other view, the three times and a half time, do not denote *three* prophetical periods, each having a character of its own which makes it stand by itself, and a fourth such period or division uncompleted; but this extraordinary language is merely a vague expression for another representing a *continuous* period in which there is no other division but the current times (be it days or years) of the almanack. It is true, the number 1260 may be broken up in this same ratio, and for $1 + 2 + \frac{1}{2}$, may give us $360 + (2 \times 360) + 180$, or $12 + (2 \times 12) + 6$; but the very doing so implies that the simple ratio is the fundamental conception on which the others have been constructed. At least, it must have been so to the mind that first entertained and uttered it. After the numbers have been given to us, we can proceed either way, from the divisors to the multiples, or from the multiples to the divisors. If the 1260 is the ground conception, then there is no significance in the *three* divisions and a half. They belong merely to the composition of the number, and do not outwardly represent a corresponding *triad* of times, definite or indefinite, in either the outward or spiritual history of the world or the Church. If so, they are utterly unmeaning as far as their trinal and dimidial ratio is concerned. But it is not easy or natural thus to regard it. The "time, two times, and dividing of a time," must have a significance, not only in its total amount, which is all that some interpreters ever look for, but in its great divisions whether those divisions denote any definite number of current years or not.

Thus, if we have made our meaning clear, the 1260 is derived from the $3\frac{1}{2}$, but it is difficult to see how, on any rational ground, the conceptual process could be reversed, or the $3\frac{1}{2}$ derived from the 1260, unless the former had been someway in mind in the construction of the latter number. Any other view makes the mind of the medium a purely arbitrary receptacle, with a blank numerical conception instead of any idea, thought, or view, out of which the conception arises, and to which it has a rational correspondence. That is not the doctrine of plenary inspiration. It would not even be verbal, but purely cabalistical.

We firmly believe, not only in the *plenary*, as the term is commonly used, but also in the verbal inspiration of Scripture. That is, the language as well as the thought is strictly designed by the Divine Wisdom. The supernatural impulse, though distinct and special in itself, and having a special purpose, yet works in perfect harmony with the laws that connect utterance, conception, and emotion. And yet there is a reason for every metaphor, for every mode of speech, for every peculiarity of style, that grows out of the individual mode of feeling and conceiving. Such metaphors and peculiar modes of speech, therefore, instead of being overlooked as no part of the true word, or treated as mere matters of rhetorical criticism, may oftentimes require the deepest study as manifesting the divine no less in the *manner* of utterance than in the *matter*. Yet still, these conceptions have their true and orderly growth in the human soul, and after the laws of the human soul. If God employs true human language, he employs also the human images that lie at the foundation of such language,—nay, more, the feelings, whether naturally existing, or supernaturally aroused, that give *birth* to such images and conceptions. The dignity of revelation is no more impaired by the one supposition than by the other. The opposite view seems to take high ground, and to honor the Bible by depressing the mental condition of the medium. It gives, however, the lowest and loosest results; for by denying any fixed and fundamental conception having a natural, and therefore, determinable place in the mind of the sacred writer, it becomes the cause of all looseness and arbitrariness in the conception of the interpreter.

But how account for the 1260? It may be regarded, without much difficulty, as nothing more than a varied expression to give it more of that enigmatical aspect which is a designed feature of the Scriptural hidha,* or oracle.

* We use this term, חידה, because of its peculiar significance in the Bible. It is not that mere matter of amusement we call the riddle, but something as significant, that is in its own way, as any other form of speech. It is used for as definite a purpose as the parable or the simile. It distinctly announces two things—an important truth, event, or idea, and, at the same time, that there is something about it which we can not know, and should not, therefore, be tempted to enquire into. The enigmatical language, or the *complication* (as the Hebrew word primarily imports) performs its office, therefore, as clearly as any other mode of speech when it is thus understood—just as Daniel *understood* it rightly, when he said, "I *heard*, but I *understood* not." It was the impression, we may think, the vision was intended to leave upon his mind in respect to this matter of current days or current solar years. It may, indeed seem a paradox, but the

Paradoxical as it may seem, there may be, sometimes, a profound revelation in the incomprehensible. There may be something higher than knowledge in the awe of the unknown. It is not the feeling of blank ignorance, —for that has no understanding, or comprehension whatever,—but rather the knowledge that knows itself, and the limits that separate it from a higher and more divine intelligence. This may be all nonsense to the Editor of the Theological Review and the Silliman Professor of Mineralogy in Yale College; but, without having the fear of either before our eyes, we must still talk Platonism. There is a *hidha*, or deep speculation of Socrates about knowing what we do not know, and the curious mystery of such knowledge. We would commend its careful consideration to both of these authorities. It might wholesomely temper the infallible dogmatism of the one, and reveal a field of thought somewhat higher than had ever been suggested by the "exact science" of the other.

But to return to the consideration of the prophetic numbers. We may not understand the precise reason of the use of the 1260—and we are perfectly willing to confess

Prophet's exclamation shows that he comprehended well the method employed to teach him impressively that he could not comprehend. Then, language is employed to conceal, some one may say. It is even so—"It is the glory of God (sometimes) to conceal a matter,"—even while revealing something most impressive in relation to it. Twelve hundred and sixty literal solar days, as one class of commentators interpret it, or 1260 current anno domini years, as another class regard it, have, neither of them anything very occult. The first is plain enough, and the second is only, in addition, the guessing at a multiple. Daniel could have entertained either view as easily as Mr. LORD. Certainly this "man beloved," so "favored with the visions of the Most High," must have been in a psychological state as favorable for their interpretation (at least so far as judging of numbers is concerned) as the Editor of the Theological Journal.

our sense of difficulty on this point—yet still no less evident are the reasons and the reasoning by which it is shown that the indefinite expression of *times* is here the fundamental one. It furnishes the ratio, and that gives us the law of the idea. It is a ratio, order, division of period and event, and not precise sun-measured duration. If this be so, then there follows a most important inference. The more simple ratio, designating the larger period, or the "time, times and a half," gives character and dimension to the day, instead of being determined by it, and that, too, both in the representative conception, and as that conception is carried out on the scale of the actual prophetic fulfilment of the common ratio. The larger designation—the "time, times," etc.,—having nothing higher of which it can be predicated as a measure or divisor, is, of course, indefinite. It would not even follow that one of these mysterious times is the same, in precise duration, with another.* God's physical movements, es-

* They may be unequal in duration as measured by solar years, but equal in historical and spiritual value. This is exemplified on the lower scale of the world's most secular history. Some periods are very brief as reckoned by the almanack, yet, contain more of eventful life,—the world, or a nation, has done more in them, thought more in them, lived more in them, than during ages of much greater extent in current years. It is true of the physical world. One period of less cosmical time does vastly more than one of greater duration, There is a cycle of *birth*, as well as of *gestation*, of quick working, as well as of repose. It is true of the individual man. He does more, he lives more, sometimes, in a month than in a year. Above all, would it hold of what may be called the spiritual history of our world. The few years of Christ's ministry, the succeeding period recorded in the Acts of the Apostles—in what ratio with these could we place the forgotten centuries that followed the Trojan war, or the stagnant centuries of mediæval Europe, or the dull, dreamy Egyptian and Assyrian dynasties, out of whose ruins modern research is striving to extract history, with so much promise and so little success,—the whole of it only serving to show how indispensable the clear though scanty light the Bible throws back upon thos: God-forsaken ages, and how little their "sphynxes" or their

pecially in a regulated course of nature, may be supposed to have a connection with astronomical or physical measures of time. Even this view, however, would have to be greatly modified when it is applied to those creative and generative acts which are concerned with the *origination of nature*, and the very adjustments of the measures by which time is afterward regulated. But in the moral, or great historical movements of God's kingdom, we have no warrant from without, and, we think, none from the Scriptures, for applying it at all. At the first serious impression, the mind starts back from the thought that the timeless One regulates his great periods by our almanacks, or by our single planet's astronomical measures of time, whether seemingly arbitrary or seemingly natural, whether reckoned by the clocks we keep in our parlours, or those that keep time for us in our sky;—for in this connection of thought one of these is as natural as the other. We would indulge here in no mere metaphysical conceit. God's purposes and workings in the universe—the moral and providential as well as the physical—have durations, indeed, and those durations, could we measure them, might be found to be certain numbers and fractions of numbers—be they more or less—of our solar years and centuries. But to suppose the divine movements adjusted to these as our movements are—that is, to imagine these great epochs as

"winged bulls," could tell us if this light were lost. Is it not most rational to suppose that the prophetic times are to be measured by this epochal value, as we may call it, in distinction from astronomical estimates, which in respect to the real historical action, may be altogether outward and arbitary? It is in the highest sense the real value, and, therefore, in the highest and truest sense may we suppose it employed in the divine prophetical estimate, and to furnish the true hermeneutical principle in our attempted estimates, of prophetical equalities and proportion.

being made exactly equal to each other through measures taken from our sun, our moon, our clocks, or exact multiples or divisors of these, so that instead of having a law in themselves determining their own durations, (as even the lower physical cycles have) their time of day and night is to be found by observations wholly outward— this is the thing hard to be believed. It is possible; and if the Bible has revealed it, we must, of course, bring our very fallible reasonings in submission to it. But it does not seem natural, it does not seem rational, it looks like a violation of all analogy; we do not see the evidence of it in the Scriptures, either as respects creation or the great epochs of prophecy, although there may be something of these solar measurements in the lesser predictions that have special reference to the merely earthly history of the Jewish nation.

We say, then, it would not follow that one of these mysterious times was exactly equal to another, although each might be represented as a great year, and a proportionate number taken from it to be divided in a manner corresponding to the divisions of our annual cycle. The prophecy, then, would denote three great indefinite periods, and the part of a fourth. If so, it is the multiple that gives character to the divisions, and not the divisions first reduced to a definite annual or astronomical duration, in current days or years, and then carried back to determine the multiple; just as though in the physical world, we should determine the day by the hour, instead of regarding the hour as the twenty-fourth part of the day cycle, whatever the length of that might be.

It may be said that in this way we get nothing definite in respect to the actual physical length of the predicted *times* in current calendar years; and to this it may be answered again, that such would seem to be the very intent of the Scriptural *hidha*, namely, to conceal the precise cosmical time from us—to put us in the very position of the prophet himself, that we might *hear* and heed, yet *understand* not,—that is, *hear* (receive into the mind, which is a secondary sense of the word in most languages) the clear epitomal outline of events, yet understand not the definite solar times it might incidentally embrace. It may have been to take away the mind from that search after current years, to which some commentators are so prone, and to substitute for this vain pursuit the higher study of cycles or periodical courses of events, whether regarded as existing in the more outward and secular, or in the more inward spiritual history of the Church;—we say the Church, for the serious student of the Bible must see that its great historical idea is, the world for the Church, and not the *Church for the world*, which is the favorite notion of our modern secularized Christianity. Commentators have followed the other method to exhaustion. They have tried every means of squaring these mysterious times to anno domini years; they have put on the fractions and taken them off; they have changed their termini, but all in vain. We would speak cautiously and reverently here. It may be the true way on which light at length may shine. We would be very far from making ill success in the application the test of falsity in respect to any method of interpretation. But this continued variance ought at least to lead serious students of Scripture to look about for some other path, and to seek the solution of the great times by means of some other kind of cycles than the astronomical. It might, perhaps, be discovered, that prophecy, like creation, has its own chronology —that is, one which instead of being measured by subdivisions from without, or in an outwardly fixed course of nature, has its own self-measuring days, and times, and seasons, with which the others may be in some kind of analogy, or may not. What would seem to aid such a view, is the use in Daniel (the fountain of this kind of language) of the Hebrew word מוֹעֵד, which when applied to time ever denotes a period whose duration is limited by its own law as constituted and appointed. It is a set time, fixed by agreement, whether of human constitution, or determined in the counsels or covenants of God, and measured by the event or appointed work which is transacted in it. This is the Hebrew word employed Daniel xii, 7—"an appointed time, two appointed times, a division of an appointed time," fixing upon the mind the most vivid impression that the trinal and semi-trinal division is of the very essence of the idea, and not to be overlooked in the estimate of another number, whether regarded as of days or years, that, when alone considered, effaces that division.* The greater *mo'-adhim* are not to be lost

* The absurdity of Mr. LORD's treatment of this mystical number is most striking. The two witnesses of the Revelations, it is expressly said, are to prophecy in sackcloth this very period of 1260 days, equivalent to the "time, times, and a half." It is his theory, however, for reasons it would be too long to state, that these two witnesses are two literal men. It is out of the question, therefore, that the number can mean years in respect to them. To suit such an exigency, it must, in their case, be reduced to literal days. In other words, it means either one or the other, just as these accommodating laws of symbolization may require. There is something, too, especially curious in the reasoning by which these two witnesses are proved to be real men, or "*symbols of themselves*." If the reader has any curiosity on the subject, we refer him to it (ch. xxvi) as one of the most singular specimens of logical circularity that the necessities of a theory ever brought out.

in this way. The prime ratio is not thus to be absorbed in the secondary representation. The Chaldaic word, Daniel vii, 25, has the same import. So also the Greek καιρός suggests the idea of a constituted, yet self-determining season, rather than any outward measure whether of celestial or terrestrial horometers.

There is another view of the "time, two times, and a dividing of a time," which gives it a more direct connection with our general subject, the Creative Days. The thoughtful reader can not fail to see that this strange expression represents exactly one-half of the number seven*,—the sacred number, the mystic number, which from the earliest period was held in religious awe as representing something of peculiar interest in the constitution and chronology of our world. Along with this may have been connected the thought of some curious inherent property which it possessed as a number, or in the relation of its numerical parts. In fact, both ideas were united; for this looking upon the world, its times and constitution, as represented in the mystic properties of numbers, is old beyond all historical date. It was a musing of the ancient mind, both oriental and occidental, long before the days of Pythagoras. In this sense of its extreme antiquity it was certainly an *a priori*, if we may not rather say, an *a primo* idea, that God made the world by weight and measure, that is, by number. It

* It comes, too, just in that order of division, from which the mathematical mystery of this number is derived. It is not $3\frac{1}{2}$, without any constitution or distinction of parts, but $1 + 2 + \frac{1}{2}$. The seven series is

$$1 + 2 + 1 + 2 + 1, \text{ or rather, } (1 + 2) + 1 + (2 + 1).$$

Daniel's number is just one-half of it, and in the same order. We simply call attention to the fact. The reader may judge, for himself, of its meaning and value.

did not wait for the slow, groping discoveries of modern Chemistry. The early mind reached out and seized the truth; whether the soul recognized it as one of its own native thoughts which it saw, or thought it saw, imaged in outside things, or whether God had given it by revelation and tradition, we may not be able to tell very clearly; but it had it in some way beyond all doubt. God made the world by number; and so the world was, in some sense, a number, a ratio, a harmony, a kosmos. The idea is everywhere in language. And then there very early followed, or rather accompanied it, the thought that the mystic birth numbers that entered into the very constitution of things might, perhaps, be somehow shadowed forth in the world's higher chronology. We have been charged with dreaming, as well as Platonism, but we beg the sober-minded reader not to be impatient here. We do not intend to discuss the truth of this idea, or to endorse its affirmance or denial. Sufficient for our argument, and for the use we make of the thought, is the historical fact of its very early and deeply grounded existence. Of the sacredness of this number seven, especially, we find traces everywhere. When men had little outward physical science to trouble them with its details, they mused much on their own ideas. Especially was the thinking mind—and they *thought* then as much as they do now, perhaps more—drawn to that strange class of existences that seem to belong alike to the objective and subjective world—the world within us, and the world without us. Numbers exist in nature; they have a still more real existence in the soul (not as mere umbræ or conceptual images, the way in which any outward thing may be said to be *in the mind*,) but as a part of its own most interior furniture* without which it could not be a rational soul, but only a sensitive life. Numbers, then, as existing in nature, it was thought, must represent something like those properties which the mind saw in numbers when it contemplated them among its own ideas. If this was not *seen* directly by the sense (as in that infant stage of scientific discovery could not be the case) then it must be *thought* as assumed by the mind. For somehow there must be an agreement, or else God did not make the world by measure and weight, that is, by number;—in other words, it did not come from mind at all.† Hence the tendency of the earliest philosophy to find out nature by the mind's own ideas—to think out the world-problem, its figurative forms in space, its great births or changes in time. It was the "a priori tendency" which Professor DANA so flippantly condemns, but understandeth not.‡ It was the view of

* Belonging to *mind*, in fact, just as truly and as inseparably, as figurative forms belong to *matter*, and forms of motion to any idea we can have of *life*.

† We are tempted to dwell on this theme, but it would interrupt our general plan, as far as our rambling book can be said to have one. We would, however, barely suggest to the men who cry out Platonism, and see so much danger and heresy in the word, that it might be worth their while to examine the Platonic mode of theologizing, or proving that the world came from mind. It found this evidence in the *ideas*; the modern discovers it in the *utilities*, or contrivances for happiness, or *well feeling* as the very essence of *well being*. The latter method can never fully answer the Atheist's objection, that the use may have grown out of the construction as an *effect* rather than a *cause*. But aside from this, we have no hesitation in affirming, and in maintaining, whenever necessary, that the Platonic mode is not only more sublimely truthful, but more pious, more reverent, more in harmony with the Scriptures, than the one now so popular both with scientific men and theologians.

‡ The consummation and most perfect result of this tendency may be found in that splendid effort of genius and philosophy, the Timæus of Plato. It is an attempt to get at the elementary *forms* and elementary *motions* of

which some of our professed Baconians, misunderstanding Bacon as well as Plato, show a sort of dreamy half-comprehension in their sneering lectures, their ignorant gibes at the old philosophers, their stale, stupid jests about the schoolmen, whilst they have no wonder for the strangest psychological fact presented in the history of philosophy and the world — the strangest, we mean, on their theory — that metaphysics should have been so much older than physics — the supernatural before the natural — the contemplation of "the things unseen" so much earlier than that study of the "things seen" and tangible that is so predominant a feature of our later times. There was an error doubtless, a great and baffling error in this one-sided a priori tendency, but there was also in it a great truth, the loss of which can never be compensated by any amount of mere physical knowledge that rejects or holds it light.

The reader will have patience with our rambling. This is a tempting theme, but we must come back to the early ideas of mystic number. There was a supposed mystery in the number 7, arising from its numerical composition. As three presented duality and unity, forming trinity, so 7 was a dual trinity connected by unity. One

all matter as derived from the necessary mathematical ideas, and the necessary dynamical laws. Plato regarded the world rather as an idea, or system of ideas, than as a power, although he fully recognized the latter aspect. Hence the Timæus is predominantly mathematical, that is—in the ancient sense of the word—geometrical; for it is the application of the term growing out of the modern analytical mathematics, that has extended it over both departments, as they are embraced in that second Timæus, the Mechanique Celeste of La Place. Of course, Plato's Timæus is a failure when judged by our college text books on Natural Philosophy, and yet we fearlessly hazard the declaration, as one we are prepared to prove, that it contains truths, physical truths, of the highest import, that are unrecognized and unvalued in our scientific conventions.

half of this corresponded to the mysterious " time, two times and a half. So it certainly is numerically; how far the idea was an element in the Prophet's vision, the reader may judge for himself. We would be content with the unquestionable fact of a sacred estimate being early entertained of this number and of such modes of dividing it. Connected with this was the idea of its being the *creative number*, which must have come from some early and wide tradition of the great creative times, and also the doctrine of the seven ages corresponding to them and which would complete the historical period of our own world or olam. This is to be found in early heathen writers;* Augustine speaks of it as a wide-spread belief; it was maintained by the Rabinnical writers as among the sacred thoughts that had come down from their forefathers, and we confidently say, that aside from the inferences that might be drawn from the passages on which we are now commenting, there are discernible traces of it in the Scriptures. The " thousand years as one day"—the thousand years of the New Jerusalem, as well as these " time, times and half time" of Daniel and John,

* The germ of this idea, we may soberly believe, exists in the Hesiodian ages, three of which had passed away, and the fourth was just gone, when the poet came upon the stage of time. Compare with this also Virgil's Sybilline traditions, as referred to in the Fourth Eclogue, 5:

Ultima Cumæi venit jam carminis ætas,
Magnus ab integro *sæclorum* nascitur ordo.

And afterwards (12) where he speaks of the *magni menses*, or *great months*. There is a similar reference in the VIth Book of the Æneid, where Æneas is shown the souls that are to be born in the great latter *day* of the earth's history,

Longa DIES perfecto temporis orbe.

The Platonic magnus annus was epochal yet measured outwardly by astronomical or cosmical movements. What are called the Chaldaean magni menses may be regarded as mainly, if not wholly, of the latter character.

show the prevalence of the idea.* Being thus a sacred thought belonging to the universal thinking, there is nothing derogatory to the idea of revelation, or inspiration, in supposing that it was divinely made the suggestive source of the prophet's conception. Neither would it at all affect this conclusion to show that it was a Chaldaism, and that it came from this source to the Prophet's mind, and imaged itself in his divine visions. The *old* Chaldea was as directly in the line of the primitive world-traditions as the Jews. There is even an additional value to the thought if supposed to have come down through an independent channel from the earliest fountains. It has a deeper interest, it becomes more sacred from the reflection that the descendant of Abraham found it among remote kindred who had preserved it since the early day when the long-parted streams of generation first diverged from the common ancestors who dwelt beyond the Euphrates. The conceptions of John were certainly influenced by those of Daniel, and yet they are to be regarded as no less truthful on that account. What danger, then, to faith, in regarding the Hebrew Prophet's conception as influenced, yet divinely influenced, by still more ancient thoughts, which had become catholic in the world for serious minds. There is, in fact, something exceedingly

* May we not suppose also that Paul's style of language was suggested by a similar mode of thinking. We refer to the πλήρωμα τῶν ΚΑΙΡΩΝ, Eph. i, 10,—the "fullness of the *times*"—the perfect seven, denoting *completeness*, as the "time, times, and a half," would seem to signify an unfinished or *mediate* period. Paul's expression would suggest the "magnus sæclorum ordo," when "*all things shall be gathered together in Christ, things in Heaven as well as things upon the Earth.*" In Galatians iv, 4, it is "the fulness of the time," τοῦ χρόνου, in the singular, and the reference is to the human birth, or first coming of Christ.

interesting in the thought of one part of the Scriptures being thus made the channel of inspiration to another. To a right thinking, the Bible becomes even more precious, the proof of its divine inspiration is strengthened, by its being thus viewed as the channel of sacred ideas that have lived in the minds not only of devout individuals but of ages. May we not rather believe that for so high and catholic a purpose these ideas have actually had their divine origin and nurture in the world?

But what, then, means the "time, times and half a time"? We answer, we know not. Prophecy in its explication has not been our study, except to note the many failures of those who have attempted to reduce it to definite solar years. But though the application may be difficult, still the reference to the creative times, and to something in the history of our own olam corresponding to them, seems more clear the more we meditate upon it. It may be an intimation that the Prophet's vision looked half-way down the stream of the *world's ages* — that it brings us to the middle of the fourth day in the world's *historical* hebdomad, when the coming of the Son of Man may be like the manifestation of the heavenly lights in the fourth creative period. This interpretation, indeed, we would not press. There is, however, a sublimity in such conceptions, a high moral value independent of all numerical correctness. One thing we are more and more drawn to believe, that prophecy does not stand isolated, by itself, measured by arbitrary numbers, but that the world's archæology and eschatology have a proportion, an analogy, both of times and events, connecting the early day and the latter day, the days of preparation, and the days of consummation, in one grand dramatic unity of action and idea.

A similar view, in one respect, is taken by Hengstenberg in his work on the Apocalypse. He regards the "time, times and a half time" as plainly connected with the number seven, but yet as possessing no chronological value. As the whole denotes fullness, completion, so the broken number denotes a period incomplete, and comparatively brief. We can not wholly accede to this. Some chronological import seems too clear, although the times may not be measurable by our solar years. It is a true chronology, but of the higher calendar. In other words, it may be truly chronological, but not cosmical, that is, not measured by present astronomical cycles, but by higher moral periods, or, perhaps, the higher physical periods that may belong both to our earth and the kosmos—periods having their cyclical law in themselves, and, therefore, independent of outward standards.

Besides the number seven, there are a few others mentioned in the Bible that belong to the same class. The chief of these are *three* and *twelve*. We need not dwell on them. Whether the latter is connected with some historical or archæological assumptions, or is supposed to possess some significant arithmetical power, we shall not attempt to determine. Was it mere accident that brought out the *twelve* patriarchs, the *twelve* tribes of Israel, the *twelve* Apostles of the Christian Church, as they are figured in the *twelve* gates of that New Jerusalem which is the consummation, or fulfilment, of both these standing prophetical types? It is worthy of remark, that there is the same historical enigma presented by other nations. The *twelve tribes* are to be traced in the Athenian and in several others of the Grecian States. They may be found in other ancient nations. There is some evidence of there having been such a division among the Etrurians. The Egyptians, too, held the number sacred. Some are ready with the explanation—It came from the signs of the zodiac. But this only pushes the difficulty of the question one stage farther back. Whence came the signs of the zodiac, the twelve houses in the sky? There is no fitness in connecting them with the moon; for although the number of lunar revolutions in a year is a loose approximation to twelve, yet she passes through the circle of the heavens every month, and, in respect to such revolution, the duodecimal division is as arbitrary as it is in respect to the sun. Both of them have phenomena presenting changes which may be brought into the divisions 4, 8, 16, etc., but nothing to indicate the duodecimal. The division was accidental, or else dependent on some fact now unknown, or some idea not now recognized.

Since we have gone so largely into this subject, a few remarks may be allowed on what are commonly called full or round numbers. These come out of the decimal notation, and owe their property of roundness to that fact, which is, in itself, entirely arbitrary as to its origin, though having this significance when established as the basis of all practical enumeration. By arbitrary, we mean, not drawn from any inherent property of numbers, but wholly from outward application. It has been suggested to every nation by the ten fingers of the hand as the most ready and obvious means of counting. In itself the *ten* has much less mathematical interest than the four, the seven, or the nine; and this strikingly shows the absurdity of regarding the exact numerical extent of such expressions, whether they are fancied to represent days or years, or persons, as intended in the fulfilment of prophecy. Thus in the case of the 1,000 years, or the millenium, as it is commonly called, Mr. LORD is not only chargeable with this fallacy, but he makes it worse by mingling the two kinds of numbers together, in one arbitrary product. Instead of treating it as one of the great *days* of the world, having a vast and indefinite extent, according to the sacred traditional chronology we have already spoken of, he makes it in current years exactly 365 × 1000. Now he might just as well have maintained the precise number of the 144,000 who stand on Mount Zion—a number made up of the round cubical number 1,000, the cube of ten, and the square of the mystical 12 the representative of both the national and the spiritual Israel. He might just as well have maintained the cubical form of the New Jerusalem, as to have regarded this cube of ten as representing that exact number of days, or years, or multiples of years, precisely measured by the number of days in our year, accurately or loosely estimated, with fractions taken into the estimate or left out. Can we suppose that the exact extent of such far distant times, and such unknown states of being, are thus dependent on an incidental method of computation well adapted, indeed, to the representative use to which we may put it, but having no other than an arbitrary numerical association with the actual ages of fulfilment? In other words, how strange the thought, that the absolute arithmetic of this higher chronology should be bound up in the precise literalness of these terms, when, as in Daniel's "ten thousand times ten thousand," and the Psalmist's "twice ten thousand chariots of God," the form of the expression would strongly seem to have been adopted for the very purpose of cautioning the reader against any such definite conclusion.

Daniel's seventy weeks has an obvious solution without any arbitrary substitution of a year of 360 days for one day. It is not 490 days, but 70 weeks, and the week of years, or seven years, was a well-known measurement of the Jewish chronology. The institution of the Sabbatical year made this hebdomad as natural and current a measure of actual time as the week of days, and the Hebrew שָׁבוּעַ, which simply means a *seven* or *hebdomad*, was as applicable to one period as the other.* It was seventy times seven, and taken as actual *weeks of years* would reach generally (though without an absolute determinable precision) to the age of Christ, as it has generally been taken in ancient as well as modern times. There is, however, good reason for believing that like

* There was another still greater hebdomad consisting of seven times seven, or forty-nine years, to which was added the fiftieth as a jubilee. It is particularly set forth, Lev. xxv, 8: "And thou shalt number seven Sabbaths of years unto thee; *seven times seven years*, and the space of the seven Sabbaths of years shall be unto thee *forty and nine years*; and ye shall hallow the fiftieth year; it shall be a jubilee unto you." What means this widening, ascending series—seven days, seven years, seven sevens of years? It had a connection with the Jewish earthly economy, we know; but has it not also a higher sense? May we not soberly regard it as giving us a hint of a higher chronology, with its greater Sabbaths and greater jubilee? Even as the Apostle soberly interprets the "ark and the tabernacle" as significant of "things in the heavens"? In connection with such a view it is easy and natural for us to believe that the thought entered into the prophetical visions and lay at the foundation of their mystic numbers.

It should be remarked, however, that if we regard the Prophet here as setting forth a definite historical time, it would be *five hundred years*, instead of four hundred and ninety; since the great hebdomad with its jubilee amounted to *fifty years*, and there is no reason why it should not be reckoned in what purports to be exact historical chronology.

the other numbers of that majestic book of Daniel, it passes over, in a higher sense, into the chronology of the Christian αἰών, and may reach to the second coming of Messiah and the New Jerusalem. If there is any ground for such a view, it might perhaps be found in the mystical form of the number connecting it with the "time, times and half a time." It is *the great* seven, the square of seven, and that multiplied by ten to denote roundness of computation, as well as that mathematical symmetry which is the symbol of chronological perfection regarded more as residing in inherent cyclical self-measurement than in any outward estimate we can make of current years.

We may be darkening counsel by words without knowledge. We would not press any such views, but we are quite confident that some other mode in the study of prophecy must be adopted, differing from both those that are now commonly employed. One of these reckons by literal solar days, carrying the periods of Daniel into some obscure times which we have to dig out of the darkness of the Antiochean dynasties, and having little or no moral or historical value, even could they be reduced to any tolerable definiteness. The other differs from this simply by using a multiple of 360 or 365. The great practical argument against the latter as well as the first is, that it gives us nothing definite after all. No commentator who has tried the experiment has ever satisfied any body but himself and a small clique of his own school. So endless have been the interpretations, so varied, and so utterly unreconcilable, so infallibly uttered too, (of which infallibility Mr. LORD is not the least amusing specimen,) that confidence in them must be seriously impaired.

This fact alone would be sufficient to show, that there had been some error here. Learned men, pious men, most acute men, have labored to give current chronological significance to these numbers, but, Mr. LORD himself being judge, have "utterly failed." If we may believe him, the best of them have failed,—to use his own very positive language so oft repeated,— they have "palpably" failed, their computations are "unquestionably wrong," their starting points are based on erroneous historical views, or historical estimates, and therefore their conclusions are utterly unreliable. Whether his own views put forth with so much pretension and such a constant condemnation of others, are entitled to any more credit, most readers will find no great difficulty in judging.* But we would not argue from failure alone.

* No men are more apt to raise the cry of infidel than this class of commentators on prophecy, and yet few things, we think, have contributed more to bring the Scriptures into disrepute than some of these books. Their distortions of history, their magnifying of obscure historical events, in order to get the termini that may agree with their hypothesis, their secularization of Christianity by connecting it with their own political notions founded on abstract ideas that the Bible does not recognize, their consequent exaggeration of events near their own times, but which, in themselves, or as they will appear when seen from afar, have really little or no historical value—as Mr. LORD, for example, in his politico-theology, so extravagantly overrates the mere mobism which a few years ago disturbed some of the capitals in Europe, and has already in the brief space of nine years subsided into insignificance—all these things have tended not only to weaken confidence, but to lead men to overlook the moral sublime of which these mysterious prophetic books are so full when contemplated with a different aim, and from a different stand point. Similar remarks are applicable to Mr. LORD's scientific allies, when they too, in their exuberant piety, attempt to raise the novel cry of infidelity. In the promoting of the real Bible-hating infidelity, next to blundering interpretations of prophecy, may be reckoned some of our scientific defences of the Scriptures. The amount of terror they have for the real infidel might be easily tested. In this very controversy, on which side, so far as they have manifested an interest in it, are the "free thinkers" of our land! Their sympa-

It would be unfair for the Scriptures, and the cause of interpretation generally. It is in the Bible itself we find a warrant, we think a clear warrant, for saying, that it is not for man to know, and it was not intended for man to know, the times and seasons. Such is the express language of the highest authority; and aside from this, the very form in which the predictions of the Apocalypse are given, show that, although it is a true Apocalypse, or un-veiling, as to great outline events not yet well understood in the ecclesiastical or spiritual history of the Church, it is truly a veiling as to the dates or times at which, and during which, they are to occur.

And this, instead of diminishing the moral and spiritual value of the Apocalypse, does in fact greatly add to it. No book bears more unmistakably the impress of the divine majesty—that "beaming and burning glory" which the old divines, to whom we alluded in our introduction, regarded as the true internal evidence of the Scripture. We do not want to know the exact duration denoted by its mysterious numerals, to be impressed and awed by it. Indeed, few things tend more to take away this effect than the frigid calculations to which we refer, and the endless controversies as to dates in history in which they respectively commence and end. It is like applying the statistics of a town and county census to the 144,000 from the *twelve* tribes of Israel, whom the Prophet saw standing on Mount Zion. It is, besides, taking our own estimate of the value of historical events (according to our poor political philosophy) for the

thies and affinities, in such cases, furnish a better test than argument; and when these show themselves on the side of the New-Haven Professor, it gives us the precisely measured probability of their being converted by his "Harmony of Science and the Bible."

divine estimate which may be something very different. It may be that in the Heavenly economy, as studied by the Heavenly Intelligences, or even as viewed from that stand point to which the unwordly or spiritual mind may attain in the loving study of the Scriptures, there is not attached that same importance to Turks and Tartars, and French Revolutions, and American Revolutions, which they possess in our eyes. Democracy may be no more the object of Heaven's care than monarchy. It may be that both are alike among the idols to be demolished, and the "plants to be rooted up," before the coming of the Son of Man. It may be that our American experiment is for a warning example rather than an encouraging lesson to the ages to come. Nothing but deep initiation into the spirit of the Bible can enable one to form the faintest idea as to what historical events, in this dark world of ours, belong most prominently to the divine plan, or have most relation to the higher chronology of the higher kingdom of the eternities. But this we can not help feeling, that in many of the common historic interpretations, so called, the glory of the Apocalypse is dimmed; its sublimity sinks; there is a weakening of that deep impression of the mighty warfare God is waging against the powers of evil, and the enemies of his Church. Such is the effect that is felt in reading some of these arbitrary yet pretentious interpretations; whilst, on the other hand, nothing is gained on the score of historic certainty. No estimate of exact times and seasons compensates for the moral and emotional loss that is suffered, when for the grand, the indefinite, the superhuman, so impressive in outline, though incapable of being interpreted in detail, we substitute the poverty of earthly calculations so little available for any moral purpose, even if not rendered altogether worthless by their endless variety and endless irreconcilability of interpretation.

And so of creation. Whether we measure by exact hours, the twenty-fourth parts of the present terrestrial revolution, or by strata and layers of fossils which we attempt to guage by space deposits and the supposed ratio of their feet and inches to supposed multiples of years — the effect is very much the same. We get nothing exact, nothing reliable, after all; but the grand impression is weakened, and, when pushed to the extent to which some would carry it out, on both sides, utterly lost. Leave it, as we reverently think Moses has left it, indefinite, unmeasured by any historical time-calendars, and we have upon the mind an effect worthy of its ineffable glory of thought, its inimitable simplicity and grandeur of expression.

But there is in prophecy (meaning by this all in the Bible that looks to the future) another use of the word *day* quite different from that of the mystic numbers, and more immediately connected with the view we have taken of the same word in the creative account. It is the distinct application of the term to some great epoch in the latter history of the world, or, it may be, to more than one. According to the definition given, there is no propriety in calling it metaphorical. "The *Day of Judgment*," "the Last Day," "the Day of the Lord," or of the Lord's coming, the "Day of the aeon," or the aeonic day, the ἡμέρα αἰῶνος, 2 Pet., iii, 18,—these are not metaphors, that is, a μεταφορά, a change for rhetorical purposes, or a substitution of one word for some other well known term that might more literally, and with more objective truth, have conveyed the required idea. There is no such metaphor here; for there is no such other term adapted to these great epochs, and whose place *day* may be supposed to take merely for such rhetorical or emotional effect. We would rank it in the same class with the creative days, only that the cyclical or periodical idea does not so distinctly appear. The revelations respecting this great time, or these great times, are not so orderly, the mornings and the evenings are not so marked. And yet, in other respects, they present the same features suggesting the same higher chronology. Hence we may style them the *epochal*, and call this the epochal sense of the word day. The first three expressions we have already alluded to, and would not, therefore, further dwell upon them in this outline view. The fourth, or the one quoted from 2 Peter, iii, 18, has some striking aspects. Its peculiar force of terminology is concealed in our translation, where it is simply rendered *forever*—a term which etymologically resembles it (that is when carried back to its kindred, the Latin ævum, and Greek αἰῶν,) but in the change of thinking has lost its ancient features. The Greek phrase, as it stands, has the epochal idea,—that is, of a great time by itself in the chronology of the universe. It is the "dies eternitatis" of the Vulgate, the "*day of euerlastingnes*" of the old Wickliffe version, and the "*day of eternitie*" of the Rheims. It may also be fairly regarded as the New Testament version of the ימי עולם of the older Scriptures. In the Old English, as in the New Testament Hebraistic Greek, the noun has the force of an adjective. The ἡμέρα αἰῶνος, the *day of eternity*, is the *eternal day*, the aeonic day, denoting *extent*, and boundless extent, yet still, in a high and perhaps truer sense, quality rather than quantity, or the character of the day as belonging to the great aeonic chronology, whether it is to be regarded as a single αἰὼν in itself, or an αιὼν τῶν αἰώνων, an *aeon* measured by aeons as lesser ages are measured by centuries and years. In any way, how different, as thus appearing, from that blank conception we connect with those withered words of ours that can only regain their life and clear impression by being carried back to be stamped anew in the ancient mint. Wickliffe's version here, though made from the Vulgate, is better than our own, and that by reason of its expressive literalness — "*the day of euerlastingnes.*" By retaining the word *day*, it keeps up the epochal idea, and suggests, if we choose to take it, the qualifying or adjective sense of the noun that is in the Greek and Latin.*

* We should have had all these ideas much more vivid in our minds, had our common version followed in this and similar places the Wickliffian simplicity of expression. That other old idea, too, of time-words used for the very worlds themselves, so that it may be taken either way, and with an increase of sublimity attending either conception, is brought out in this pure Saxon English with all the force and clearness of the Greek. The reader may see this in all those places where Wickliffe's translation, following the Latin, has *world* or *worldis* for αἰὼν and αιῶνες, whilst the common version has the general epithets *eternal* and *everlasting*. As in Gal. i, 5—" To whom is worschip and glorie into *worldis of worldis* (αιῶνας τῶν αιώνων)—Eph. ii, 7, "In the *worldis aboue coming*"—Col. i, 26, " Hidden *fro worldis.*" So also the Rheims. The other English versions have the singular, "before the *world* began," notwithstanding the Greek plural, and the Hebrew plural from which the mode of expression is derived. The translators did not recognize the idea of time-worlds, and so took those plurals collectively. We have other examples—1 Pet. iv, 11, " Glorie and lordschip unto the *worldis of worldis*"—Rev. iv, 9, " That lyueth into *worldis of worldis.*" The same Rev. xv, 7, xxii, 5—" They shall reign *forever*, or *forever more*," say the other versions. The Wickliffe has it—

But the word day is consistent with its absolute unending everlastingness. And so we are prepared to view it in this passage of Peter. Not only is it applied in the Scriptures to the great olams that divide the chronology of the created universe in its cosmical ongoings, but to the whole that preceded, and to the whole that may be thought as coming after. Thus we may reverently think of three great days, or greatest days, which may be described as the ante-time state, the kosmos that now is, and the ἡμέρα αἰῶνος or *all* that succeeds this world or the worlds that now are. Taken all together, they would be the "*yesterday*, *to-day*, and *forever*," of the Divine

"And thei schulen regne into *worldis of worldis*." But perhaps there is no passage in which this Old English version is more striking, or more instructive, than in its rendering of 1 Tim. i, 17—"Now unto the King Eternal, Immortal, Invisible, the only wise God, be honor and glory forever." This has, indeed, a grand sound, though having only the general imageless adjective; but it is not equal, either for truth or effect, to the old Version that follows so closely the Latin and the Greek—"Now unto the *Kynge of worldis*, undeedli and vnuysible, God aloone, be onoure and glorie into *worldis of worldis*, Amen." It is the counterpart of Ps. cxlv, 13—"Thy kingdom is a kingdom of *all worldis*." This kind of language is the source of the grand expression in the Episcopal Prayer Book, "*world without end*." Surely it is not too much to say, that if the form and spirit of these early translations had been preserved, (and certainly they are nearest to the original,) the mind of the common reader would have had something far more true, as well as far more vivid, than the blank conceptions that are given by the current terms. One style of language gives us *one* world with a waste continuity, undivided and undivisible, before and after it. The other fills them up with *worlds* and *worlds of worlds* stretching on in either direction as far as the mind can go towards the boundless complement of the Divine Kingdom. We surpass the readers of these old Versions, and of these old originals, in our space conceptions; but how far we are behind them in those of time, is shown by the change of language and the disuse of the old vivid forms. We may seek to compensate for this by rows of decimals, and frigid conceits of solar systems turned into sand-glasses to measure eternity, but it is all a blank as compared with those mighty pluralities, the *æons* and *olams*, and *worldis of worldis* of the earlier mind.

Existence. There would seem, then, good reason for ranking this expression (2 Pet. iii, 18,) in the same class with that in Psalm ii,7—the ancient day of the "Eternal Generation," and the day Isaiah xliii, 13, where it is said "Before the *day* I am He," that is, before the whole cosmical manifestation. We might regard these as belonging to a still higher chronology than the days of creation and the days of prophecy, but any attempt to name them would be only a repetition of the same language, and a reduplication of the same inadequate conception. We may be content with the idea as sound and Scriptural, where the conceiving faculty utterly fails to present it to the sense or the imagination. There was an ante-past eternity, before time began, "or ever the earth or the world was." Of its mode of being we can know little or nothing; of the *fact* we may reverently inquire if we guide our thoughts, and our imaginations, by that only light, the interpretation of Scripture soberly conducted, but with an aim bearing some proportion to the acknowledged divinity and consequent grandeur of the Book.

CHAPTER IV.

Kedhem or the Ante-time State—Psalm LV, 19, *"He that Inhabiteth Kedhem"—Sadducean Interpreters—Psalm* LXVIII, *"The Heaven of Henvens of Old"—Spiritual in Distinction from a Cabalistical Sense—Space Sense—Messianic Character of the Psalm—Where is Kedhem?—The Rationalist—The Twenty-four Hour Interpreter—The Timeless State—The Question of the Eternity of Matter—The Absurdity involved in the very Inquiry.*

BUT what do we mean by an ante-past eternity, or ante-time state, as with good Scriptural authority it may be named? This may be called a purely speculative question. It is, however, one of exceeding interest; and, therefore, we would beg the reader's indulgence if we devote a chapter to its consideration—most scanty and inadequate though it be. We can not help feeling that there are allusions to it in the Scriptures, although in all such cases he who seeks nothing higher may find plausible ground for being content with a lower sense. Of such ante-past eternity there seems to the writer a vivid recognition, Psalm lv, 19, rendered in our Version "*He that abideth of old.*" The Sadducean interpreter may take it of some old historical time upon the earth, some forefathers' day of the Jewish genealogies, and should he be determined to adhere to it, it would not be easy to refute him, or drive him out of it. It certainly may have that sense if a man chooses to see nothing higher, but to others in another state of mind the Hebrew suggests a thought sublime beyond all expression. It is יֹשֵׁב קֶדֶם, "He that inhabiteth Kedhem;" with which we may compare Isaiah lvii, 15—"He that inhabiteth eternity." Kedhem denotes the most ancient state of anything, or rather that which was before the most ancient state of anything. It would mean etymologically the *antiquity*, not in the sense of the oldest part, but rather as the anterior or the *before* state. Compare Prov. viii, 22, 23, where it may be rendered "the antiquity before the world was." So here—"Who inhabiteth the antiquity,"—the ante-mundane state—the *day* before the world was. Compare also מִקֶּדֶם as spoken of the Logos, Mich. v, 1,—"Whose outgoings are from Kedhem,"—*egressus ejus ab initio, a diebus eternitatis.* There is something very striking in the whole expression, especially in the other word יֹשֵׁב, as applied to God—"who *sitteth* kedhem." It sounds very strange, and the interpretation may be condemned as strangely literal; but may we not soberly look for "wondrous things," when such a term, and in such a connection, is applied to Deity?* May it not intimate to us that ineffable divine *repose*, that transcending quietude, that preceded all worlds, when God *sat* alone, dwelt alone, in the ineffable glory of his triune existence. It may be said there is something anthropopathic in such conception of the word; but what can we do? In what other

* The thought comes out far more vividly in the old versions. The LXX, ὁ ὑπάρχων πρὸ τῶν αἰώνων—"*Who subsisted before the ages*, or *the worlds*, if we take the New Testament sense which we may certainly give to the word in the Septuagint. Vulgate—Qui est *ante* sæcula. The Syriac is clearest of them all—"who was *before the world*,"—קדם עלמא,—and there can be no doubt of the sense in which it employs the term, as, elsewhere, for the world idea.

mode is the conception, or the idea, to have a place in our minds? The *conception may* be anthropopathic, yea, *must* be anthropopathic, and yet the *idea* the conception represents may be one that transcends all philosophy.

There was certainly an ante-mundane state, whether near or remote; for such terms are merely comparative. Their power of affecting the mind, or producing religious emotion, depends on other associations. But where was Kedhem? It is a question we may reverently ask. Certain commentators who call themselves sober or rational, and who neither seek nor find anything profound in the Scriptures, especially in the Old Testament, would carry the word back, perhaps, to the period *before* the Saul dynasty, or, it may be, to some such respectable antiquity as the days of Nahshon the Prince of Judah, the grandfather of Boaz, who was the great-grandfather of David—about as far as from the present generation to the days of the Pilgrim Fathers. This to their minds satisfies the language, "*He who abideth of old*," or "He who inhabiteth Kedhem." It does pretty well; and is a tolerably fair sense, we say, for those who choose to take it. But we would desire to bear in mind that it is the Book of the Eternal God we are reading, and we would remember the reproof Christ gave the Sadducees for their narrow yet plausible interpretation, when they found nothing but matter in the Old Testament, and spiritual nonentity, and a few fleeting generations of miserable creatures who had not even a dream of anything beyond the dissolution of the body, and yet were arrogant enough to claim the undying One as their God and the God of their fathers who had long since gone down to Sheol. "Thou art our dwelling place in all generations." This, as the Sadducees maintained, was said by men, and of men, who had long since "been laid like sheep in the grave," where "their beauty," their mortal forms, the only real beauty that ever belonged to them, "had been consuming" in their eternal "dwelling place" of mortality. So the Sadducees held, and they had some respectable grounds for their Sadducean doctrine; but, Christ himself being witness, they were neither sound nor profound interpreters. There were those in the Psalmist's day who believed in the ἡμέραν αἰῶνος, the "day of *euerlastingnes*," and such minds could readily admit the thought of a kedhem or pre-existent state *before the day when the world was.*

There is another similar passage, Psalm lxviii, 34,— לָרֹכֵב בִּשְׁמֵי שְׁמֵי קֶדֶם,—"To Him who rideth on the *Heavens of Heavens of old*—the *Heavens of Heavens of Kedhem.*" Here, too, may the word present its radical idea of *antiquity*, or a time or state *before*, and yet in perfect consistency with a gradation of senses (according to the taste or reverence, or views of inspiration, or spiritual mindedness in the interpreter,) until we ascend to that highest and oldest to which the hyperbole or upmounting form of the expression would seem to carry us. It may thus be taken for the old skies on which God *rode*, or, as the word may be rendered, *sat throned*, on the desert! It may refer to the Heaven of storms which he gathered around the awful peak of Sinai. Either of these is a good sense, a most important sense. It may be taken—preserving, too, the same old radical conception of *antiquity*, or the ante-state—for an old heavens before the Mosaic heavens, and belonging to the times before the earth was; or it may signify for us that most ancient state before there were any mundane heavens, atmospherical, stellar, or nebular, if we may use these terms by way of accommodation. Or if we give the conception another form, (yet preserving its essence) it may suggest to us degrees of heavens in what we have elsewhere called the altitudinal, or degree aspect, in distinction from that of space and time. It may carry us through all these heavens until we come to that oldest timeless state, and that ineffable height which we have regarded as ultimately set forth in language like this. A man, we say, may take the lower, but why may he not also take the higher sense, if it comes fairly out of the ever widening conception, and if it be really the case that this book, we are venturing to interpret, is truly a book of God's thoughts, as high above our thoughts as the heavens are high above the earth.

Such a higher or spiritual sense, is the one taken by a spiritual mind building on the old fundamental conception. We may freely call it the spiritual sense of Scripture, without fear of its involving us in any cabalistical fancies; for it is the great difference between it and any cabalistical or Swedenborgian spiritual sense, that the latter has no such fundamental conception capable of being fixed by philology, but in the foundation as in the superstructure is wholly arbitrary, built on a supposed second lexical revelation, or "dictionary of correspondences," to which it is not even pretended that the rules of philology have any theoretical or practical application. This cabalistical or fancied spiritual sense, too, is ever dry; it has no more warmth than light; it has as little to do with feeling as with the intellect; whereas the other is the rational expansion of the "spiritual mind," under the influence of pious emotion which we may regard as giving breath to the thought, whilst the understanding remains ever anchored on that ground idea which is the same for all. It is the same, in this respect, with the Old Testament as with the New. Being γραφὴ θεόπνευστος, "inspired Scripture," it must be capable of the same expansion from lower to higher degrees of the same fundamental thought. There are those who contend earnestly and ably for it, as a true part of the sacred canon, and yet somehow adopt a view which renders the position in a measure worthless, even after such great pains to establish it. The course taken by the "liberal" commentator is certainly more logical, if not so pious. If it is God's inspiration it must be every where full of life — "the Divine breath," to use the words of M. Guizot, "must everywhere animate" it. The thoughtful reader must especially feel this when he fixes his mind on the sublime terms of which we now are treating. But there are others every where that expand themselves, and legitimately expand themselves, in the same ever widening, ever ascending manner. Take, for example, such words as *life*, *salvation*, *righteousness*. It may be the *life* of the body when the Psalmist says, "Thy favor is life," but what prevents its being taken for the life of the soul? "Thou wilt show me the path of life." It may mean here deliverance from temporal death; the rationalist has good grounds for such an interpretation, but how much higher ground has the spiritual mind for interpreting it of the *life of the spirit* in this world, or for the life of the spirit as the spirit is the life of the body — and even for carrying it out to the eternal life in the olamic kingdom of God. Salvation may mean, —it does mean,—temporal deliverance, but what shall forbid its being understood in a true, yea a truer sense, of *soul health*, the true σωτηρια even here, and the everlasting salvation both from Satan and from sin, from condemnation and from depravity, when Christ shall have put all enemies under his feet. *Right* or *righteousness* may be the vindication of a temporal justice, and so it may be, and truly is, a pardon, nay, more, an absolute *robe of righteousness* which shall fit one to appear in the very heaven of heavens. All these senses flow out of the words, and to the mind that can receive them are as real in themselves, and as truly the *meaning*, as any lower significance that may be discovered by the dry light either of mysticism or neology. Those who choose may feed on the husks and throw away the fruit; for the lower senses are really there, and the mind that is satisfied with them may rest in them without seeking anything higher or more free.*

* In close connection with this there is, in the next verse, another expression that invites comment,—"*Ascribe ye power unto God whose glory is upon Israel, and his strength in the skies.*" The word שְׁחָקִים is rendered in our version the clouds; but it is more usually a word for the visible or space "heavens." The primary sense of the root is to *make thin*, attenuate, and hence to expand. Hence it is applied to the æther, or the substance that was regarded as filling all space, and which, on the same etymological ground, is called by Aristotle ἡ λεπτομερὴς καὶ φλογώδης οὐσία. Thus etymologically regarded, it would be equivalent to the classical expression *in summo æthere*, or the frequent Homeric phrase αἰθέρι ναίων. The word is also used for dust (Isaiah xl, 15,) from the radical sense of *attenuation, fineness* or *rarity*; and hence, as some think, is applied to the clouds, either from their rarity, or from the fancied resemblance which the dark *nimbus*, or thunder-cloud, may be supposed to bear to a rolling bank of dust. As in that sublime passage, Nahum i, 3,—"His way is in the whirlwind and the tempest, and the *clouds are the dust*

The word Kedhem, it must not be overlooked, has a space as well as a time sense; but the former would seem to come naturally from the latter. It means the East, the *ould countrie*, the fatherland, where dwelt "the men of *yore*," the men who were *before* us. So afterwards Phœnicia was *Kedhem* to Greece, and hence they said *Kadmus*, or the Eastern man, brought to them the letters of the alphabet. Thus it never loses its time idea of *beforeness*, if we may use such a term, or *die vorzeit*. Both the LXX and Syriac versions have adopted this space sense in the passage. They render—"Who ascendeth upon the heaven of heavens *from the East*," so as to correspond to the translation of v. 5, where, instead of our rendering, "who rideth on the heavens," or the more correct translation, "who rideth on the desert," they have, "who ascendeth *on the West*." But the LXX and Syriac version of v. 33 will not suit the accompanying expression "*heaven of heavens*," which must evidently refer to degree either of altitude or time.

Should any feel a misgiving at such an expansion of these phrases, let it be borne in mind that this Psalm is distinctly quoted by the Apostle, Eph. iv, 10, as one of the Messianic prophecies, and, therefore, there must be a higher and holier sense to it. Let "rationalism," with all its learning, go to the winds; we must hold to this, or give

of His feet"—although in this place a different word is used. In its primary sense, as well as in its applications, it resembles very much an Arabic word *habaon*, signifying *atoms*, or the fine particles of dust that float in the air, and of which kind of "star dust" the Mohammedan Doctors say God made the world. The Hebrew term arrests our attention here, because it seems to give us the space aspect of God's power, or kingdom, in distinction from the time and height aspect. So Gesenius on this word—*Designat cælum ab expansione ut* שמים *spatia alta.*

up the whole Scriptures ; and the more a man heartily studies them, the more he will see that such a holding is not a mere blind faith of necessity, but one which commands (not asks in aid) the firmest assent of all that is highest in his spiritual perceptions. But "rationalism" is more consistent than that Biblical criticism among us which so bravely proves certain Psalms to be Messianic, and then is perfectly content with such a barren work, making no use of the position after all, seeing no more in the Scripture, sometimes even less, than the rationalist himself, and perhaps (after having thus saved its evangelical credit) showing its learning and its hardihood by going to an extreme of frigidity of which the more spiritual German mind would be ashamed.

This sixty-eighth Psalm describes a triumphant procession of the theocratic Israel, and a transfer of the ark into its Holy Place. But it also has reference to a higher Israel, and a mightier Conqueror, who has entered into the highest and holiest Heavens. "Wherefore he saith, He hath led captivity captive, He hath ascendeth up on high, *far above all heavens*, that he might fill all things." Why should we be simply content with acknowledging the Psalm to be Messianic, and yet give it no proportionate width and height of interpretation. Let us for a moment see what is involved in the position. If it be a Messianic Psalm, then it refers to the Πρωτοτόκος, the same who is said, Psalm cx, to have been "before the birth of the morning," who is called by Paul the Απαύγασμα, or First Out-beaming,—that manifestation of the Divine which preceded all physical creation. "Who is it that descended but He who ascended up *above all heavens*," to that timeless "glory which He had with the

Father *before the world was.*" Our argument is very simple and very brief. If the Psalm refers at all to this higher Conqueror, and this higher victory, then may the time words applied to him swell out to their higher, yea, their highest dimensions. If, however, the neologist is content with the lower meaning, no objection need be taken to his philology.

The authority of the Apostle is sufficient for styling this LXVIIIth Psalm Messianic; but the thoughtful reader must see, on the very literal face of it, the evidence of the greater triumph and the higher heavens. Ever as the triumphal song advances there is a rapturous swell, an uplifting higher and higher, until it becomes a gloria in excelsis, a *Halleluiah bamromim*, a Hosanna *in the highest.* How it continually ascends from the lower to the upper spheres! He who rode on the skies of the desert, who came down on Mount Sinai with twice ten thousand angels, who ascended into the heavens leading captivity captive—He it is who ascended far above all visible, all conceivable worlds, and sitteth throned in the *Heaven* of *Heavens* of *old.**

Similar to this is the view of Venema, the soberest of that sober race of Dutch commentators. We always feel strong in quoting this profoundly learned writer. In all that is substantial in Oriental scholarship he was

* The sense of *riding* given to the verb רכב, is, in fact, a noun sense, from the noun signifying chariot, as this is from the older architectural sense of the root we find in the Syriac and Arabic. The primary idea is that of *putting one thing upon another*, so as to hold it in its place—*imponens—superimponens.* Hence, in the Syriac version of the New Testament, it is applied to the compact joining of the spiritual temple, Eph. ii,20, Col. ii, 19. According to this view, the imagery would represent God as *throned* upon the Heaven of Heavens of Kedhem, thus giving the idea of permanence and stability, rather than motion.

the equal of the modern Germans, while he was far beyond them in what may be called Biblical unction, or the power of discerning profound ideas in the Scriptures. In commenting on this remarkable expression, he says: Had it been *the heaven of old*, in the singular, it might have been referred to the heaven of the Mosaic creation, or to Sinai and Zion, those terræ sublimioria which were to the Jews as Olympus to the Greeks; but as it stands, in the plural, it must have the older and all transcending sense—"Quia ipse nunc in *supremo cœlo*, non sicut antea in cœlo inferiore et supra terram in loco sublimi residet, sid in *cœlis cœlorum antiquorum*." And again, —"Sed nunc Deus adpactus dicitur in *cœlo cœlorum ante-rioritatis:* adeoque *supra cœlos illos* residens, in loco sublimissimo, purissimo, et summæ gloriæ ac tranquillitatis, in sede quæ respectu *cœlorum inferiorum* est et ipsa et dici potest *cœlum*. Plane quemadmodum Eph. iv, 10, Christus legitur *adscendisse supra omnes cœlos:* et Heb. vii, 26, *sublimior cœlis factus*, et iv, 14, *pertransiisse cœlos*.

There is something inexpressibly sublime in this thought of Heavens rising in ever mounting stories one above the other. We have said, that while the time conceptions of the ancient mind surpassed those of the modern, its space conceptions fell short. But the latter remark needs qualification. We may distinguish two kinds of space conception, the emotional, and the mathematical. Of the first kind, are the ideas and images of the Scriptures; to the latter belong the numerical estimates of modern science. In Psalm cxiii, 5, God is represented as having his throne so high that he looketh down upon the Heavens themselves as into a depth immensely below. High as are our visible heavens, there is a loftier dome as far above them as they are above the earth, and so on, Heaven above Heaven, as far as the imagination can mount. But what is all this, some may say, to the calculations of modern science? What are these conceptions of apparently vaulted domes thus rising above each other, to the distances reached by the calculations of Herschell and Leverrier? We can not give the mathematical ratio; but if we may judge of the real magnitude of the conception by its emotional power, the latter bears no comparison to the former. We rest the opinion, too, on the most undeniable facts. The scientific estimate has ever been cold, emotionless, productive of the feeblest religious influence. Pious men—pious from other causes—have endeavored sometimes to extract from them their pious uses; but some of the greatest names connected with such mere numerical calculations have belonged to men who have manifested but little fear of God, but little reverence even for the true greatness of the universe. The fact, we say, is undeniable. Let the psychologist, or the historian of philosophy, account for it as he may. Sines, cosines, tangents, and logarithms, ever so powerfully applied to the cosmical distances, will not make men religious, they will not keep them such. Neither has the telescope any more converting power. Atheists, or what is not much better, mere scientific theists, have looked through it and remained atheists and scientific theists still. But what good, it may be said, can come out of fiction? One of these may be called a false conception which science has exploded. True—but this image, though false, still represents the most truthful of ideas. It is that of the ever ascending glory of God, of which time worlds and space worlds are both but the visible or conceptual manifestations. The scientific estimate, on the other hand—as one of them of highest note has impiously said—"represents the glory of the astronomer." The heavens are his diagram, the stars his figured points. It is most frequently "a knowledge that puffeth up," instead of making men devout, and hence in proportion to its scientific accuracy, is oftentimes the enormity of its spiritual falsehood. Here we find the explanation of the fact so strange, yet so susceptible of proof, that men who thought the skies came down upon the mountain top, have had thoughts of God so much greater than were ever generated in the proceedings of academies or the discoveries of science. David and Pythagoras have, in this way, had a higher conception of the cosmos and of the divine glory in it, than men who have calculated eclipses, made tables of the planets's motions, or spent their lives in astronomical observatories.*

* The force and majesty of such sublime Bible images are at once impaired, whenever we attempt to give them a scientific interpretation, or connect them with any scientific notions. The thought is fettered, compromised, restrained to a view which after-science may show to be inadequate, and kept within a sphere where the petty scientific interest is predominant at the expense of the higher and the emotional. We may cite, as a striking example of this effect, Mr. LORD's interpretation of Rev. xx, 11,—"*And I saw a great white throne, and Him that sat thereon, from whose face the earth and the heavens fled away, and no place was found for them.*" There is a sublime here that nothing, even in Scripture, surpasses. Creation would hide from the Holy Presence, but finds no place where it is not. Who can add to this? Who can make it more clear by any scientific filling up—who can increase its effect by any rhetorical or hermeneutical illustration? The right-minded reader must feel that all science here is out of place, and most especially a science which must have been unknown to the writer. Whatever may be its pretensions, it is too small a thing, (to say nothing of its imperfection and inadequacy,) to be allowed any weight,

We are dwelling too long on the spatial view. It is the time aspect of these cosmical phrases with which we are chiefly here concerned, and especially the fair meaning of the term so expressive of the most remote antiquity. But where, then, was Kedhem, the oldest Kedhem ? In what earliest principium of time, or rather, if we follow out the thought, in what unknown, inconceivable, yet faith-apprehended state of being, of which we are compelled to think as of something that was ere time began or any of those finite acts and finite thoughts of finite beings, by whose successions alone either time or chronology can be conceived of as having any existence ? We have alluded to the rationalist's idea of Kedhem. Mr. LORD would go a little beyond this. He would carry it back to a date about three thousand years before the Psalmist, and nearly six thousand years, perhaps, from our own time. Here he finds not only a young

and any place, in the awful picture. The splendor of its sublimity pales at once when we begin to talk of orbits, and aphelia, and the statistics of the solar system. But let us hear Mr. LORD's interpretation. "The flight of the earth from the presence of the Judge, indicates that the scene of the judgment was at a distance from its orbit. In other visions it had been exhibited as stationary in order that the symbolic agents might exert their agency in the Apostle's sight. But no such reason remained for its continued presence, and its *flight* accordingly, and *that of the planets*, was that *doubtless*, of their real motion around their orbits. *That no place was found for them, simply denotes, therefore, that they continued in motion.*" Think, for a moment, of the language thus interpreted—*From whose face the earth and the heavens fled away.* This means the planetary motions in their orbits. *And there* was found no place for them—This means that "they continued in motion." Such is the interpretation he would give of the Greek ἔφυγε—*they kept moving on,* in exact obedience to the laws of centrifugal and centripetal forces! We would indulge in no disparaging remarks on Mr. LORD's scientific view of this remarkable passage. It is sufficient to present it to the consideration of any thoughtful reader who can feel the inexpressible sublimity of the Scriptures.

Tellus but a young Kosmos new created, or rather, just brought from absolute nonentity. To this six thousand years, or thereabouts, add six solar days, of twenty-four hours each, and all is gone; earth, sun and stars *are not*, in any sense—not even an *idea* of them, or law, or force from which they might arise, or any "unseen things" from which they might be created. Matter has yet no being, the hyle or mother of matter is not yet born, or, if we may not allude to such a dangerous "Platonic conceit," there is not even an embryo existence of the "highest (or most elemental) part of the *dust of the world*." Even the light has not yet had its birth. It has not yet, in any part of the universe, commenced that long journey of which the books tell us, as requiring millions of years to reach our own planet. There is no light anywhere; for there is no outward divine glory to be revealed, and no kosmos to reveal it to. This "robe of Deity" is still unwoven, and God has not yet began to "dwell in light inapproachable and full of glory." Angels and Archangels, Thrones, Dominions, Principalities and Powers, yea, all the celestial hosts are yet nonentities; for all this results if such be the true date of the beginning mentioned by Moses, and that beginning is the great principium, with nothing before it but the very being of the Divine or uncreated essence. On such a view of dates, we must look for the evidence of such prior existences alone in Milton; we search in vain for it in the Scriptures.

Such an estimate of times may be perfectly consistent with piety. It may be perfectly consistent with sublime views of Deity. We find no fault with it on that account.

As well six thousand years ago, as six million ages. Since the world, regarded as all that is not God, must have had a beginning, an absolute beginning, a precise beginning of a beginning, then it would be, at a certain date after that absolute beginning, just six thousand years and six days old, and why may not that be our own terrestrial date? No reason to the contrary could be given if the Bible had clearly revealed it. Science might raise some objections to trouble us, but science has ere this dealt in phantoms. The answer then is, We do not find the evidence of it in the Scriptures. We find things that look the other way, and which, the more we study them, assume more and more the opposite aspect. Not that the Scriptural writers were ambitious to give us cosmical knowledge, but the manner in which they speak of the great times of God's kingdom — their language of olams and olams of olams, of ages and ages of ages, of eternities in the plural, of great chronological divisions in the past and future, instead of blank continuances after the style of much modern thought — their use of these pluralities and these swelling reduplications in a manner inconsistent with the narrow bounds into which the historical times of our planet would cramp them — all these produce strongly the conviction that the Bible does not represent our world, or olam, as an isolated existence with a cosmical blank before and after, but as connected with an ongoing series of ages stretching immeasurably back as they reach onward to a distance immeasurably future.

But where is Khedem then? Some of his clerical friends, alarmed at the rebuke received at the same time from orthodoxy and science, have manifested some concern for the writer's sanity. There is a bugbear which haunts their minds on his account. It is the frightful idea of the eternity of matter. Hardly any heresy has such terrors for them as that. A plurality of Adams, or the dual "theology of the intellect and the affections," or even a development theory of Christianity, would not be half so frightful. Do you not, they ask, teach, or, at least, are you not in danger of teaching, the eternity of matter? We would set this friendly solicitude at rest, once for all. There are two sides to this matter, or this question of the eternity of the universe. One is clear, positive, and capable of a most clear and positive statement. Let us state then, very sincerely, our firm belief that this world, kosmos, or universe, (using the terms for all dynamical existence that is not God,) has a certain finite age, as certain and as finite, although unknown, as the known age of an individual man or an individual tree. That is, —there is an exact number of minutes (by which is meant a measure of time determined by a certain known space, or pendulum of a certain known length) since this world, kosmos, or universe as above defined, or any seed, or embryo, or element of it, began to be. This number of minutes is theoretically, if not practically, assignable, —that is, it is a finite number capable of being expressed in a certain extent of decimals, if we had space or room to put such decimals, either in our own known world, or within the bounds of any distance that has been reached by the highest lens of Lord Rosse's telescope. We hope the answer is clear and definite, and that we shall be relieved, hereafter, of the odious heretical charge, and of the consequent odium theologicum which a very pious science has so scientifically, and so magnanimously labored to fix upon us.

But now there is another side of the matter. Let us see what definite ideas, or if there are any definite ideas, we can get about it. We travel up this road very easily; for ten billion years are as easily passed over as ten seconds; and so we go back, back, in our conceptions, without any difficulty, till we come to that point at the head of all undivine being which we term the beginning. On this side lies all created δύναμις, (whether matter, or force, or each as inseparable from the other,) with all successions of *acts* or *facts*, and all created spiritualities, with all successions of *thoughts* and *ideas*. In other words, we have got to the point beyond which time is inconceivable, unless we suppose that God's thoughts are as our thoughts, which the Bible tells us expressly they are not. Well, what then? If there was no time before this, then this was the beginning of time. Hence, there was no time when the universe was not. This may have a very bad look to some, and we would not press it upon the nervous weakness of some men's orthodoxy; but yet it is a position which need not occasion much anxiety whilst we hold fast to the other. We are safe as long as we do not drag the anchor that is fixed sure and steadfast in the first and firmer ground. No one need be unduly alarmed at what they might call a perilous ascent; it will ever be easy to get safely down with such a foothold as was first secured in the exact numerical age of the world as seen from our own or the finite side. But why, then, stop at all in the finite? We can only say it is because we can not help ourselves. We can not get out of the laws of our own thinking, even though they give us certain evidence that there is something above those laws, and that it must be inconceivably more glorious than anything they can directly think or conceive. There is certainly great gain in this. Even though it be an unknown and unthought world, it is much to be certain of its existence;—it is much that our finite powers can reach the point that assures us of the necessity of the infinite, of that which not only "eye hath not seen, nor ear heard, but which it hath not entered, and can not enter, into the mind to think or conceive." Still, it may be asked—What do you mean by the timeless state? We answer: We have no conception, no thought, no idea of it in its mode of being, and yet some idea of it as a glorious reality inseparably connected with the divine as distinguished from finite minds. It is the ante-time, as well as ante-mundane state, when God inhabited Kedhem, dwelling alone, and yet not alone, in the glory of his triune existence. But may not the question be turned against the interrogator? What do *you* mean when you say there was an eternity of time before this principium of the universe? What succession of facts existed before this,—what succession of thoughts? Your conceptions of it are a blank. When you attempt to fill them up, it is only the poor cheat of figuring over and over again *our* successions, our years, our chronology,—out of which we can not think,—and carrying them out of cosmical time into what you are pleased to call a past eternal time before the world began. Such objections, with all possible respect for their makers be it said, are not only unsound, but senseless. The man who talks of matter, or the material universe, as eternal, meaning thereby co-eval, co-existent, and, therefore, co-essential with God, talks impiously. The man who affirms that time was before any cosmical, or undivine existence,—employing the term in the usual and only conceivable sense of finite divisible duration, measured by *succession of events* in an outward finite physical, or by *succession of thoughts* in an inward finite spiritual world—that man talks, not only impiously, but ignorantly, absurdly. His only defence against profanity lies in the fact that he knows not what he means. He has good sonorous words, indeed, but all soul, whether of sense, conception, or idea, is wanting there. Let us cease our prattling. What can such worms as we are know about the mode of existence of the Infinite, or what is possible for the Infinite, or what he ought to be? The writer is willing to take the rebuke to himself. Neither of us know what we are talking about; yet stil lit may be maintained, that *he* is most reverent who contents himself with negations or exhausting positions—simply affirming, in the language of Scripture (our only light here,) that "God's ways are not as our ways, nor his thoughts as our thoughts," but heaven-high above their highest reach. The universe is finite; for it is not God. It is finite in time and space. It has a certain age; it has existed a certain whole or fractional number of our years; and there is a certain number of decimals, if we knew them, or could write them, by which it is expressible. We both think so, because we can not help ourselves—we can not think otherwise. Our reasonings about eternity and infinity are worthless in themselves, and whatever relative value they may possess is only on that side which proves their worthlessness. With the Scriptures in our hands, we can go directly to truths which philosophy feebly announces, and of which science knows nothing. One of these is that time and thought are not to God what they are to us. In going beyond this simple announcement, or in dwelling upon it, one may "darken counsel by words without knowledge," but his error is not so great as that of him who wholly rejects this transcending truth, or whose reasonings claim the merit of common sense and intelligibility only by being directly opposed to it.*

* There is one thing connected with this matter of the "eternity of matter," that really tries the patience. We allude to the bugbear of Platonism, raised by such writers as Mr. LORD and Professor DANA, and the stereotyped charge they make that Plato taught this doctrine. It has come from Church historians either confounding, or, as is the case with the more respectable, writing so carelessly as to lead their readers to confound, the old with the neo-platonism. Now, we affirm, that Plato never taught the doctrine in any such sense as they would attach to it. We can only mention here three heads of argument that might be conclusively urged in refutation. There is,

1. Plato's labored argument against the atheists, the fundamental position of which is that "*soul* is older than *matter*," either in its essence or its properties. It is sufficient to say, that the whole foundation, as well as superstructure, of this elaborate argument is destroyed at once by the least admission of the idea of the eternity of matter, as such writers understand it. There is,

2. The important distinction so clearly made in the Timæus, 27, D, between the two great classes of existence, τὸ ὂν ἀεί γένεσιν δὲ οὐκ ἔχον, —"the ever being that hath no origination," and το γιγνόμενον, or "that which hath birth," and beginning, as well as change and end; the one uncaused, uncreated, unchanging,—the other *born in time*, continually changing, having of necessity a cause, and that cause the pre-existent *being* which he calls τὸ ὄντως ον. To the first class belong *God* and *truth*—God as the oldest *soul*, and truth as his mind, or Νοῦς; to the second, all that falls, in any way, under the cognizance of the *sense*, as distinguished from the νοητόν, in short, the world, the world of matter, in all its forms from the most elementary up to the most organic. We may say, too, the world with all its dynamical phenomena and physical life; for nothing is more clear than that Plato represents even his *anima mundi*, his soul, or

life of the world, as a distinct creation (whether absurdly or not, we do not now enquire) made by the Eternal One before its material body.

3. The eternity of the material world, or of matter in any sense, would be irreconcilably at war with that doctrine of ideas by which Plato is so widely distinguished from the Aristotelian philosophy of old, and the Baconian of modern times. Both of these latter are perfectly consistent with the idea of the eternity of matter and of a world of eternal causation; nay, more, they can not disprove it;—nay, more, they are compelled to admit it, if they remain true to their fundamental law of induction without unconsciously bringing in, from other sources, a light that of itself forms no part of their lauded science The Platonic, on the other hand, is the only philosophy with which such a doctrine is fundamentally and irreconcilably at war. The very essence of the Platonic system is involved in its great gradations. Matter is younger than life, life is junior to law, law is junior to ideas, ideas belong to mind, and mind, in the order of conception, if not of time, (for here all time is transcended,) is born of the Αγαθον, or the ineffable essence. We can only here present the points of an argument. It is, indeed, an attractive theme; but its full discussion would demand more space than can be bestowed upon it in the present volume.

CHAPTER V.

THE FOUR GREAT IDEAS OF THE MOSAIC ACCOUNT.

The Word—The Work—The Rest—The Day—These must be in Harmony with Each Other—The Old Arabian View—The Patriarchal View—Theory of Guyot—Of Mr. LORD—*Of Pye Smith—The True Scriptural View is the One that has least Need of Science.*

THIS subject of the Creative Days has been pursued at great length; and we would, therefore, only add to the present argument a synoptical view covering the whole ground, yet capable of being set forth in the clearest and briefest terms. To the writer's own mind it is irresistible, leaving not a shade of doubt as to the general force and aspect of the passage. It is hoped that it will so strike the mind of the serious reader. The thought has already been alluded to; but it is one that will bear to be dwelt upon. We say, then, that to one carefully reading this remarkable chapter, (Gen. I,) as it ought to be read, there must present themselves four important ideas, standing distinctly and prominently out from the face of the narrative. There is,

1st. The going forth of the Word and Spirit, each time in wondrous conjunction, and making the division of each wondrous day.

2d. The Divine *Work.*

3d. The Divine Rest.

4th. The Divine Day of Working.

Now, we appeal to Mr. LORD himself, blindly determined as he is to peril the whole veracity of the Scriptures on his narrow notion of twenty-four hours. The first three of these ideas, he, of course, admits to be ineffable, that is, above all human standard, both as to manner and degree. The Word, the Work, the Rest—they are extraordinary, to say the least. The divine Spirit was not a wind, as some say, both among sciolists and commentators. The divine Word was not an audible voice. Even Mr. LORD would not dare to call a man an infidel for thus interpreting. The divine Work was not a mere exercise of power, a huge Cyclopean, upheaving, earth-moving strength, differing only in degree (however immensely) from human work. We cannot repeat it too often—"His ways are not as our ways," *His work is not as our work.* It is not the mere quantitative energy of "the God of Forces;"* it differs from ours not only in dynamical potency, but wholly in some transcending mode or series of working. And then that sublimest of all ideas, the divine Repose; we can not get words for it; the Hebrew *Sabbath* furnishes the simplest conception for the human mind; other terms might mar and pervert, as well as fall short; but no language in respect to it could be hyperbolical. The divine repose after the creative days! Are all these, then, the Word, the Work, the Rest,—are all these extraordinary, ineffable, in a word, divine?—and shall we not extend the same scale of measurement, and the same mode of thinking, to that fourth term, and that fourth idea, which is ever in such immediate connection with them? If we refuse to do this, why not bring it all down to the same anthropomorphic

* Daniel xi, 38. Deum Maozim, as the Vulgate calls him.

level? The one view is no more metaphorical, no more forced, no more an accommodation than the others. Where all else is superhuman, divine, shall the day be a human day—just such a day as we now see constantly measured by the sun and divided by the clock? The work might have been instantaneous, and that would also have been wondrous, ineffable. True—but it is clearly revealed to us that God has in some way taken times for his manifestations; he has employed series; and shall not these times be in admitted harmony with other features of the grand succession? In the contemplation of such a *work*, and such a *rest*, can we without a discord mingle the idea of days of twenty-four hours each, and especially when we are expressly told that in the first four of these mysterious days the sun had not yet appeared in the heavens, nor any outward astronomical phenomena by which such time-periods could be connected with any outward cosmical standard? Shall all else, then, be in such splendid proportion, and yet this held to be of such withered dimensions? It is out of all keeping. The discord of such a view must have been felt by Moses, and the earliest readers of Moses, as well as by any modern mind. Science has given us no advantage here. The world-problem, and especially as it presented the thought of great successions of ages, was a favorite of the earliest east. The grand conceptions of cycles, and series, and olamic periods, came as easily and as truthfully to the Idumean sages as to the Yale College Professor of Mineralogy and Conchology. To those sons of the desert, the thought may have been suggested by astronomical cyclical appearances, or it may have been the voice of old traditions that had come over the waters of the great flood, but it was none the less grand and free that it lay in their minds unconnected with any puzzling positions of the rocks, or any doubtful, ever-changing statistics of exhumed fossils. They needed nothing of this to convince them that the Great Allah had been working, not from an absolute eternity, (a metaphysical notion with which they did not trouble their devout, practical brains,) but for ages, and ages of ages, running on to an extent so vast that our own age, world, or olam, (for all these words mean the same thing,) was but as a passing *day* in the mighty series. There can not be a more frigid conceit than that modern science either gave birth to, or has enlarged, or is at all necessary to, this conception. It might have been entertained by any thoughtful son of the thoughtful Shemitic race. In perfect consistency with what we know of the Patriarchal character, may it have been thought by Abraham on the plains of Mamre, or by Jacob on his stone pillow at Bethel. Above all would it be familiar to that same Moses, "the man of God," who has given us this history of the creative days. Who can have a doubt remaining, as he reads that sublime Ninetieth Psalm, which all antiquity, with all modern assent, has ascribed to him as its author—"We spend our years as a tale that is told, as a thought, as a sigh,* but thou, O Lord, art from olam to olam, from world to world! A thousand years are in thy sight but as yesterday when it is past, and as a watch in the night." We have advanced on the ideas of the ancients, it is vauntingly said. Compare this conception of the Mosaic Psalm with Mr. LORD'S

* Such is the expressive rendering of the Syriac.

narrow interpretations, and you have all the answer that the case demands.

Thus we have the simple yet grand conception as it lay in that imaging mind to which the Divine Spirit first gave it. The *Times* are as extraordinary as the *Word*, the *Working*, and the *Rest*. When we come to examine it closely, we are astonished to find what an absence of all support there is in the Scriptures for this narrow conception of an exact twenty-four hours. Yet once off this contracted ground, we have room enough. There need be no concern about the length of these creative times. We may dismiss alike from our thoughts the clock measured solar days, and the stratified eras of the geologists. We find ourselves among the aeons and olams of the Bible, those *worlds*, or *ages*, that we are told, Heb. xi, 3, were *framed*, or put in order, by the Word of God bringing out the visible from the invisible. There is ample space both for revelation and geology. Science may fill up the details as she pleases; she may shift them as she pleases; she may make as many seeming "harmonies," or seeming discords, as she pleases. The great and threatening collision was in the idea of the earth's remote antiquity which science claimed to have discovered. The opposite cramping view removed, —the Bible suffered to speak in its own majestic style, —the times once conceived of, and most rationally conceived of, as in harmony with the other sublimities of the narration,—the indefinite, the boundless once admitted, —we need not be troubled about other difficulties. The grand outline order must, in the main, remain unaffected by anything that any induction from existing appearances can ever present. There may be unexplained appearances of overlapping, in some details, but the great periods stand out in bold distinctness,— a dark world of waters — light thereon — an atmosphere, or sky *appearing* — land appearing — vegetable life — celestial manifestations — animal life — Man — the world-rest. These must remain in their grand chronological order, whatever face science may put on or off. Here, beside the beginning and the rest, are the six great ineffable workings, each commencing with a new utterance of the Omnific Word. Here are the six great *divisions*, each supernatural, or *God-made*, in distinction from the natural or sun-divided days. Here are the six great *appearances*, each making a new morning; and all followed by that wondrous repose of Deity which distinguishes the present among the olamic times.

On this we take our stand as opposed to the most narrow anthropomorphism, on the one side, and the ever-shifting theories of science on the other. The grand objections to the view of Guyot, as advocated by Professor DANA, is, that it either makes Moses a mere mechanical revealer of facts of which he had no *conceptions* at all, or gives him a science which we are certain he could not have possessed. He no more thought of nebulæ, and nebular rings, than he did of sun-risings and twenty-four hours for the first great day, or for any of the great days that followed. He thought of no other world than this, and the sky around it which he called the heavens, and in which the heavenly bodies *appeared*. These heavenly bodies are presented, not in their far-off unknown localities, but as they are optically manifested in the near visible firmament. It was that sun and moon, and not the sun and moon of modern science, with which Moses had to do. He may have known more or less about them; but he describes the "things that are seen," and their origin *as things seen*, instead of their essential birth from nonentity, or the causations that are connected with their phenomenal change. The second day's working had no reference to nebular condensations or the throwing off the nebular rings of the solar system, (if there ever were such rings,) but to the forming of our earth's atmosphere, and its phenomenal sky. His chaos was a chaotic earth covered with waters, and not the first immeasurably extended matter of the universe. His stars were luminous points in the firmament, such as they appeared when the arrangements of the fourth period first suffered them to shine upon the earth, and not the far off suns whose light it has taken millions of years to travel down to us.

Thus stands the Mosaic narrative by itself, unique in its sublimity. The views we have rejected, on both sides, are so rejected, not because of their agreement, or disagreement, with science, but because we can not find any place for either in the written narrative. Especially do we fail to find that awful chasm that Professor DANA makes in the work of the second day, and on which we would dwell more fully in another part of the argument. Mr. LORD's scheme is at war with the obviously remarkable or extraordinary character of the first days. It is tested at once by the conclusive fact, that it has to bring in more explanations, or rather guesses, from modern science, than the view which he falsely charges as being held in deference to science. It has to talk of shifting axes, and changed ecliptics; it has to falsify the account, and go right in its face, by giving the heavenly bodies their earth-enlightening, day-measuring, and day-making office in the very beginnings of the periods, and before the fixed date that Scripture assigns to them. It has thus really no work at all for the fourth day; it is a blank in the creative calendar, occupied simply by an empty announcement of what had been done long before. Its opposition to well settled science we would not dwell upon, since it forms no part of our plan. Still, since Mr. LORD has so much to say of science, it justifies the remark, that no man of ordinary intelligence can now regard his view as agreeing with the most common observations which go to prove the earth's antiquity. The Pye Smith theory is at war both with science and revelation. It is opposed to the manifest idea, that the Mosaic account was meant to embrace the whole earth and the whole sky or atmospherical heavens regarded as above and around it. Equally obvious is it that the Mosaic narrative means to commence with our world in a state of comparative infancy, and to conduct it through a series of ascending toledoth, or "generations," up to its present condition as the abode of man. Although not cosmological in the widest sense, so as to embrace the remotest universe, it is evidently occupied with the history of our planet from a period before which it had not been a world of life or light. There is no intimation of any previous history known or thought of. There is no evidence that would justify, on any philological ground, the throwing back the first verse away by itself, and separating it by a chasm so out of all proportion with the shorter times, and comparatively modern dates that come so long after. Like Mr. LORD's guesses, it is a mere deference to science, and one, too, which creates more scientific difficulties than it removes. The indefinite-time view of the creative day falls in easily with the spirit of the account, and proves itself to be the true interpretation by the little need it has of any scientific support, or of any cosmological conception that might not have been entertained by the earliest minds. It is the Scriptural view, and science, instead of demanding a forced conformity, must seek a reconciliation within the broad limits it allows. She must not ask Biblical men to be ever putting ahead their hermeneutical landmarks every time she chooses to change her oft-shifting positions.

CHAPTER VI.

SCIENCE AND THE BIBLE.

Spirit of the Scientific Patronage—Professor DANA'S *Apothegm—The Bible "the Boat, Science the Current"—The Natural in Creation—Claim of Prior Discovery—Claim of Science to have Proved the Supernatural—Science can not find the Supernatural—Must ever assume a Law for a Fact—Can not even find a God—An Atheist as good a Scientific Man as a Theist—Secret Wheels and Cogs in Nature—The Greater Durations—Science can not disprove Development—Can never refute the "Vestiges of Creation"—Bible alone can slay "The Vestiges."*

IT is the spirit thus manifested, that is more anti-Biblical than any particular difficulties raised by science. Without wishing to judge harshly, we can not help regarding it as in its ultimate effects more injurious to a true and hearty faith than the unmistakable feeling manifested by the avowedly unbelieving geologist. The advocates of this pious talking theism mean well undoubtedly; but there is in their prominent position in respect to the Scriptures, and their favorite talk about nature as a parallel revelation, as real an undervaluing of the true and only Divine Word, as is contained in Auguste Comte's utter rejection of the idea. The author of the Vestiges of Creation, as far as we can see, has as good a theory of revelation as Professor DANA. When he comes to the proper place for it in his book, the latter writer talks just as piously as our scientific friend, and as we expect to show, with as much consistency. The Bible is the boat—the New-Haven authority lets us know, in his significant comparison—the Bible is the boat, and geology, or science, the current in which it floats. There is no mistaking the meaning, or certainly the spirit, of the representation. The writer did not intend to be impious. The professed orthodoxy of his literary position would lead him to speak well of the Bible, and to be rhetorical about " the harmonies," etc.; but he is sometimes off his guard. He becomes so in the passage to which we now refer, and which may be found on page 93 of his review. It had been remarked in the book, that " geology had been driven more and more to acknowledge the mixture of the natural and the supernatural in the production of the earth." This is taken up as an insult to geology, and the champion of geology and science in general must repel it with indignation, and not only that, but even " carry the war into Africa,"—and there he forgets himself. It had not been said, at all, that Geology had been driven to this by any Biblical interpretations. We never supposed her so pious as that. In fact, the thought was the other way. She had been driven to it by the pious feeling seeking it in her own discoveries,—the pious feeling which, although no part of science, and, in truth, no effect of science, yet was vital in many most excellent scientific men, and controlled their scientific reasonings. When it was thus said that Geology had recognized the supernatural, it should have been regarded as something of a compliment to this youngest daughter among the sciences. But the word "driven" was perhaps the offensive term. It would seem to convey the impression that Geology is not *naturally*, as some claim, very religious, that she is not ever seeking the supernatural and rejoicing exceedingly to find it. And yet such a suspicion might be pardoned in one who had only read the works of Lyell, and knew how scientific men in Germany and France — men certainly every way the equals of Professor DANA — had rejected this whole notion of supernaturalism which he claims to have been a discovery of science. But such a thought, it seems, can not be allowed at all; Geology, as such, must be cleared of every suspicion. It is not enough to concede to her the supernatural as a frank admission joyfully made by pious geologists, and on evidence piously sought in deference to so respectable an authority as a divine revelation, but it must be an original or independent discovery of science, which Bible men must take on her authority, and bring their Bibles up to it, easily if it may be, but forcibly if no other method remains. But to give the quotation — This, says Professor DANA, in reply to the bare suspicion that Geology had been influenced by revelation, (a false suspicion, too, of his own as to the meaning of the passage in the book,) this "is very much, we think, as a current is driven by the boat it carries; for Geology *first* proved that the natural was involved in creation, and with a rare exception has always admitted the supernatural; and she has *finally drawn off exegesis* so completely into the same course, that some, as they are hurried on by the current, exclaim in great glee over their wonderful progress, and in their remarkable self-complacency look down frowning upon the current that they imagine is trying to keep up with them." There is no mistaking this language, nor the spirit from which it proceeds. It is a spirit, we say it boldly, that is more odious than the avowed infidelity that has led scientific men (some of them, perhaps, in deep sorrow,) to regard the Scriptures and scientific discovery as hopelessly irreconcilable. It is a language, moreover, we say it fearlessly, which is and ought to be regarded as an insult to the Christian world. It was an insult to the Biblical Editors of that Biblical Review in which, by a circuitous route, he sought to obtain an influence for his criticism which it never could have had on its own merits. It was an insult to every clergyman, unless it be those who regard this mode of defending the Scriptures as better and more available than interpretation. Such are pleased, doubtless, because it so piously patronises Moses, and makes him so much more scientific than they had ever imagined. But what is their occupation, not to speak of their vocation, if the above paragraph be true, either in its letter or its spirit? What are the clergy, what are orthodox Professorships, what is Yale College, or Andover theology,—what are Biblical Reviews, if the Bible is indeed such a nose of wax, which can be made to suit any countenance, and Biblical faith such a "floating boat" on the current of science, as this writer has so unmistakably represented it? There is no misunderstanding the language, or the air of scientific pride, with which it is brought in. Biblical interpretation is "the boat," and science is the broad directing current in which it floats, and by which it is carried down. The contrary idea that in revelation may be found the permanent, whilst science sometimes floats, and shifts her place, is treated as a hypocritical pretense. An honest and hearty study of the Scriptures, with a conviction deep as life itself, that all the treasures of human science and human philosophy could never begin to pay for the loss of that first chapter of Genesis — or of the deference which is its due — such a study, and such an expression of opinion is treated as a hollow ruse on the part of these men of exegesis. It is all a false pretense to save their waning credit. They glorify the old book, and "exclaim in great glee over their wonderful progress," when, after all, they are only sailing down that current which they "imagine is trying to keep up with them," and which "has drawn off exegesis so completely into its course." There is no mistaking, we say, the meaning of this language, or the temper which gave it utterance. We have battled some with the infidels, perhaps, at times, with too much acrimony, though ever with an irresistible feeling of the life and death nature of the controversy,— but there is a patronage of Christianity, and of the Bible, compared with which unbelief is entitled to our sympathy. We say it fearlessly, there is no form of Bible rejection we would not respect more than the spirit of the above quoted passage; there is no position of infidelity we would not openly avow rather than be the author of such a declaration. To see how this petty science assumes to lord it over the Scriptures, and the men of the Scriptures! for there is no proof that the author of the book assailed is alone referred to. A class is described. It is the friends of exegesis, who pretend to find in the Bible evidence of what Geology claims as all her own. The sneering remark has an equal application to all who study the Bible with the expectation that it will teach them any thing on the great questions of origin and destiny that would certainly seem to fall so appropriately within its revealing province. All such men are invading the domain of Professor DANA and his friend AGASSIZ. Their exegesis is all a mockery. They are in a "floating boat," and that boat is in a current from which they can not get out. Their Biblical studies are all a mere pretense to enable them to make the best of their poor position in the rear of science. Strange how apparent extremes do sometimes agree! Mr. LORD from *his* stand point has a similar view, and expresses precisely the same feeling. Any man who ventures to think that the wondrous creative day was not exactly twenty-four hours in duration,—neither more nor less—he unhesitatingly sets down as insincere. Their deriving such a view from the Scriptures, he modestly says, is all a pretense. They would have us believe that they have anchored their exegetical boat, when they are only floating down the current of science.

We have had mainly to do with the spirit of the above extract, but a few words may be given to some of its statements. "Geology," says Professor DANA, "*first* proved that the natural was involved in creation." Here there is something very sweeping. No room for modifications or exceptions. Has he traced the consequences of this far-reaching assertion? What, too, must we think of its modesty, when we keep in mind the connections in which it is said, and the references it invariably suggests? Geology *first* proved!—It is a claim of priority. Against whom? Against what? Who is the rival in the case? It is no one of the fellow-sciences; it is no dogma of philosophy; it is no competing theory, professing to rest itself solely on human reasoning and human scientific discovery. It is certainly a strange assertion; but it reveals the whole spirit of the article in which it appears. It can have no meaning unless the supposed rival claimant be the Scriptures, or the Scriptures so interpreted as in any way to teach the natural in creation. It reminds us strongly of the comparatively petty disputes which so often arise within this jealous field of natural science, such as the question — Who first thought of steamboats, or who first invented the cotton picker, or who first discovered the principle of the daguerreotype. Such questions may amuse us, but the competition here presented is revolting to every true feeling of faith and reverence. "Geology *first* showed the natural in creation"! Then it is not taught in the Bible at all. If so, what becomes of "the harmony," that boasted "harmony of science and revelation," which Professor DANA takes as the running title of his article? Does he mean that Geology first discovered this exegetically? That would be nonsense. But by what other possible process could she find it out?— we mean, not simply the natural, but the natural *in creation*. This is the essence of the vaunting proposition. Geology might discover the natural in the rocks; but how does she know whether this is *creation*, or any part of creation? It is mainly a Scriptural word and a Scriptural idea. How does she know at all what creation is, or what cosmical acts are included in the word, unless the Creator reveals it to her? How does she know that creation, whatever it may be, is not now going on? How has she learned when it ceased, or where it began, or in what processes or periods it consists, unless by a revelation from some higher plane, or from that higher ground the Scriptures are assumed to occupy.

If it is not taught in the Scriptures, then Professor DANA is in opposition to them; for there can be no middle ground here; the ignoring so important an element in the creative process, is equivalent to a denial of it. Such opposition would not give much trouble to some men; for we boast of being a free thinking age; but the Professor must, in some general way, be on Bible ground. He would not wholly discard the old boat as long as it floats so conveniently and so quietly down the current. It may have been in the Scriptures, however, one might say, yet undiscovered, "until science found it elsewhere." That would be strange, especially since the idea of the *natural*, and the words by which we express it, date from the earliest times, and from the very roots of language. Their primary images fade away and the words are laid up as fossils or dried plants in the cabinets of science and philosophy. But the ideas both of nature and law are very old. There are two reasons for this. The most common observation discloses the fact of a regular ongoing in this world in which one thing is continually coming out of another, and, secondly, it is one of the inward laws of the mind's thinking, if it think at all, that there must be an outward law,— a harmony, unity, call it what we may, that *binds* these ongoings together in one kosmos as the idea of one mind. Thus every particular organism is thought of as having its life and law, without which it could not be an organism, and the same mode of thinking is irresistibly carried out to the law, or unity of the great whole as far as it is known to the sense, or conceived to be. It is the foolish boast, and stale story of the modern scientific lecturer, or college orator, that this idea of universal law was never in the world until Newton saw an apple fall from a tree; but long ago Socrates spoke of it as an opinion held by the sages of old, and he might have said the men of old, that "harmony and order (κοσμιότητα, law, or regular harmonious arrangement,) held together heaven and earth, and that for this very reason *the whole* was called kosmos." It was a "geometrical equality or harmony," he says, indicating that it was a higher mathematical law which after-science might trace a few steps farther, but no science could ever hope to sum in all its glorious completeness. The idea of Socrates' ancient sages is no where more clear, to one who will look for it, than on the pages of the Old Testament. It is the חָק־עוֹלָם, the *law of Olam*, and the particular manifestations of it, are the חקות עולם, or the חקות שמים וארץ, *the laws of the Heavens and the Earth*, Jer. xxxiii, 25, Job xxxviii, 33, the "laws of the moon and the stars," Jer. xxxi, 35. It is the "*word* or law of the Lord (Psalm cxix, 89) that is established in the Heavens" In æternum Domine, verbum tuum permanet in cœlo, in generationem et generationem. Ordinatione tua perseverat dies; quoniam omnia serviunt tibi. "All things stand according to thine ordinances." How much better and nobler is the mere recognition of such a law, however taught or acquired, than the science which, in its extravagant boasting at having traced a few of its links, loses all the moral grandeur of the idea, in the petty, selfish, scientific interest.

It may be thought by some that the author, led away by a favorite idea, is finding too much in the Scriptures that would seem to him to have a scientific or philosophic aspect. But this would be an altogether mistaken view of his aim and thought. There is no science in the Bible — God be praised for the fact. But there is that which is deeper than science, broader than science; we mean in respect to nature and the world. There is that which is fundamental to all sound thinking, and which science, in its modern acceptation, instead of having discovered or made more clear, oftentimes confuses and obscures. It is so with these ideas of *law* and *nature.* Men thought as distinctly about them, and as truly about them, with a limited, as they do now with a multiplied knowledge of physical facts; and the reason is, that such thinking does not depend on *amount* of facts, or *quantity* of discovery great in one aspect yet ever most minute in another, but derives its strength, and its certainty, from those broad and universal views that lie upon the honest, intelligent face of nature, those views that require not so much the experimenting crucible, as the musing, meditative mind. Modern science would have us believe that these ideas are all her own; that the terms belong to her vocabulary. To listen to the rigmarole about "physical laws" which so often furnishes the whole warp and woof of a scientific lecture, one might almost suppose that the idea, and all connected with it, had been before utterly unknown to the world, instead of being interwoven, as it really is, into all language, and all thinking that deserves the name. We mean a *true idea of law,* with its two inseparable thoughts — both of which some kinds of science have a tendency, either atheistically or pantheistically, to obscure — the thought of a lawgiver who imposes the law, and of a true *subject,* or nature, made capable of obeying it. As well might the discovery of the mighty ocean be claimed for those, and by those, who had made a few shore soundings on the edge of its unfathomable depths. This "great and wide sea" of causality had been gazed upon, and mused upon, by the human soul, just as effectually (as far as the higher ideas of philosophy and theology are concerned) before physical science, so called, raised its head, as since it has filled the age with its noisy claims. The assertion is made because truth demands and can sustain it; even if the interest of sound thinking, and sound philosophising, were not both concerned (as they truly are) in the abatement of these one-sided, blinding pretensions.

No man can carefully study the Bible without finding the fullest recognition of a *nature*, or *order of things*, universal and particular. Yet Deity is ever represented as working *by* it, and *through* it, and *over* it. It is not the sentimental notion of "God in nature," the pretentiously pious, yet pantheistic idea of the Power that

> Warms in the sun, refreshes in the breeze,
> Glows in the stars, and blossoms in the trees.

No, the Hebrews believed in a real nature that God had made to "go of itself," as He had the right and *power* to do. It was a real nature under the control of One who sat above it in the skies, and who made use, not alone of the matter he had originated, but of the *laws and forces he had created* (as well as the matter) to accomplish his good pleasure in the world, and to bring to pass what he had eternally decreed should be done. They distinguished, however, between two modes of action in the divine government. They made a more practical and clear division than is conveyed by our terms natural and supernatural, especially as now used in their clouded philosophic sense. It was more properly a distinction of mediate and immediate. It was the mediate action employing the established ordinances of the world, or it was that direct immediate action which they called by the expressive term, "the finger of God." And this contented them. The careful student of the Bible can not fail to see, and to be struck with, the manner of the sacred writers in this respect. How boldly, and with how little fear of inconsistency, they set forth these two agencies, evidently regarding the one recognition as being as pious, and as honorable to Deity, as the other. Whether He employ "a strong east wind (Exod. xiv, 21,) to make the sea go back," sending his own divine agency into the linked causalities of nature without breaking one of them, or make the water gush forth from the arid rock in crushing defiance of all the laws of solids and fluids, it is still the same unmistakable divinity. These primitive men — though with a clear recognition of nature in its true idea — see no more danger to faith in the natural, or semi-natural, in the one case, than in the immediate supernatural of the other. They went farther than this. They recognized this divine agency as controlling, not only nature, but something else which God had also, in his might and sovereignty, made to "go of itself" within certain limits, and for certain purposes which he meant to accomplish. They did not hesitate to recognize him* as interfering with the law and

* This idea of a divine intervening causality directing, controlling, *turning round*, events that depend on human volitions, is most significantly expressed by a curious Hebrew word which sometimes occurs. They called it סִבָּה, *Sib-ba*, a *revolution*, *conversion*, or *turning* of anything out of its course, or, as we would idiomatically say, a *bringing about*. There is a

liberty of human wills, turning them this way and that as important agencies in the bringing about the issue of his sovereign counsels. This, also, was sometimes mediate and sometimes *direct*. He employs the ambition of Nebuchadnezzar for one end, the weak vanity of Hezekiah for another. Whether it be a vindictive, or a disciplinary purpose, to punish an individual or a nation, or to show a man "what was in his heart," still it is the divine agency, and distinctly recognized as such. There is, too, the same bold assertion of the fact when he acts *directly* on the conduct of human agents; — as when, for example, he "hardens Pharoah's* heart that he might

striking example, 1 Kings, xii, 15, where, of Rehoboam's most impolitic answer to the people, it is said—"This was a *sibba*, or *bringing about*, from the Lord, that he might establish his word which he spake by Ahijah the Shilonite." The LXX call it a μεταστροφή, or *turning aside*. The primary image of the verb, which is very common, gives us the favorite ancient idea of a wheel, or wheels, (cyclical movements,) as denoting mediate and circuitous in distinction from *direct* or straight causality, and yet without any breach of the laws of human thinking or human feeling. The verb is used in the same manner, 1 Sam. xxii, 22. Hence in the cognate Arabic, and modern Syriac, a noun of causality *sababun—Res qua aliquid cum altero conjungitur—vinculum affinitatis*—and hence, as a conjunctive particle—*causa, propter*—denoting *motives, reasons*, as links in a spiritual chain or circuit of events. See also 2 Chron. x, 15.

* The old Jewish writers had as tender a moral sense as we have; but they never seem to shrink from such expressions and such an idea. And why should we? The Hebrew חזק, the verb employed here, does not mean creating evil where evil did not exist before. We stear clear of that inexplicable problem in this case. It does not mean that a tender conscience was indurated either directly or mediately, positively or permissively. It does not mean, that a good and pious nature was forced to evil, or that a good and holy will was turned into a bad will. Let any one examine carefully the Hebrew verb, and he will see, we venture to think, why the moral sense of the writers was not shocked, as ours should not be. The term has no moral or even spiritual meaning in the higher import of the word spiritual. It means, *to strengthen, make firm, bind hard*. The influence was on the sensitive or lower nature. God nerved this wicked coward do his own wicked will, and so carry out the righteous purposes

not let the people go." Whether he acts directly and positively on the heart of Pharaoh, which is the only sense the passage will bear, or employs the evil nature that is already in that vessel of dishonor, it is equally the Divine power acting according to the high and most righteous counsel of the Divine Will.

But let us state the bearing of this upon the main argument. We would say, then, that it is this distinct recognition of each, and yet this fearless mingling of the ideas of the natural and the supernatural in the divine action, that forms a peculiar feature of the Old Testament, and renders easy of belief, and easy of interpretation, the assertions which look like setting forth natural processes, growths, or *generations*, in the creative account. The inspired writer, and his old readers, were not concerned lest it should seem to detract from the honor of Deity. They acknowledged the natural in creation, as easily as they acknowledged the supernatural in their subsequent history. Whether our modern tendency to crowd all of the one kind into the early days, and to recognize as little as possible of it anywhere else, comes from a stronger faith, and a more reverent sense of Deity, may well be doubted.

If, then, the natural is in the creative account, it may certainly have been discovered by some minds. If so, it should not be insulted as a pretense, even though brought out so late as the nineteenth century. But, in

of a divine and holy will. He made him *strong*, which he had as good a right to do as to keep him alive. He made Pharoah no worse, but gave this bad man *courage* (heart strength) to act *out* what was *in* him. Some may stumble at this, but those who get their theology from the Bible must regard it as a divine prerogative, righteous in its exercise and glorious in its display.

fact, it was discovered long ago. If there is no idea of the natural in the First of Genesis, it is nowhere in the Bible, for there is employed there the same language of *birth*, of *growth*, of succession, of *generation*, in a word, of *nature*, that in other parts is applied to what can be taken in no other possible sense. It is not a new discovery. Old interpreters saw it, and saw it clearly. St. Augustine is explicit upon it, as we have shown. He calls the creative periods by this very name of *natures*, and founds his idea of the days on this very distinction of the natural and supernatural. We might fill pages with decisive proof of the utter falsity as well as recklessness of the assertion. The idea of creative generation is more prominent in the patristric writings, but it has ever been in the Church as an opinion that might be orthodoxly held.

But let us look again at the spirit of this boast. The Scriptures have no meaning, no ascertainable meaning, at least, on this and kindred questions, until Geology brings her fossil-lighted lamp for their illumination. It is the spirit the writer is ever so full of, and which he can not disguise. And yet how odd it is that those very passages where a natural growth is most clearly set forth, if any language can set it forth, he wholly ignores, and not only so, but in his exuberant piety brands the interpretation given them (and that, too, without even an attempt at refuting such interpretation,) with the opprobrious name of naturalism—that bugbear of "the religious world," so well adapted to carry with it the narrow odium theologicum. Grand work this for our man of science! It might not be so strange in the narrow polemical theologue, but science boasts of its liberal spirit, its

Baconian progress; it is ever talking of Galileo and free thought. It would be easy to show that, according to Professor DANA'S easy rhetoric of "God in nature," which he has endeavored to employ against the author of the book, there could be really no essential distinction between the natural and the supernatural, or between creation and rest from creation, between origination and subsequent ongoing—but of that more fully elsewhere.*

* A clerical critic in one of our religious newspapers, asks with great simplicity, and yet with an apparent feeling that the question is unanswerable—"If Moses meant growths, births, natures, gradual processions, &c., why did he not call them so?" This is the substance of the question, although we do not give the exact words. Why,—we would say to our clerical friend (for he professes to be a warm friend, and we do not doubt his sincerity,) Moses does call them so—exactly so. Root meanings of words must have had some force in the early day, if they ever had force at all; and the primary ideas of the Hebrew words Moses employs are just the ones involved in this question of yours. Study carefully your Hebrew Bible, and you can not fail to see it. "Let the earth *bring forth*, and the earth *brought forth*." They are the same words that are applied to vegetable and animal parturition elsewhere. In their radical meanings they imply some kind of *birth* and *natural growth*, as much as the language used Gen. iii, 18,—"Thorns and thistles shall it *bring forth* unto thee." In this post-creative act, also, was there something miraculous; the earth would not have fulfilled the curse and *brought forth* the thorns and thistles (there mentioned) of her own unvisited energy, or by the old nature (then old, we mean, but once new,) which she had received on the third day of creation. But though miraculous, it was evidently connected with a nature still—a process of birth and growth divinely and miraculously initiated; but a growth, a birth, a nature still,—for all these words and ideas, as we have elsewhere most abundantly shown, are radically the same. "If Moses meant births, growths, natures, why did he not call them so?" He has called them so, we say again to our anxious friend. That is the very word and idea, neither more nor less. "These are the *toledoth*," he says, "the *Generations*, γενέσεις of the Heavens and the Earth," Gen. ii, 4. Examine your Lexicon in respect to the meaning of the verb from which this noun comes. What is better, take your Hebrew Concordance, and trace it in all its applications, and see if you can discover any radical difference between it and the Greek γίγνομαι, γεννάω, (with other words of the same family,) and the Latin *nascor*, *natus natura*. "Why should

We allude to it here to show how inconsistently science may sometimes talk, especially when it turns pious and forgets itself. "Let the earth bring forth,"—"Let the waters be gathered together, and let the dry land appear"—these passages are interpreted in the book, (whether

we be wise above what is written?" We would retort the language of our friendly interrogator. But the word is not now so taken by readers in general, it may be said. *Generations*, as there used, may be held perhaps to be an accommodation, a figure of speech, a comparison, or it may be explained in some other unmeaning way. The same method, too, may be employed to take all significance out of the language of Job and the Psalmist, especially where the earth is said "to be brought forth" and the "mountains *to be born*"—in which expression the root of this very noun *toledoth* is thus used for the generations, births, natures of the creative periods. But "why should we be wise above what is written," we say again, or put our own faded abstractions, our own lifeless metaphysics, on these fresh Mosaic words, and then cry out metaphysics against the man who attempts to restore them. It does not at all follow because we now, in the old age and dotage as it were of language, use *nature* and similar words for anything and everything, that therefore Moses employed *toledoth* in the same loose way, or meant to depart (least of all in this creative account) from its clear radical sense of one thing, or one state of things, successively *born*, or generated out of another. And yet Moses in his simplicity, and those who thus faithfully interpret his language, may have had as high and as pious an idea of the divine power, the divine miraculous power, originating a nature, controlling a nature, working in, upon, or through a nature previously made, as those over-wise and over-righteous critics who think that the honor of the Bible and of the author of the Bible is tarnished by the use of any such phraseology.

Those who would well take exceptions here, ought carefully to inform themselves in respect to the difference between the ancient and modern modes of thinking. Even down as late as the times of the Christian Fathers, there is a style of language which sounds strange to many. It will not do to call Augustine a heretic, and yet he sets forth the creative successions by this very word *naturæ*. From our self-sufficient modern stand-point, we may call it a figure of speech, or skip it easily over in any way as of no theological or exegetical importance; but he used it strictly as a translation, and true representative, of the Greek γενέσεις, even as the Greek means neither more nor less than the Hebrew תולדות. Had our translators instead of it used *births* or *natures*, they would have expressed radically no other idea.

correctly or not,) as denoting prolonged processes, and successions, to which we can give no other name than *nature*, or *growth*, or the *birth*, or being born of one thing or one state from another. It is, however, with the most distinct recognition, derived not from any outside philosophising, but from the direct Scripture testimony, that each of these growths, or natures, was commenced by the supernatural going forth of the Divine Word and Spirit, with a new command, and a new energy. This is the φύσις which our orthodox Professor regards as so dangerous. He brands it as naturalism. His science, liberal as it would be thought to be, is excessively alarmed at the heresy, and hence he deems it his painful duty to warn the good people who may not have the science and experience of the critic in such matters, against the dangerous infidel tendency of the work. This might seem truly ludicrous to those who well understand the theological latitude both of the critic and the Review through which he gives the alarm; but we would refer to it here as a beautiful specimen of consistency. This man who is so disturbed for the cause of orthodoxy, when one finds a φύσις, or nature, in the Bible, actually claims for Geology the honor of having been the first to discover this same φύσις in the rocks, or as he calls it, "the natural in creation"! It can only be explained on the ground that when a writer has no other or higher motive than to assail a fancied adversary, he must forget himself. Consistency becomes, in that case, a lower virtue which he cannot be expected to preserve.

What does he mean by "the natural in creation?" With truly intelligent minds this whole matter of naturalism may be brought to a short and decided issue. What does he mean by "the natural in creation," and his empty boast of its having been *first* discovered by Geology? Is it a nature that had no beginning—a nature unoriginated, unmade, uncontrolled, uninterrupted, unvisited? That were indeed an atheism at which Plato would have shuddered—an atheism

μεσονυκτίης μελάντερον ορφνης,

blacker than blackest midnight. Is it, on the other hand, a nature which God created, which He made to do just what He had eternally foreordained should be done, to which he gave *laws* that should bring out in chronological order his own everlasting *ideas?* Is it a nature that had its birth in a Divine Word, that is ever and anon quickened by a new Divine Life, that both in its general and its particular ongoings, is visited by repeated, *oft-repeated*, Divine interpositions? Is it such a nature as this he means? Then the writer is defied to find language in which it can be more clearly set forth than it is in the book he has, either so ignorantly or so perversely, misrepresented?

It is not enough, however, for him to brand as infidel, when brought out as an interpretation of the Bible, that which is most scientific and most pious when found written in the rocks. The religion of Geology demands a further concession, and still higher honor, and so the Professor ventures upon another assertion. Not only has "Geology *first* discovered the natural in creation," but, "with rare exceptions, she has ever admitted the supernatural." This we can not help regarding as more perilous ground than the other, although, perhaps, not so insulting to the Scriptures. If he means by the supernatural some far off First Cause brought in as a logical necessity, or some prime mover, or something like a first originating power without which we can not reason at all about creation, the proposition is hardly worth any serious notice. Auguste Comte, much as he has been assailed by inferior men who are no better believers than himself—Auguste Comte would admit that. The author of The Vestiges would admit all that. In such a sense, and in some still nearer senses, he willingly concedes the supernatural.

But if, taking it in its true, and higher, and more special sense, the reviewer means that leading geological minds have been fond of the idea of the supernatural, that they have *not* preferred to explain everything by uninterrupted natural causality, and that the leading authority among them does not regard this natural causation, as, of itself, sufficient to explain all the phenomena that science now discovers in the rocks and formations, —if he means this, he could not well have made a statement more at war with known and indisputable facts. There are men now of highest name in the science who would laugh at him for the assertion, if so made, and so understood in the only sense that gives it any importance, especially any importance in the present argument.

But to examine the position more upon its essential merits. By its own Baconian boasting, then, science (we mean as the naturalist employs the term) can never really reach the supernatural. *Its* laws, of which it talks so much, are, and can be, only generalizations of facts or appearances. Repeated, or usually recurring facts, make settled laws—that is, settled in science, not *in re.* Unusual facts or single appearances can only suggest some law of less frequent occurrence, or less understood; and so they all may be natural; the contrary supposition would be unscientific, and even irrational, as far as science is concerned, or in the absence of any higher light. All may be nature, an eternal causality, as far as she knows or ever can know. She goes by observation and experience,—this is her boast,—and there can be no scientific proof, or even ground of belief, that any fact or appearance is isolated, or stands out single, and unconnected with the combined causalities of the universe;—there can be no scientific admission of this except from the experience of an eternity. Revelation and all a priori ideas once shut out, there is no evidencce short of this she can consistently admit. There may be hidden springs touched once in an immensely long time. She has no right to deny it. Nay, more, she is bound to assume it, as long as she remains truly upon her own ground. The more usual manifestations of forces she finds in the coils of the seemingly eternal spring she is seeking to unwind; she has no right, therefore, to say, and, when not "driven" by something from without her field, she never does say, that the less usual appearances, even the very rare appearances, are not equally so contained in its everlasting folds. Professor DANA himself, unphilosophical and even unscientific as he is, betrays a consciousness of this, although his eagerness to magnify Geology prevents its standing out objectively and distinctively before him. "*Admits* the supernatural"! he says. But what language is this for science? It is worse than the Professor's "*physical nature*"; that was simply an absurd tautology; this is absurdity itself. Science does not "*admit*"; she proves—such is her claim. She discovers; sometimes she graciously *accepts*—as Professor DANA accepts the Mosaic account—but *admitting* looks like a force of some kind, an influence from without. It suggests the thought of a reluctation;—it has something of the appearance of being "driven"—to use again the word that has aroused so much indignation—or at least of "floating" in some boat carried down the current of certain opinions, higher or lower, true or false, which are not science, nor any effect of science, but belong to another sphere.

Let everything keep its own place. We are not reproaching science, but exposing the false claims of some scientific men. Science can not be expected to see what she has no eyes to see. She makes good use of her natural vision, short sighted as it is, when she confines it to her own field. She sees *appearances*, facts, events; she observes how they come and go, and deduces laws which are but the summings,—nothing more,—of these her observations. Where the facts are numerous, she has a very strong probability, such as the inhabitants of Plato's cave might have deduced respecting the laws of the shadows that were ever flitting across the rear wall of their prison. Where the facts are few, she must do the best she can, and make a theory; where she has but one, she must guess and wait for more, or consult some higher authority of philosophy or revelation in respect to it; but, as far as she is concerned, and in her own province of observation and induction, she must ever, as we have said, assume that there is, somehow and somewhere, a law, a natural law, for every phenomenon, and so she can not get out of nature,—she can not look out of nature—she can not find the supernatural. But science, we repeat, is not to blame for this. We can not expect to see these things through her lens, any more than we could rationally hope to discover spirits in the crucible, or see angels through the telescope.

Natural science, then, it can not be too firmly maintained, both for the cause of science as well as for that of all sound thinking, is a seeker of law, of natural law, in her own sense of the term, as a generalizing of appearances ever assumed to have come from one universal force. Atheism can not exclude from her brotherhood. Piety can give no title to admission. Auguste Comte would have a fair right to a seat in any convention. A man may deny the existence of God, and be just as scientific as the most devout Professor. Experience has shown this by most abundant evidence, if there were not the strongest a priori proof of the fact in the very laws of ideas. Science, natural science, is a hunter of natural causalities; that is her business, and she can never legitimately find anything else. If she does so, it is out of her line; she "admits" it from some influence more or less distinctly felt, of some higher authority. She "accepts" it, more or less willingly, but can never be said to discover it, without violating, or, at least, ignoring for the time, her own essential law. We want no better proof of this than Professor DANA's own article. Will he pretend that he has not been influenced by the sound theology of New-Haven, and the old standard orthodoxy of Andover; or, in other words, that the "currents" setting round these venerable institutions have not "driven" his own geological boat in a pious direction, it might not, perhaps, have taken in Germany or France?

Now we have no fear that the drift of these remarks can be mistaken. It is not denied that scientific men have maintained the supernatural truly, religiously, biblically, in its real and divine sense. There have been those who were scientific men, and, at the same time, something more, and better. There have been many such, we rejoice to say it, who have found the supernatural, and recognized it *among* their scientific discoveries, but not *from* them. There was something better, higher, yea, stronger than science, that led them to it. It was a mental temperament, original in some respects, but more truly produced by revelation either in its direct or social influence. It was devout religious feeling which never would have been developed, to say the least, without revelation in some form. That of which we speak is of itself a supernatural state of mind, acting as well as acted upon, and leading men to believe truly in such a revelation as the great first supernatural fact of facts, the solid ground of credence in all other supernatural. The evidence of this suggests itself in a supposition which comes home to every mind. Let revelation die out of the souls of men (if it ever can die out,) and how long would science find the supernatural? In certain regions the old habit of believing might retain some of its power for a generation perhaps; in others, we may say, the experiment has, to some extent, been already tried. There are parts of the world, there are schools of thinking, where faith in any objective or supernatural revelation has in the main already died out. They are able schools, too, most scientific thinkers, as good thinkers as can be found among us; but where do they find the supernatural? As far as science is concerned, or their rank in science, these foreign free-thinking naturalists ought to be, at least, as pious as Professor SILLIMAN or Professor

DANA. But "faith comes from hearing," the hearing both of the ear and the heart. "By faith we understand that the worlds were built by the Word of God;" by faith we find the true supernatural,—by faith, itself a supernatural state of soul as well as a supernatural gift. Even the false or superstitious belief in the supernatural came originally from the same divine source. It is an echo, broken, indeed, into wild and wizard sounds, yet still an echo from the earliest revelations made to the human race. Most true it is, therefore, that science, natural science, proceeding on its own fundamental principles, can never get out of nature, unless "driven" by some power lying fairly beyond its own domain.

We dwell on this because the position is a cardinal one, and it is of the utmost importance to keep separate the bounds of ideas that are so absurdly jumbled together. We should closely distinguish between what may be found by some scientific men, according to the latitude in which they live, or the outside theological currents in which their "boat is floating," and that which is found by science per se. Prof. DANA should be careful here. With all his fine talk about "God in nature," and "laws and types," he may, if he lets go revelation as the only revealer of the supernatural—itself a supernatural work—or treats it as a secondary authority, have a development theory before he is aware of it. That is, for all he knows, or for all his science can affirm or deny, there may be reserve laws of nature, which, in this vast machinery of law and types, may be represented by little cogs or springs going round and round unseen by the sharpest science, because they are touched, perhaps, in the revolution of some greater wheels, only once in ten thousand or ten million years, but which, nevertheless, when the clock strikes the true time of the *magnus annus*, may bring out species from species just as certainly as the ordinary wheels that go round visibly in our times, or the less ordinary whose movements we can trace, bring out individuals from individuals;—there being no more, or, we may rather say, no less a priori mystery in the one form of generation than in the other. "Knowest thou the way of the spirit, or how the bones do grow in the womb of her that is with child?" Nothing can be more absurd than the claim that any mere science can disprove the fact of such a more interior law in nature, or of such a rarer and more occult form of generation. But do you believe it? it may be retorted on the author. Alas, we have little or no belief about it, unless as we can get some glimpse of evidence from a divine revelation. "We are but of yesterday and know nothing." Individuals, species, and all, came from the creating will and power of God. That is quite clear from the Scriptures. There is also pretty fair evidence, if we can interpret language at all, that this creation of vegetables, and of the lower animals at least, was some how connected with a new word or command, and a new power given to the then nature, or the earth. But which law of generation God saw fit in the first place to create, (for in spite of Mr. LORD and Prof. DANA, we must still continue to regard the *creation of laws, principles, and ideas*, as sound common sense as well as sound metaphysics,) or whether he created many such laws acting successively or concurrently, there are the scantiest means of knowing from revelation, and none at all from science. God made the plants and lower animals by some created law, or laws, of generation, connected originally with the earth. This is all we truly know. Any theory of generation that is consistent with this, or does not contradict this, a man may orthodoxly and Biblically hold.

We care nothing about "The Vestiges of Creation," or its degree of piety. It is the famous book, we know, of which some clergymen are so afraid—a fear that does not argue much for their firm belief in the Scriptures—and on which certain scientific men of a certain calibre, and placed in positions peculiarly favorable to a kind of orthodoxy, are ever and anon trying their steel. It teaches development, they say, and that is impious. But what do they know about it? If the author of that book means an eternal development which God did not in time originate, and from time to time control, then we refute him very easily—not from science, but from Scripture. Goliah as he is, or is said to be, with that shepherd's sling even a Sabbath-school child can overthrow him. But if it be development without this impious, unscriptural idea,—if it be development as a more remote and interior form of generation simply, then his theory, as a theory, is as good as theirs, and they cannot refute him from any science built on present observation. Their mode of attempting it is certainly very curious. These hidden wheels, or cogs, or springs, of development have not acted, or even been visible during their inch of time and space, and therefore, say they, there are no such wheels. God could not make them; for such a creation of laws and principles is all Platonic nonsense. Creation, they hold, is ever of hard matter made right out and out,—of matter in some way, hard or soft, of a certain density, of a certain shape, of a certain extent, and in a certain place. In other words, it is a creation of death before life, inert mass before organizing law, *eidolon* before *idea*, effect before cause, or shadow before substance;—unless our consistent nominalists should say, as they doubtless would, that hard matter is the real being (τὸ ὄντως ὄν) next in birth to deity, whilst life, and law, and idea, have but dependent, shadowy, and unreal existence.*

But there are no such wheels. Of that they are certain, for the best of all reasons—they have never *seen* them. What is more, they have never seen, they say, a trace or vestige of them—the reason of which we may give in another chapter. They go wholly by experience and induction. The clock has not struck in their *day*—their *minute* we might rather say—nor for many a day before them; in other words, they know no other nature, and therefore, there is no other nature—never has been, never can be.† And so they claim the merit of having

* Should any be disposed to come half way, and say that laws and principles are in their being and origin independent realities, but have not existence *in time* before the material things or movements, manifest or concealed, of which they are the organic laws or principles,—it would be sufficient for our argument. They are before the matter, then, in the order of being, if not of time. They are independent existences that do not *grow out of* the matter, but come into it from some other source, or are put into it by a higher Power who made them as really as he made the matter,—and made them, too, of immensely greater variety and higher workmanship. This is sufficient. In this sense they are *creations*, true independent creations, of a higher order than the matter, and from which (as we go farther and say) the matter derives, if not its substance as matter, yet that organization which makes each material thing that is, what it is.

† Had our present olam, or the *whole day* of the race been a single revolution of the earth upon its axis (a supposition neither incredible nor absurd, since the race might have been made so as to live as much in such a period as in the one allotted,) then these immutable laws of science would, on such a view, have been altogether different. The natural, or what is the natural now, would become the supernatural, because the scientific men of such an age had seen nothing like it. The generation of a tree, or its revival

slain The Vestiges of Creation, when, in fact, it is their cowardice, or their prudence, that stops short of conclusions following plausibly from their boasted premises, and which that writer has had the boldness to carry out. Their "floating boat" is driven timidly in by currents which his stronger oar enables him to stem. Their orthodoxy here is not owing to any science so much as to other influences, for which, if they have any real piety, they should thank God and the Church. It is the Bible-nurtured and Church-nurtured belief in a supernatural revelation that has made them find the supernatural where the author of The Vestiges has not discovered it, and where their Baconian induction never would have discovered it, never *could* have discovered it, whilst remaining true to its own boasted fundamental law of laws. The Professors of this pious naturalism wofully deceive themselves when they thus attempt to patronize the Scriptures, and give them the benefit of their discoveries. It may be said, too, that they fight The Vestiges of Creation in very much the same feeling that leads men in the Church, whose orthodoxy is but a shell, and whose position, therefore, lies nearest to the infidel camp, to be ever writing books on the evidences of Christianity, and assailing the infidels. These fight valiantly against Hobbes and Paine; they are ever running a tilt against Hume and Voltaire; when the earnest believer looks upon Hobbes, and Paine, and Hume, as being actually of great service to the Church, by showing men — at least all thinking men — what they must come to if they will not docilely and

after a season of torpor, or a new tree springing out, either like or unlike the old, would be as incredible as anything we now denounce under the name of development.

reverently, and most thankfully receive the Scriptures. And so they slay The Vestiges, these valiant men!—yea, thrice do they slay the slain, and yet the ghost will not be laid. The book still lives and has a deep hold upon the common mind. The reason is, that whatever may be its errors, it presents that thought which—revelation gone, or once supposed to be gone,—presses so heavily upon the soul. It is the thought to which every true thinking man feels he must come if he has to give up the Bible. He may dread it as a sane mind sometimes dreads the horrors of apprehended insanity, but he knows of no true security against it unless it be a voice from heaven believed through a supernatural faith whose essence, incipiency, and power, is heaven's own gift readily and lovingly bestowed upon all devout and docile minds. It is the thought so feared by some, so loved by others, because it is so *natural*,—the thought that perhaps all is natnre, and nature all,—eternal law, eternal nature—unmodified by anything that has ever come into it from any higher world of being. When faith in revelation once wholly departs from an age, or a country, or an individual, there will not long remain any belief in the supernatural. Geology can not cure this, even if it does not aid it. Science can not help the matter. Its times are too short. Long as they may seem, as compared with shorter cycles, yet when reckoned on the greater scale they too vanish like passing shadows. On this illimitable field of an ever outstretching eternity, or olam of olams, the geological epochs disappear like the solar days of the literalist. A stand point may be assumed from which the difference between them becomes too small for metaphor. The æonic and the solar times come to seem alike literal, alike figurative, alike evanescent, when regarded as measures of the still greater cycles in the kingdom of all eternities. Alas, we are lost! In such a survey of an immeasurable universe of space and time, we can have no assurance, no hope, except in a voice from the highest heavens, a voice of God coming very nigh unto us, speaking by direct communication of mind to mind, whether primarily or through mediate minds, instead of the ever uncertain vestiges of nature, or the illegible book of the rocks which some are so fond of placing in rhetorical comparison with Heaven's written volume.

But this whole question of the greater durations, lies away beyond the fair field of scientific induction. The scientific naturalist examines present appearances. He examines them very carefully. This, he says, was before that. He is pretty safe in saying, that if there has been no disturbance — a caveat he can never wisely neglect — the lower deposit, or the lower fossil, most probably went to its rest before the upper. When he would assign periods, however, he measures the times of nature *then* by its movements *now*. But this is all a guess. He can never get an expression, or a formula, for a *time*, except through a *space*, or effects appearing in such space; but what was once the rate of that efficiency he can not know. There is no hypothesis that he can prove, none that he can render probable. The time pendulum, the comparative time pendulum (for all time measured by space is thus comparative,) varies in its measuring movements so that the variation is perceptible even on the narrow field of this earth; it changes with the latitude; the sun minute and the same pendulum minute do not always and everywhere agree. Even the sun minute is shown by certain discoveries in astronomy to be not a constant quantity. Our years vary, and with them all subordinate degrees of all subordinate arcs. Now, if this be true, as we may say, right around us, in phenomena that come home to the observations of our own fleeting sense, or our own fleeting historical reminiscences, what calculus of variations shall be applied to time and causal succession (the only real measurement of time) in those far off regions of space, and those immeasurable remotenesses of eternity, where the imagination utterly faints, and even reason reels and staggers like the inebriate in his delirium. Even the Koran here is better for us, has more light for us, than science. "We flee for refuge to the King of the Worlds, the Lord of the day-break." But we have something better than either. It is the sure Word of the Lord, revealing the true supernatural, revealing the creative process, whether it be of all worlds, or of our own world, whether of all times, or of our own olam, whether of the great cosmical principium, or any nearer beginning on our own earth—revealing just what God deems best for us to know of earthly or mundane origin,—above all revealing Himself, as having his abode in "Light unapproachable and full of glory," and yet "his peoples' dwelling place in all generations." It is this Word of the Lord, faithfully interpreted, heartily believed, and placed in its proper rank, before all science, and all philosophy—it is this, and this alone, that will effectually slay "The Vestiges," and all other forms of naturalism that come, whether innocently or not, from the modern extravagant boasting, and extravagant estimation of physical science. For it is this spirit, more than any particular difficulties now and then raised by science, that is to be dreaded. It is this putting nature and the Bible on a seeming par; a practice of which some are so fond, though all the real deference is in reality paid to science in every case of seeming collision. It is this patronizing parallel, now so commonly run between the "two books," as they are styled, "the book of Nature and the book of Revelation," and of which we have such a fine specimen at the close of Professor DANA'S article. These are the things most hostile to the Bible, most injurious to a true and hearty faith. This is the real naturalism.

CHAPTER VII.

WE KNOW NOTHING OF ORIGIN EXCEPT FROM A DIVINE REVELATION.

The Vestiges of Creation—Who Killed the Monster?—Individual Generation as Mysterious as the Generic—Revelation itself the Highest Supernatural—Why should we be afraid of the Natural in Creation?—Animalculæ—Agassiz's Doctrine of Man—The Primus Homo—Science Occupied with what is, and how it is—The Cosmical Movement—Science does not take it into Account—Hypothetical Discussion between the Vestigian and the Anti-vestigian—Nature's Gestation long, her Births sudden and complete—Doctrine of Types—No Meaning in the Language as used by some Scientific Men—The Atheism of "The Vestiges," in what it truly consists.

WE KNOW NOTHING OF ORIGIN EXCEPT FROM A DIVINE REVELATION. This we would take as the motto, not only of the present chapter, but of all that we have written on this and kindred subjects. God may make things directly, or he may make natures, laws, etc., through which things and phenomena are produced, or he may combine both methods, and work by them concurrently or successively. We know here only as he has told us. In pursuing this theme, the reader will pardon us for dwelling a little longer on this famous book entitled The Vestiges of Creation. The bugbear that has been made of it in the religious world, the dishonor which the alarm about it has cast upon our faith in the Bible, the unfair and disreputable efforts to excite odium against certain opinions by connecting them with this unpopular name, all demand some further consideration of the grounds on which it is assailed, and especially of the manner in which others are assailed under cover of a protest against it. Aside from its fairer and more effective theological opponents, certain men of science* have felt it their interest to keep up a batrachian clamor about the honor of slaying the monster. Who killed the Vestiges? may come, in time, to excite as much interest as the famous question of the nursery book with which we are all familiar. The author, not being a man of science, can not engage scientifically in this melée; but having some general information on such subjects, and a little reading in the Scriptures, he would respectfully venture the opinion, as one among many others, that this terrible book must be overthrown by the Scriptures, or not at all. If the Bible does not refute it, or furnish any means of refuting it, then its doctrines should not be the cause of any great alarm. They become in that case indifferent to a true faith, whatever aspect they may assume. Now, aside from what a supernatural revelation may affirm of these primordial matters, all that we can say with any tolerable safety is, that a certain theory of generation may be true, or it may not be true; or it may be partly

* It is just that we should speak in terms of the highest respect of the writings of Hugh Miller. His attack upon the Vestiges was the most effective, as combining more of philosophy and theology than can be found in any other scientific argument. Although we do not wholly agree with this writer, yet no one can be more sensible of the great good he has done in this department.

true and partly false; or the whole region of speculation may be regarded as a land of shadows of which we know less than we know of the constitution of the monstrous shapes that go under the name of nebulæ in some late maps of the astronomical heavens. In other words, science can no more disprove than she can prove any such theory of origin. Both sides of such questions, we venture timidly to think, lie out of her clear domain of observed facts and laws generalized therefrom. To speak with any certainty here, as science, she must have had an immensely greater space for her observations, and an immensely greater time for her inductive experience; unless she insists upon intuitions, or something like a priori ideas which must not be contradicted; and then she is clearly out of her record. There *are* some such a priori ideas, or laws of thinking, that have a bearing upon these questions, but science has nothing to do with them; she does not acknowledge them; she regards them as shadowy and unreal as compared with her own "exactness." So that we may safely say, that the author of The Vestiges has a science as good as that of Professor DANA, and we think the theology of the book will also present a fair comparison.* The superiority, however, in this latter aspect may be freely given to the Yale College authority, if he will only frankly admit that his pious notions may have had their birth in his Scriptural education, rather than in his geological and conchological researches.

* It is a number of years since we read this book. The impression left upon the mind was not favorable to its piety. It appeared to us decidedly anti-biblical in its tone and spirit. Its style, both of thought and expression, is very different from that of the Old Testament. It does not talk like Moses. If we may judge, however, from its very confident manner, so much resembling that of certain other productions of a similar Baconian genus, it must certainly be considered a work of respectable science.

But to keep to the issue we have presented. If the Scriptures teach anything of origin, that is conclusive for the believer. He sits down to the study of them, knowing nothing as far as the facts to be revealed are concerned, and prepared to receive whatever they may teach,—even should it be found that they reveal something like a development doctrine in some form, or after some of the varied uses of that wide and much abused word. For development is simply the outgoing of one existence, whether individual or generic, from another existence in which the first is supposed to be contained or wrapped up. Such a development may be single and almost immediate, or it may be varied and multifold. It may have one, or more, or many supernatural beginnings, with ongoings after each determined by laws which God has made to do that very thing just *how*, and *when*, and *where* he has foreordained it should be done. Thus should the Scriptures say, "Let the earth bring forth," "Let the waters bring forth," he will not be frightened by it, or set himself to work to devise some way in which he may consult the honor of the Scriptures by relieving them of this odious appearance of naturalism. He will not attempt to be wise above what is written, if he can only fairly get its meaning. He will frankly admit the fallibility of his own particular interpretations; but the principle he will never surrender—the principle that we know nothing on these subjects except what we may get from the divine teachings, given to us in such way, and *after such measure*, as the divine wisdom may prescribe. Even should the Scriptures seem to teach a growth, a nature, or what some would call a development in its narrower or wider senses, the reception of it is still as much a matter of faith as though it had disclosed an instantaneous transition from not-being to perfect or finished being, or a succession yet consummated in the twinkling of an eye, or in twenty-four seconds, or twenty-four hours, or six indefinite periods,—or had revealed to him any other method in this unknown and unknowable region. It satisfies the true believer either way. The mere fact of a revelation from God of what is otherwise inscrutably hidden, is the great supernatural for him, the warrant for believing in all other supernatural. Has a voice truly come to him from the All-knowing? Then its revelations as to the origin of lower things will have for his faith enough of other supernatural, whether that supernatural is presented in the origination of the general order, or orders, of vegetable and lower animal life, with the creation, at the same time, of laws and types for their development,—or is taught as coming more specially in at the generic birth, or specific *making*, as some would say, of every species of animation *by itself*, or of each individual progenitor of such species by itself, from the "great whales" (which the Bible seems to speak of as a special formation) down to the lowest and most invisible forms of the million-formed animalculæ that have their habitation among the closest particles of other matter animate and inanimate, or that are found in every globule of living blood, and in every drop of stagnant water. Let him have for it something which he can trust as a "thus saith the Lord"—some word from the supernatural sphere itself—speaking not to his science but to his faith, and he will believe the natural, or the supernatural, without confounding either, and whether the latter be rare or frequent,—revealed only as acting in the most general beginnings of life, or, as the Scriptures would seem to intimate, and science would perhaps deny, carried clear through in some cases, so as to be present in some part of the quickening process of every individual, at least every individual human generation.

What, then, has Scripture revealed in respect to the *origin* of the earth,—the origin of things that grow upon it— the origin of man? Our object here is not so much to answer these questions, as to state certain principles in relation to them. If the Bible has something to say on these matters, let us hear it and thankfully receive it. We shall never get any reliable information from any other quarter. If Scripture says little here, we know little; where it says nothing, we know nothing. If its language is general, our knowledge is general; if it gives us but an outline, we can be only certain of the outline facts, although it will be no irreverence, we think, to suppose a filling up, if we are careful to keep out everything that may be inconsistent, or may seem inconsistent, with such outline view. It may be, and it is, rational to think, that the account is limited to an outline view because we could not comprehend the more detailed processes, or their ineffable rationale, as given, or attempted to be given, in any human language. There are such ineffable processes in the generations that are constantly taking place around us, even in this settled condition of things; how much more full of them may have been the *primordia rerum!* There is something which all the science on earth can not explain, and never will explain, in the life germination of every garden seed; there is an every day mystery, O! how much higher and more hidden still! in the wondrous transmission of the human vitality, even considered in its lowest sensitive form, and aside from the rational and divine element in our being! If there are such inscrutable hiding places, impenetrable chasms, we may say, in the links of this ordinary causation as it is passing continually under the eye of our sharpest science, what an abyss of the unknown, and to us unknowable, must there be in the awful transitions from nonentity,—in the *principiis principiorum*, the transcending primeval births, the *quickening*, not of transmitted life, but of vitality itself. "*Vestiges*" of Creation! Who shall dare talk of them, except as his way is illumined by the lamp of God's own Word? In opposition to such a claim of science, how appropriately may we accommodate the grand Vulgate version of the LXXVIIth Psalm?—Tu es Deus qui facis mirabilia; in aquis multis semitæ tuæ, et *vestigia* tua non cognoscentur. עקבותיך לא נודעו, "Thy *footsteps are* unknown."

Why should we be afraid of the idea of the natural in creation, or of the *mediate* as distinguished from the *immediate*. If God chooses to make a nature, give it its laws, ideas, potencies, times or periods, and then work by it, making other creations by this creation, what have we to say against it? Whose pious science, or scientific piety, "shall touch His hand and say unto Him, what doest Thou?" This hyper-religionism is not for the honor of the Scriptures. It is to save to science, or to certain aspects of science surrounded by religious influences, that honor through which it especially claims to patronize the Scriptures, and to assume a controlling voice in its interpretation. What does such science know of physical life, or the conditions under which it may be developed? To deny that God could make a provision by which it could be brought out in some manner different from what we call ordinary generation, is to run into a Charybdis of materialism worse than the Scylla of which they affect so pious a horror.

We are naturally in the same condition of utter ignorance in respect to the origin of man. The Bible represents it to have been specially supernatural — something not to be resolved into a wider life that had a beginning in some former supernatural, but, standing by itself, a special isolated act. The creation of other animate existences is given generally and generically. It is represented as somehow connected with nature or the earth. Nothing is said about the making of individuals, even in multitudes, much less of pairs, or any individual progenitors. There must have been some reason for the absence of this kind of language in the one case, while it is so marked and peculiar in the other. The origin of man in two individuals — one of these created out of the other — is the great and striking feature of the account. And yet this sacred region, too, has this false science lately invaded, whilst, as has been already intimated, some of the religious world who are determined to have a harmony at any cost, are preparing, as usual, to strike in tune with whatever key-note she may sound, or to follow wherever she may make her move. But here, again, this kind of science has undertaken something clean out of her inductive province. She can only define a species in one of two ways — *theoretically*, by the philosophical idea (that is, borrowed from philosophy,) of generic unity of life, or *practically*, by the scientific law of a certain amount of resemblance held together by a greater or less permanency. This latter, or the mode which though the more defective more truly belongs to science, has been chosen. As thus given, it is strictly a matter of quantity, and in this direction the science that employs it can never get out of the ever changing quantitative idea. But all such definitions grounded on quantity or degree, whether of resemblance or anything else, must be ever inconstant, continually varied by new facts,—these facts, too, changing even within the range of our very narrow known, but which, when compared with the unknown in time and space, become absolutely worthless terms in the series, too vanishing to enter into any trustworthy analysis. Thus an amount of resemblance that might make a pretty fair probability for one extent of time and space (supposing that to be all that is, or is to be, affected by it) could afford no ground for a classification demanded for another. The application of the rule to a short historic term might make many separate varieties of man,—a vastly longer time might shut up, not only man, but all the lower animals with him, into one universal brotherhood. Mr. Agassiz, for example, defines as difference of species, all differences that were distinctly such when known history commences. Put back this date of history, or put it forward, and the definition is good for nothing. If science defines a species by the other mode of a supposed once existing *actual unity of life*, from which the whole species has diverged, that will do; but in the case of the human race, such unity, or want of unity, is a fact necessarily transcending human history, and only capable of being made known to us, or disproved to us, by a supernatural revelation. To find this historical point of unity, we must take the Bible account, or step back to some antiquity that may furnish the time necessary for such a back convergency of varieties into one. But in doing this we have no guide in science. The amount of it all, then, is this—*of the origin of our planet, of the origin of life upon it, and of the origin of man, we must have a revelation from the Creator himself, or remain in impenetrable ignorance.*

In respect to these matters, therefore, our only business is to study that revelation. If what it reveals is scanty, it must be either because God did not deem the knowledge omitted as of any great importance, or did not deem us capable of fully receiving it. With sunlike clearness has it made known to us the most important, but, otherwise, undiscoverable, fact of a *primus homo*,—the very fact which modern science, or that which claims to be most scientific, is taking upon itself to deny. It gives us, with like clearness, the fact of his divine supernatural birth; it teaches us something, less distinctly, of his physical origin, but still the Bible does not make the dignity of man to depend so much on his mode of origin, especially his material origin, as on the divine dealing in the important covenant transaction made with that *one man* as the physical, spiritual, and forensic representative of all his posterity.

But of all this, and of all that relates to the origin of man and the world, we repeat it,—and it will bear to be repeated—we know only from the Bible. By the living Word of the Lord alone can we refute The Vestiges. Just as the Bible is firmly believed, will the latter book, and all similar books, have but little hold upon the common mind. With such hearty and general belief in a Divine Word, there will be no need of any geological aid to faith, and without it, powerless will be all the efforts of one kind of science to lay the evil spirit which another kind of science has been so efficient in raising.

Such must ever be the position of science in respect to revelation. And even in regard to cosmical knowledge in general, we may safely say, that from the very nature of man, and his confined position, natural knowledge must ever be relatively very small. It looks large to some who are in the midst of it, but to a true thinking it contracts with its own discoveries. Paradox as it may seem, it grows darker with every addition that is made to its feeble light, because, in fact, that light, if we have no other or higher, must ever reveal mysteries faster than it can solve them, and so continually throw a denser and still denser gloom on the dark back ground of human existence, making more and more inexplicable the problem of human life and the enigma of the vast and terrible nature in which we seem to be sunk and lost. So, we say, it must be to the thinking; but there is a great deal of science that never thinks, strange as the assertion may seem; it only watches for phenomena, makes experiments, adds to its little heap of curious facts, attends scientific conventions, reads scientific papers thereon, and therewith is content. Take it in its widest field, science is legitimately occupied only with what *is*, (or rather is seen to be,) and how it is. The future and the past belong to her only as she can safely carry the present into them and measure them by it. But the moment she begins to do this her boasted exactness begins to fade. She can calculate an eclipse, but it is only on the supposition that not only the observed phenomena remain the same, but that the rate of movement, and the rate of the rate of movement, remain the same; just as we tell the time of day by the clock, or predict any future position of the hour and minute hands, if its rate of motion does not in the mean time suffer any variation. This does well enough for a relatively near past, or near future, such as the time of day, or the movements of the clock, in respect to the astronomical changes, and the visible astronomical changes in respect to some great cosmical movement that may be neglected in ordinary calculations, but which it would be very unscientific for us to leave out of the account when we are rash enough to apply present scientific observations to the measurement of the great olamic times. Thus viewed, in either case, whether it be that of the clock or of the eclipse, the changes in the cosmical time-table become infinitessimals in regard to our magnified present. They imperceptibly vary the result. But move off either way, advancing into the future, or receding into the past, and the unknown comes pouring continually into the scale, faster and faster, until it forms quite a disturbing quantity,—yea, so as to affect the very balance of fact that must be known and taken in to form anything like a true induction. Carry it still farther, either way, into the very remote, and unless we fall back upon revelation, or some unscientific a priori principles, as some would sneeringly call them, all becomes a guess, a fool-hardy assumption that has not even the dignity of a conjecture.

But when we keep our thoughts upon our own world, and our own race, the ground assumed becomes still more sure and incontrovertible. On the supposition of no supernatural revelation having ever been made, or of its being lost to knowledge or belief, it may be safely affirmed that the real darkness hanging over the problem of human life, yea, of existence in general, would be greater now than in the days of Pythagoras, and that the increase would be in the direct ratio of the increase of natural knowledge from that time to this. It would be like the traveller lost in the wilderness. He collects specimens of herb and mineral, he examines the curious positions of rocks, he gazes upon the stars above his head, and explores the earth beneath his feet, but he is ever *more* lost still. The multiplicity of objects only adds to his confusion and perplexity. Darker and darker grows the interminable forest, or wider and wider spreads out before him the blinding bewildering waste of the boundless desert. In view of this, there is no trifling like that of certain kinds of science, especially when regarded in connection with its inane boasting. "Is it not true," asks Professor DANA, "that science (meaning of course natural science) is ever tending to the clearing away of doubts"? No, we answer boldly. We take a direct issue here, and we have proved our side of it. Natural science *alone*—let the qualification be ever remembered, for it is of the utmost importance in the argument—natural science *alone*, and with all that the widest claim can bring within her province, is ever, to a thinking man, breeding difficulties and doubts inexplicable. There is enough darkness in one magnified drop of water to lead such a one to implore light from a higher world, or to flee for protection to the least evidence of a revelation from above the sphere of the natural. Again he asks—"Is there no foundation for full faith in the teachings of nature, or the deductions of the human mind therefrom?" The sentence is ambiguous; it may mean *faith in nature* as the object of belief, (for which there is certainly a foundation, a blessed foundation, though not in nature herself,) or it may mean a foundation in nature for faith. If such be the meaning, again we answer, no. There is darkness in nature, there ever will be darkness in nature, growing ever, the more we explore her by her own light alone. God meant it should be so,—we may reverently say it—to drive us to himself without this endless circuitous mode of seeking him. It is for our moral discipline that we should walk in the wilderness, but the true light that shines on nature, and renders scientific progress any thing more than a blinding maze, is not from nature herself,—as would soon be found should there ever be a setting of that ancient Star in the East, whose beams so many mistake for their own or nature's illumination. " The Heavens declare the glory of God," but it is to those who receive the " higher law" than nature, that " law which is perfect, converting the soul, that *testimony* of the Lord which is sure, making wise the simple." How different this " *declaring*" is from that search for links without beginnings or ends, that tracing of utilities and designs ever terminating in nature, which is boasted of under certain aspects of science and " natural theology," may be elsewhere shown. It is alluded to here, simply that our meaning may not be mistaken. There is, indeed, an outward glory in God's *works* to those " who seek Him in his *Word*." But from nature alone there ever comes forth to the thinking soul that query she so solemnly suggests but never answers—" Where, then, shall Wisdom be found, and where is the place of understanding? The Deep saith, It is not in me; the Sea saith, It is not in me." Nature can not tell why God made her, or why He made man. She might give up all her secrets to science, if that were ever possible, and yet be as far as ever from revealing the secret of the universe, or that wisdom which alone makes nature herself intelligible.

But though we say *no* to Professor DANA'S queries, we can not subscribe to the conclusion he would attach to such denial. "If such," he says, "be actually the end of man's contemplations, he would be forced, in just indignation, to write FALSE over the whole face of nature, and to replace the word GOD with that of DEMON." Who charges nature with being false? *They* put lies into her mouth who find in her what God alone can reveal, and has chosen to reveal in some other way. They make her false who would place her at the foundation of what she can not support, and which God meant should be the foundation, the available support, of any true living faith in her. They thus "write false over the face of nature," when they should rather write *ignorance* and *folly* on their own boasting knowledge of her revealings. They "replace the word *God* with that of *idol*," we will not say *demon*, when they make nature the fountain of light, and all but worship this veiled power, or talk of her as in any sense a parallel revelation. There was once a pretty thing they called natural religion, with its five moral articles, after the style of the Herbert and Bolingbroke school. Some even thought they could have it, and, at the same time, the written revelation, too, as a sort of reflection of the higher creed. Butler swept this all away. There has since grown up what may be called, not so much natural religion, as the religion of nature, or of natural science as a parallel revelation, to say the least, with the written Scriptures. The same service is demanded by the Church in respect to this assumption, and when it is done, then may we expect the "restoration of the old belief," in something like its old strength. When this confused middle ground is all cleared up, or men are shown that there is, in truth, no such middle ground between revelation and atheism, we may trust the better feelings of humanity, fallen as it is, for a return to the book of God with a firmer hold, and a faith more strongly anchored, perhaps, than any the Church has ever before possessed.

We are not defending the author of The Vestiges, or adopting his theory. We know not how that theory might strike us, if compelled to give up revelation. After such a sad event, there would be but little difference in value between any systems of science or philosophy. But we have not come to that yet. We hold the doctrine of one Moses, "a man of God," who derived his facts from the mind to which there is no unknown in time and space, or height of being. Yet, still, since there has been so much said about it, it might be expected of us to state briefly some of the objections that might fairly be made to such a doctrine of development of species from species. There are two principal ones that we have read of, or that occur to the mind as of chief importance. The first is physical, the second metaphysical. It is not the law or mode now, and from appearances that we discover, or, rather, the want of appearances, we infer that it was not the law or method in the long geological epochs. This is the physical objection. The proof of it is supposed to be found in the absence of all transition marks, transition forms, or half-way stages, such as there would have been remains of had there ever been such a thing in nature, creative or otherwise, as species changing into species, or a new species coming from some natural. We think we have stated the position fairly, and since our stand point as followers of Moses renders us perfectly impartial here, we may also give a reply that may be offered, if our scientific friend, Professor DANA, does not find in such a "hypothetical statement" the seeds of another alarming heresy. It might be said by the man who has found, or thinks he has found, the vestiges, and whom for the sake of distinction we may call the Vestigian, that analogy, as he reads it, is against such an objection. In the individual birth, he might say, nature is sudden, though her gestation is comparatively long, silent, secret. Even in her most remarkable changes, as we know they take place, you do not commonly find marks, at least any visible or prominent marks, of the transition state. The preparation is made slowly, imperceptibly, stilly; the consummation, when it comes, is quick, clean, and complete. There is much analogy to show that in her mysterious births, nature modestly vails her face, and chooses the night, whether it be of the shorter or the longer day. So may it be, he would say, in the still higher mystery of specific generation, higher, it may be called, in some respects, and yet, in itself, no more a mystery than what is called ordinary generation. Gestation is long, but birth is sudden and mysterious. He finds many curious facts in evidence of such a general law. Nature may now be carrying in her womb embryo powers, and embryo laws, which no naturalist hath seen, or can discover, and yet as really there as the power that sends forth the new life in the spring after the long torpor of winter, or quickly ripens the new fruit in every recurring autumn. True generative powers are never wholly inert, although they may lie long apparently dormant. There was something *going on* all the time in the grain of wheat that lay three thousand years in the cloths of the Egyptian mummy, and then grew again in English earth. It was *doing something* all the time; for we can not conceive of a physical power that is not, in some sense, doing, energizing, producing *some effect* in time and space; and yet no science could discover such an energy. And so in nature on a wider scale. The process may be too noiseless, too deep down for any scientific lens; it may be too slow for the watching of any experience though it be that of successive generations; it may be too hidden for any science to find any of its links, and tie them together in any inductive series; and yet, when the hour of travail comes, the evolution may be as rapid and as sudden on the transcending or the wider scale of generation, if there be such wider scale, as we know it to be comparatively in ordinary or more usual growth. In nature, thus contemplated, even though there might be transition movements, there would not be intermediate transition forms, or, if so, rare and obscurely visible. When the long cycle of gestation is drawing to its close, and the long invisibly revolving wheels (invisible because science can only see powers in their effects) touch at last the hidden springs to which they have been coming nearer and nearer at every successive revolution, then comes forth quickly, and perfectly, the new birth, the new growth, which may have been as truly in the original law, or great wheel of the cycle, as any of the more usual powers and forms of reproduction.

We need not give at length the rebutter to this, or the surrebutter. The anti-Vestigian who sticks to nature *as he sees her*, may talk of polywogs and tadpoles, and collect his statistics of transition marks that nature, the present nature, leaves when she does, or seems to do, her present work irregularly. For she does sometimes blunder,—it must be confessed,—and make *faults* in generation, as well as those that are found in geological strata. Though possessed of artistic skill of the highest order, yet, like other finite and imperfect agents whom God has made, she sometimes works out an idea badly. And this, says the other party, or he might say it, shows that had there been any such strange transitions in the olden, the very olden time, there would have been left in the rocks some visible traces of such abnormal, or to us abnormal ways. He might maintain, also, that the birth in its highest outward completeness, may be throughout discovered in the gestation if we watch it close enough, and have glasses powerful enough; and he may be right, wholly or partially right; we think he is right in the main; especially against any Vestigian opponent, who, like himself, is content to appeal to no higher authority than inductive science. Yet still we decide not dogmatically between them—

Non nobis tantas componere lites.

Our only business here is to get, if we can, the fair meaning of the Scripture teachings, be they full or scanty, on these *primordial* matters into which neither of these contending parties have either right or power to carry their speculations. If revelation gives us something, be it ever so little, by which we may hope to reach a conclusion, we will make the most of it. If it gives us nothing of the kind, then we have scientific and philosophic liberty to adopt either side, without fear of any charge of heresy, or of any hard names that either the scientific or religious bigotry may cast upon us.

The other, or metaphysical argument, has a still stronger look against the Vestigian, and yet we can not pronounce it perfect. To talk of the higher coming out of the lower, it says, and says truly, is something worse than any contradiction of nature's laws; it is a contradiction of ideas. "What is not in, can not come out." It would be *plus* e minore, *more* from *less*, and that is the same as something from nothing. This is well taken, we say, if we assume a certain hypothesis, or adopt one which present facts seem to establish. What is not in, can not come out. True; but in the absence of any facts to the contrary, it may be said that it is *in*, and therefore may come *out*. There are, however, such facts, furnishing proof which we can not deny without danger of universal scepticism. There *is more* in the man than in the monkey, and, therefore, man never could have been *in* the monkey. We need not be troubled about man here, as we have special Scriptural proof in his case, and in conservation of his dignity, but some consideration is also due to the nobler species among the lower animals, who can not be so well shielded by direct Scriptural interpretation from this derogating suspicion of development from seemingly inferior natures. To develop the mammalia from the reptiles would also seem like getting *more* from *less*, or bringing *out* what was never *in*. So the dog seems to have a higher nature, to have *more* in him in fact, than ever could have been supposed to be contained, dormant or otherwise, in the stupid masses of half-animated flesh that inhabit the water or the mud. In the same manner might be stated many other cases. And yet this is a difficulty for geological science rather than for a development theory, or partial development theory, which might be so framed, and on pretty fair Scriptural proof, as wholly to escape it. We say partial development theory, for it would have so far to depart from uninterrupted development, (a thing which any one who holds it would very cheerfully do,) as to admit the Scriptural idea of a divine Word, or a divine interposition, supplying this higher or *plus* quantity, every time there was such an ascent in the animal scale, although building each time on the lower physical. We do not maintain, and have not maintained, even this in respect to man; we were rather cautious about carrying so far this super-building of the higher upon the lower, although we speculated and hypothesized some about it; but if our scientific friends are shocked at it, will they, pray, tell us, in all clearness and honesty, what they mean by that doctrine of types of which they say so much, and which Professor DANA is so fond of exhibiting, even at the expense of all consistency, in his charges against the author. We would enquire of him elsewhere what he means by his "*laws;*" but we would ask here, and with a deep sense, too, of the difficulty of understanding him,—What *does* he mean by his types? If he does not find the man in the fish, he certainly finds the fish in the man, the mammalia in the man, the monkey in the man, the whole caravan of lower animation, we may say, in this single all-containing homo. We have no particular objection to this speculation of Geology; on the whole, we rather like it, although the special Scriptural account of Adam contents us; but does not this look something like development? If it is not a development of man out of the lower animals, it is certainly an envelopment of the lower animals into man; and that equally affects our dignity by making them physically bone of our bone, and flesh of our flesh. But we need not be humbled at that thought, or, if humbled, it should be with joy and penitence, when we remember how a higher and heavenly nature (if we may use the word nature in this connection) took upon himself, or rather *into* himself, the nature of man, thus raising us from our deep abyss of animality, internal and surrounding, to a dignity which no psychological rank could impart, and no connection with lower orders of being ever diminish. Geology teaches,—Professor DANA teaches,—that the lower nature of the fish is the ground on which is somehow built (in type at least the most important part of the process) the higher nature of the reptile, whilst this becomes the ground of that which is next above, and so on until we come to the upper stories of the scale. Has this doctrine of types any meaning as taught by science? Or what does it mean? If we would have anything more than a most inane figure of speech, it can denote nothing less than an actual stream of life flowing on without breaks in its continuity, and yet, from time to time, receiving from a higher source a new energy and a new elevation. In this stream, as their constant *materiel*, (to use the term in its philosophic sense,) the types are impressed,—each time with a higher beauty, a higher finish, and a higher life. It is, in fact, when rightly viewed, precisely that doctrine of Platonic ideas against which Professor DANA attempts to excite the easily excited religious odium. Under another form of language, and without knowing precisely what it is, he admires it greatly, and is never tired of introducing it into his article. Some scientific men, of highest note abroad, had brought this mode of speech into the scientific dialect. Others have adopted it, pleased with the pretty sound, yet with so little clear knowledge of its real force that they are ever running into inconsistencies in the use of it. Plato represents these types or *ideas* in nature as something distinct from her laws. They are the σπερματικοὶ λόγοι, the *spermatic words* sown in the stream of natural causality. It is a figure, indeed, and yet something more than a figure. The type is an impression sinking into the nature *as it flows*, and not merely a material mass separately originated, outwardly affected, and artificially formed, each time, in *imitation* of something outward that was not vitally present in its organization. The lower type is carried by the stream into the higher life, and there it receives a real addition of beauty and design that is transmitted to the next, and so on—becoming more *ideal*, that is, less gross, sensual, utilitarian, merely animal, at every step. Above it all is the great Architect of Ideas carrying on the creative work—making a nature,—that is, originating a nature, sustaining that nature against the necessary deterioration of its own finity, making it the mold to receive the divine ideas, and, as the plastic stream flows on, impressing upon it continually a higher and still higher idea from that eternal paradigm, that timeless thought, which was with Him πρὸ τῶν αἰώνων, "before *the ages* or the *worlds* began."

Whether this doctrine of types, or ideas, be true or false, the view we have thus presented is the only one that makes it anything more than an unmeaning simile. We have endeavored to put some meaning into this language Professor DANA is so fond of employing. *Types* sounds well; it is, indeed, a beautiful, as well as most significant word, but, then, as he uses them they are not really τύποι, but μιμήσεις, not *types*, but *imitations*, not the true *in-forming* architectural design, as wrought in and constituting the real molding, but a mere delusive fresco painting. This cheating fancy can only make itself intelligible at all by representing each work of God as separate, and Deity as each time separately *imitating* in every after production of his creative hand something which he had done in earlier efforts. It represents the Great Printer—with all reverence be it spoken—as making over and over again the same type or types, not only at the printing of every volume, but for every impression of every page, and word, and letter,—nay, more, as casting again each time, and for every letter, a new metallic mold. This is not printing. In such a process there are really no types, no molds, but only imitations of them. All this results, if ideas, and types, and that in which they flow, the continuous life, are not by themselves, *in natura rerum*, as real existences as the matter hard or soft,—yea, more real in any true and proper notion we can attach to the word reality. In the other view, or rather want of all definite view, which prevails among some scientific men, there is nothing truly typical or ideal—nothing even that can be called comprehensible, or of which we can perceive any idea or meaning. All comparisons we know, and all words fail here. There is no difficulty in taking exceptions to any expressions, however carefully guarded. Still there is a fitness in this language of types that has struck the most religious as well as the most philosophic minds, although as sometimes used they are mere sound and shadow from which all significance and all ideas have departed.

We may well ask, again—Has this doctrine any meaning as taught in scientific books? If it has, then what consistency is there in branding with an odious name a statement which only attempts to bring out that significance, and in holding up as a bugbear that Platonism from which the idea has been filched, although, it may very well be, without any definite knowledge on the part of some who make the greatest parade of the language.*

But we would not lose sight of the only conclusion we have sought to establish in this chapter. We may guess, we may fancy, we may philosophize, we may pursue analogies clear or dim; but, after all, we *know* nothing of origin aside from revelation. The writer would say for

* The author, in that passage of The Six Days of Creation which has called out one of Professor DANA's most pious rebukes, did not go as far as this. He was very cautious—more cautious, perhaps, than he need to have been. Instead of thus building the man on the fish, as this scientific doctrine of types must do, if it means anything, he simply said that *if* the Scriptures had taught that the human body had been a growth from lower to higher, he would not pronounce it monstrous or incredible. Pretty safe this. And then he proceeds to show some reasons from Scripture which would seem to be against it. Professor DANA has only left out an *if*, that most unimportant word in a hypothetical statement. The amount of it, then, is simply this. The author said he could believe *with the Scriptures*, what Professor DANA holds *without the Scriptures* and, we may even say, without any intelligible idea. This is the ground, too, on which he pronounces the book "decidedly infidel in its tendency." It is hard to decide which is the more striking here, the unconscious inconsistency, the gross absurdity, or the extreme narrowness of the charge as coming from one who would be thought a liberal minded and liberal thinking man of science.

himself, that away from this authority he has no theory of development or undevelopment; none, at least, that he would not surrender, in a moment, to any fair demand of interpretation against it. For the doctrine of ideas he must confess an exceeding fondness. He thinks Scripture is not against it, if there is not rather something which, although in the Hebrew or Oriental way, looks very much like a recognition of at least a similar view. "Thine eyes did see our substance yet unformed,* and

* Psalm cxxxix, 16. LXX, Ακατέργαστόν μου. Symmachus, ἀμόρφωτόν με, *when I was formless.* Vulgate, imperfectum meum, my *unwrought* or *unfinished.* "*In the days.*" This is not expressed, although significantly given by the words in our translation, "*in continuance.*" The passage, doubtless, refers, in the first place, to ordinary generation in the maternal womb, but it suggests the greater sense; and may there not be a transition to the greater sense,—in other words, from the individual to the mysterious creative generation? May not that remarkable language, "*the lowest parts of the earth,*" be exegetical of the words in Genesis ii, 7, "And the Lord God formed man of the earth," מן האדמה? Was there a process in this primitive formation, or generation, of the first humanity in the perfecting of the first individual man? Those who say that the brevity and tone of the language excludes such an idea, should compare with it the expression, Jer. i, 5,—"*I formed thee in the womb.*" Had we known as little of ordinary, as we do of primitive generation, or the creative תולדה, some zealous advocate of literality, as he styles it, might call a man an infidel for suggesting that the language in this latter text might be consistent with the idea of a process, long or short, or a gestation, that is, a formation, or making, through a system of law and causal agency. It may be as much outline language, in the one case as in the other, and should render us cautious how we make our knowledge, in fact our ignorance, the infallible measure of the meaning of God's brief yet mysterious language. There are difficulties, certainly, attending this view of Psalm cxxxix, and the mere suggestion of such a transition sense is offered with great diffidence; but there are also difficulties, which every commentator has felt, as existing in some parts of this language, when we attempt to confine it wholly to the first view. Especially is this the case with that strange expression, "the lowest parts of the earth." If a figure for the maternal womb, it is no where else so employed in Scripture. Still, in either view, our leading thought of a super-material formation, in some

in thy book our members all were written when as yet there were none of them"—"*in the days*" when they had not yet come out in outward being, but were being formed and "curiously wrought" in the divinely formed womb of nature, amid the *interiora* of generic causation,—in the very depths—"*the lowest parts of the earth.*" Is it true of the maternal gestation, (which would seem to be the first meaning of the passage,) and is it not also true, and may we not suppose it to be affirmed as true of the higher and older birth of our humanity? God made the tree "before it was in the earth,"—that same tree which the earth afterwards so mysteriously *brought forth* individually and specifically into outward materiality. He made it "before it grew,"—that same thing, in one and a most important sense, which afterwards did grow. He made,—from no material seed, or outward material substance, as

way transcending the material, and going continually before the material, receives the same support. Just as the tree is made before it grows, so here something is made and regarded as truly *in being* before it *ex-ists—stands out*—visibly, tangibly, outwardly. Every one who studies the passage closely, must feel, we think, that the idea of foreknowledge, simply, of a future event, or of events as future, does not come up to the mysterious strength and breadth of the language. Not fore-knowledge, (*pre-science*,) but *omni-science*, is the great thought of the Psalm. "*No darkness can hide from Thee.*" "*The darkness is light about Him.*" He looks through shades which neither our optical nor our spiritual vision can hope to penetrate, and sees what IS—sees it directly, not only in the timeless ideas, but in the very natures he has made to bring it out in chronological existence.

We might say, in addition, that such a thought of human origin, if we could suppose it entertained by the Psalmist, could not be called scientific or philosophical. Though inspired, it might still lie naturally in his mind, and in perfect harmony with the ancient thinking about man as the child of *earth*, formed somehow in her womb, yet having, at the same time, a high and heavenly origin not only of his spiritual being, but also of his physical existence. "He is of the earth earthy," and yet we are not driven by this to suppose that there was not an unearthly, a supernatural, a transcending process even in his physical creation.

we can learn,—that same potency which afterwards produced its first material seed, and had its first material semination, after the manner which nature has ever since exhibited. Did he make the tree by outward plastic shaping, leaves, branches, roots and all, with its perfect seed fully formed, a tree that never grew, a seed that was never born from any parent stem, and then place it in the earth, just as a human gardener makes a place for the transplanted oak and gathers the earth around its roots? If the strangely mysterious language will not allow us to hold this, then must we take a view, which, whatever may have been the duration or manner of the growth, involves all the difficulties about antecedent laws, and types, and organizing seminal powers, which some men would so easily and so ignorantly avoid under cover of the opprobrious name, as it seems to them, of Platonism.

But the whole ground is too serious and too sacred for any rash speculation. We are greatly attracted, we say again, by this doctrine of ideas, and that corresponding doctrine of types whose adoption by modern science we would regard as one of its highest glories; yet, still, we can as truly say, that, if demanded by any clear authority of revelation, we would yield it, at once, to the higher teacher, if not without a passing regret, yet with a conviction that the truth which comes in its place must far more than make compensation for its loss. The Bible here is everything or nothing. On this great question of origin, as well as on that of destiny, there must be no thrusting it aside on the ground of its province being solely the *moral*, as some would define the term, in distinction from the physical. Who gave them power to run this line, or what peculiar qualifications have they for settling this boundary? In determining the line, and on both sides of the line, as far as it assumes to teach, the Bible is everything or nothing. If we can only establish this position in the minds and hearts of our readers, we shall have done some service to the Church, for the sake of which we would yield any of our own particular interpretations, however prized as falling in with certain views, or whatever of personal value they may have acquired as the fruit of severe labor and some faithful study.

The atheism of "The Vestiges" is not simply in its doctrine of development of new species in nature; for all science may be defied to show why God might not have made such a law, and put into nature such a continuation of life, as well as the equally wondrous, if not in some of its aspects still more wondrous development of individual life from individual—certainly more wondrous when predicated of the higher organisms, and especially of humanity, than any mere growth of animalculæ out of conditions hitherto unperceived by science. The atheism of The Vestiges, we say, is not in this, but in its studied exclusion of the divine and supernatural, as far as in conception they can be excluded, although barely admitted from a logical necessity at one and that the remotest end of the scale. It is, along with this, the ignoring of the Bible, although the author professes all respect for the Scriptures. We have no right to say that this profession of respect is any less sincere than that of the writer in the Bibliotheca. In both, Biblical interpretation is the boat, and science the strong current in which it floats, and by which its course is to be controlled and harmonized. The religious world may, perhaps, get its eyes open to discover that if the helm is to be thus surrendered, it will make but little difference in what direction the boat drifts. Faith is as truly gone in the one case as in the other. It is this claim of science, and this giving up of the pilotage that is the real naturalism, the more dangerous, perhaps, the more piously it talks of harmonies. These have not been made from interpretation. In fact, the very thought is contemptuously discarded as a false pretense—as a "clapping of the hands in great glee at the thought of keeping up with the progress of science," when they are only carried along on its triumphant wave. Have we not some grounds for saying, that there is really less heart in such an easy harmony than in doubt itself?—the sorrowful doubt, it may be, that rejects all hope of reconciliation. The writer feels that he can never stand on any other ground than that of the plenary inspiration of the Scriptures in the most common sense of the term, and of the absolute verity of the Mosaic account. If forced from this, he must "walk mournfully beneath the sun" in utter despair of any satisfying light from science or philosophy on the great questions of origin and destiny. But he would not judge others by his own temperament, or his own position. If any can hold on in some other resting place, God keep their feet from slipping. It may be that one who, pressed with difficulties, takes the Mosaic account as mythical, or adopts the theory of partial inspiration, may really have a more honest and hearty love for the Bible than others who claim a higher orthodoxy. It may be, that he sees not, or that he shuts his eyes to the difficulties that press upon his own lower path, but it is very possible, too, that he may have a deeper sense of the preciousness of the Scriptures, and that he would feel more grief for their total loss, than many, whether in the scientific or religious ranks, who prattle away about harmonies, and yet have too little hearty interest in the great question of a written revelation, to make them feel a doubt, or gird themselves to the encounter of a serious difficulty.

CHAPTER VIII.

THE SIX DAYS AS FOUND BY SCIENCE.

The Writer in the Andover Bibliotheca—His Nebular Theory—The Reviewer finds no Difficulties—A hearty Faith is not so easily satisfied—The chief interest of the Mosaic Account—1st. Its Supernatural Character—2d. Its Hexameral Division—The true Greatness of the Mosaic Account—Greatness of Moses as compared with Aristotle or Bacon—Professor DANA'S *Seven Points—Of the First Three Geology knows nothing—Her Protests or Acceptances of no Value—Rests in Nature—The Scientific Scheme of Creation—As well Six Hundred Days as Six—The Reviewer's Boat driven by two Forces—The Word Beginning—Sudden leap from the Birth of the Light to the Growing of the Mosses—Immense Distances from which Light travels—Want of Chronological Harmony—Immense Hiatus in the Second Day—A Modest Note—Spectral Light of Geology—The Rakia or Firmament—Was it the Breaking up of the Nebular Rings?—Had Moses any such View, either as Fact or Conception?*

IT would seem to be a part of Professor DANA'S plan, in his two Andover articles, to give a scientific theory of Creation. The book reviewed is condemned, not so much for a failure in the only thing it professed to do, that is in its interpretation of the Scriptural account, (for of this the reviewer has not a word to say,) as for some deficiency in not coming fully up to that nebular hypothesis of creation which has become so great a favorite with certain scientific writers, and with which they so please some of the religious people delighted as they are to be taught that Moses is so much more scientific than they had ever imagined, and still more delighted to find the Bible actually believed by such wonderfully clever men. It strengthens their faith greatly. The testimony of a mere theologian, or of a mere Bible student, would not have half the value. It is this assumption of the widest cosmological view, that in the estimation of some minds gives the article in the Bibliotheca Sacra a credit, perhaps, that would not have been conceded to a less ambitious attempt. And yet it is not easy to make out what the outlines and features of this hypothesis truly are. It is presented in such a rambling method, and there are so many ambitious suggestions that lead the writer away from any regular path, that it is very difficult to determine what it really is in itself, and still more difficult to determine that "harmony" between it and the Scriptures, without which the title of the article is all a deceptive misnomer, in other words — a pious fraud. He makes the Mosaic creation commence with the very beginning of matter and all worlds. It is cosmological in its widest sense, embracing the nebulæ and nebular condensations, the throwing off the rings that formed the solar system, and that whole process which belongs as much to the material formation of the remotest visible or invisible bodies, as of our earth and moon. There is no other meaning to be attached to his remarks on the author's use of the word beginning. He is altogether hypercritical, or this word "*beginning*," as employed in the Bible account of creation, is taken by him for the absolute beginning of all material existence, the widest in space, the remotest in time. But it is folly to talk of Professor DANA'S views of the Bible account. What he presents does not lean upon the Bible at all, and he takes no pains even to give it that appearance. In general it marches on independent of the Scriptures, all along assuming a harmony, but made out on no Bible grounds. It is taken for granted that it must be so, and this, perhaps, to a careless reader, might look like a reverence for the Scriptures too profound to allow the question of difference to be even so much as raised. Now we have not the least doubt of Professor DANA'S sincere belief in the Scriptures, and yet we venture the paradox that a very hearty faith would not have been so quiet, so calm, in its undisturbed assurance of a hypothetical harmony. The immeasurable importance of the questions concerned would have made it more anxious. It would have found more difficulties, such as a hearty study of the Bible ever finds, although, at the same time, it gets from the same source a light, and strength, and grace, we may say, to overcome them. Now this is a peculiar feature of Professor DANA'S articles; there are no difficulties in them, none whatever; everything is as easy as the latest geological theory. All he had to do was to weave in his nebular hypothesis in the way best adapted to show off this latest science in some of its more specious aspects. To look into the Bible, and to study the Bible with the hearty purpose of seeing how all this really agreed with the language of Moses, would have been troublesome. It would have been to meet with perplexities. There would have been some danger, too, of running on positions that certain minds might, perhaps, call infidel. It would have required, moreover, let us boldly say it, a patience and a discrimination of mind that are not demanded by the easy natural sciences, and we do not except even Geology from the remark. It is easier to form theories here than to get at the fair meaning of old words, and to lay a good foundation for the interpretation of an ancient document. It is this absence of all difficulties in the Andover articles that we would especially present to the reader's notice. If he is intelligent he can not help drawing the right inference. It must be seen, however, that it gave their writer in some respects the advantage as a critic. Having nothing in his own way, he had the more leisure to make objections, and find difficulties in the way of others. To use the language of a gentleman of high scientific standing—"having no real disagreement with the ultimate conclusions of the work, he had the fairer opportunity for charging on the book faults and deficiencies which, even if real, had nothing to do with its true design. Had there been a hearty antagonism on the merits, instead of a spirit of mere scientific petulance, it would have given a different tone to the whole article. Such a hearty antagonism on the merits, would naturally have compelled something like a fair statement of the real positions of the book assailed, for the very purpose that they might be the more squarely and availably met."

But to return to Professor DANA's theory of creation. We see but little of outline or feature in it any way—nothing but that which the next general change in geological language, and geological speculation, may destroy as easily as it has created. But how does it agree with the Scriptural account? This is here the question, the only question. Where is the Omnific Word, the Brooding Spirit, the *naming*, the *dividing*, the working—the rest? Not but that these ideas, or some of them, may be suggested by the scientific theory if such theory is read by the lamp of the Bible,—but are they words or ideas that would have ever come out of any discoveries of science alone, and upon its own ground? He has much to say of light and life; talks eloquently of *types* and *laws*, taking good care, however, not to have much meaning in the phrases, and specially avoiding all the great and real difficulties connected with these most mysterious ideas. He preaches finely about "God in nature," trying to represent the author as very heathenish on these points, or at least far less orthodox than the Reviewer. He tells us why God made mammalia, when he did, and why he did not make them before. He has much to say,—in fact he talks everywhere about "the harmony;" but where do we find the six days? No man can read this pretentious article, so ostentatiously entitled "Science and the Bible," and derive from it any reason why there should be six days any more than sixty or six hundred. In the book they are the prominent feature. In interpretation they could not be overlooked. They were the *res gestæ*, the real matters of fact narrated. In the scientific theory they are made entirely subordinate. They are to be taken only in a very loose and general way. It is one of the points of the harmony where we must not be too pressing. The scientific side is so taken up with that other idea of antiquity that it almost wholly overlooks the remarkable Scriptural feature of the hexameral succession, so distinctly defined by the regular supernatural division, and of so much more importance, both in itself, and for the consistency of the narrative, than any duration be it long or short. It is just as much a *succession*, whether passed through in six very long days, or in six very short days. The six-fold aspect preserved, nothing more need be asked for the integrity or consistency of Scripture ; but take this away, or render it confused, or indefinite, with nothing but forced arbitrary lines to mark the divisions, and the fair face of the narrative is blotted ; that by which we know it is no longer recognized ; its identity is gone.

The other idea of duration is subordinate to this. We believe the Bible language to be fully and fairly consistent with the most remote antiquity,—using the term relatively as compared with historical times now measured and passing upon the earth ; yet still short times might satisfy the same language, especially in the absence of any outward view that might give interest or importance to one or the other aspect. Now, it is this idea of antiquity that has been regarded as the legitimate prize of Geological science. Hence the absurd sensitiveness at the claim of discovery from any other source, even though that source be the Word of God. Hence, too, the strange disposition, not only to sacrifice to this every other feature of the Mosaic account, but even to assail with unfair criticism and odiously disparaging epithets any effort that may arrive at the same or a similar conclusion by the hermeneutical road.

We have spoken of the six day division as being a very prominent and indispensable feature of the Mosaic history of creation. But it is not even here we are to look for its highest interest. This lies rather in the fact of its being a supernatural revelation from God himself. It is its own supernaturalism, whatever it may reveal of the natural, or of any other facts. In some previous remarks we may seem to have disparaged the objects both of science and of revelation, by representing our greatest times and spaces as such comparative infinitesimals. But, in truth, such a view does not at all affect the latter, or diminish its true greatness. We might say the same of science when considered in a proper light. The true grandeur of science is this discovery of its own littleness. It is most sublime when most lowly, most truly great, when, instead of boasting of its exploits in the spirit of our scientific Reviewer, "it puts its hand upon its mouth and its mouth in the dust,"—if not in the true fear of the Lord, at least in the awe of the Infinite and the Unknown. But taking science as exhibited to us by such writers, it can never have any real or absolute greatness. It must ever be a quantitative thing, and can, therefore, never be certain of anything more than an infinitesimal rank. It has no other rule than that of amount in some aspect—amount in time, in space, or in power. This is the only value it knows or can know,—how *long* a thing exists, *how much* space it occupies, *what* it does, or the amount of dynamical action it manifests in such space—and these are all comparative. Their rank ever varies with a supposed extent of the universe. Their value, intellectual as well as physical, ever sinks with the supposition, the rational supposition, of an unknown immeasurably if not infinitely exceeding the utmost that is known or can be known respecting them. In the same ratio sinks the intellectual rank of minds whose utmost attainment in the knowledge of the universe can only be measured on the same comparative scale. Hence it is no dream, no fancy, but a most sober deduction from the seeming infinity we see stretching out around us and above us, when we say, that the times of the scientific man may be infinitesimal moments, his worlds, of which he has so much to say, miscroscopic motes, himself an animalcule, and his boasted knowledge, as compared with higher intelligences, but the dullest instinct of the worm. This *may* be true. Leave him to his science alone, and all her boasted laws and analogies would go to show that in the immensity of space, time, and power, it actually *is* true.

Such is its greatness on its own favorite scale of measurement. Nothing can protect it from the rigid application of its own rule of quantity in one of these three degrees. Such is the greatness of Geology, in itself considered. But the Scriptures have a different greatness, an absolute greatness not depending for its rank or value on any known or unknown size or age of the universe. It has the same greatness whether there be one earth, or billions of solar and stellar systems, whether its creative times be six solar days, or a thousand years, or ten thousand times ten thousand ages. It has a greatness differing essentially from this, and which no comparison, or mere quantitative relations, can ever affect. In what, then, does it consist? We answer,—Not in its times and divisions, great as they are, not in its antiquity, or its revelations of antiquity, comparatively vast as we believe them to be, but in the fact of its being a revelation. This takes it at once out of the inconstant and ever depressing rule of quantity, by connecting it directly with the Eternal and the Infinite. It is the fact that it is God speaking to us worms of the dust—the Great Soul of the Universe (we are not afraid to use the language) throwing nature aside, taking off her vail, manifesting his ineffable personality by talking directly to us, not waiting till by searching nature we find out God, but finding us who were otherwise eternally lost,—graciously coming down to us through all space and time and height of being, telling us of himself, and how he made this world in which we live, giving us some of the steps in the process, and that, too, in language wherein the common mind is on a par with the most scientific, revealing to us wherein he made use of nature, and how from time to time (be they long or short) he came forth personally from his own supernatural celestial sphere. This is the interest of the Mosaic narrative, an interest, we say, remaining the same constant quantity whether there be none, or billions of other worlds beside this, or billions of other ages before our mundane history commenced. There is a sublimity in the other features; but it sinks in presence of this fact that the wondrous history itself is a voice from the sphere above nature, from the "firmament that is over the heads of the living powers," a voice from the Eternal and the Infinite, talking to us and telling us what science never could have told, and for which she never would have had even a language, had not revelation, from the earliest times, furnished the ideas and conceptions on which such language is founded. She might have found the same facts she now finds, and traced the same phenomena, and the same sequences of phenomena; but she would never have known creation, she would never have found the supernatural, she would never have risen above the sphere of physical causation. As long as men kept this early light, the "visible things did manifest to them the Eternal Power and Godhead." When they lost it, as Paul tells us, the religious instinct remained, but it sank into that nature worship of which all heathen mythologies, and nearly all heathen philosophy, were but the direct or mediate products.

This, then, is that other kind of greatness which the unphilosophical science, if we may employ the term for an important yet too little recognized distinction, can never reach. This is the greatness which is dependent on no real or hypothetical size of the universe sinking every part into nothingness by its comparison with the whole. This is a greatness which is measured by no flowing terms of quantity, but by a constant equation giving the constant term of nearness to God the great central heart of the world. It is the value that never changes; it is the theo-centric position that has no parallax. It is that which made Moses so much greater than Aristotle, or Archimedes, or Galileo, or Newton. This is the greatness that makes one verse of the revelation given through Moses of more value, and its right interpretation of more real importance, than all the demonstrations of the Mechanique Celeste, and all the discoveries of all the Geologists. It is not the extent of the supernatural announcemeut, nor the amount made known to us respecting the world; for when we are once assured that the divine voice has truly broken through nature, there may be as much ground for faith in the scantiness as in the abundance of the revelations. The silence in respect to that over which the vail still remains, may be even more expressive, more sublime, having more religious awe, and thus producing a closer confidence, than might have come from its removal, even if our souls could bear the unveiled aspect of what God has not seen fit to make known. This might be our reply to some who think that the creative revelation is degraded, and made unworthy of Deity, by being supposed to be confined to our inferior earth instead of taking in the whole universe in space and time. The rational soul longs for the supernatural; it listens for the supernatural; yet let it be assured of the voice and a whisper may suffice it. A revelation thus given may have respect to the smallest part of the kosmos, to a satellite, or a satellite of a satellite, and yet, on this very account of its being a revelation, have something for us more precious, immeasurably more glorious, than all that any inductive science has discovered, or may yet discover in the widest fields of space and time. The most astonishing thing of all, is the fact that this poor natural knowledge — poor, we mean, in the attitude assumed by the Reviewer, though having a beauty and an honor when it chooses to be modest — should so dare to put itself face to face with the Scriptures; not in the attitude of a manly though impious antagonism, but in the far more insulting spirit of petulant rivalship. For we can give it no other name than this when it pretends to have superseded the necessity of interpretation, and claims priority of discovery, as though it were some contemptible quarrel about the invention of a new machine, or the first sight of some shower of meteoric stones, or of some broken asteroid, or some worthless comet still roaming among the unsettled irregularities of nature. There are scientific men of noblest stamp; we have professed our sincere respect for them, and can not be repeating it for fear of being misunderstood. But it may be also said, that among all the wonders science reveals, there is nothing so truly wonderful as the fact that some of its professors can stand in the presence of these four great Scriptural ideas, the Word, the Spirit, the Ineffable Working, the Divine Repose, and yet babble away about their "rock written revelation," when their highest decypherings of these old palimpsests, even where they reveal some clear and orderly ideas, do not so much as make an approach to these transcending verities of the Mosaic account. They are still in a region far below, if not in space and time, yet in the rank and grandeur of idea. We have a specimen of this in what may be called Professor DANA'S summing up. He makes seven points. The first three refer to the great primordial questions—the true ideas of nature, of matter, of natural causality, or growth as having its *origin* in a Divine Word, and its *efficiency* in a Divine Spirit. The others relate to the phenomenal facts as they occur in the order of the Scriptures, or the supposed order of science. With regard to the last four points, "Geology," says the Reviewer, "can make little exception to the author's conclusions;"—implying that she differs from him on the first three. Geology is very gracious here; but need any intelligent reader be told that all this parade of points is shown to be absurd, and all this graciousness of Geology is nullified at once, by the simple consideration that these first three must, from their very nature, lie entirely out of her domain, so that her protests, or her acceptances, should she make any, are really of no value whatever. Revelation may settle these points, or leave them unsettled. Philosophy may legitimately entertain them as matters of abstract speculation; but to Geology, or natural science, in the common acceptation of the term, they belong not at all, and no true man of science who is, at the same time, philosophical enough to understand what truly falls within her province, would ever think of claiming them as subjects of any inductive or scientific decision.

In a similar absurd tone of authority, the Reviewer asserts that "the intervals of rest in nature which Professor L. speaks of, are not in the records of the earth." Has he decyphered those records? Has he clearly interpreted even their title pages? Is he sure that he understands the language in which they are written? Men may get hold of an alphabet to some imperfect extent, as is the case in respect to some of the Assyrian inscriptions, and yet the words, much more the meaning, remain a deep enigma. Does he certainly know what really is retrogradation in these movements,—what part of the cycle is directly onward and upward, what is the reverse, or the apparently reverse direction, or what is the standard by which up and down, higher and lower, are really to be determined? He contradicts himself, moreover, in the very next sentence; or else it has no meaning. "The longest suspension of life in North America took place, as nearly as we can learn, between the coal period and the middle reptilian." There the reader has it as exact as it can be fixed by the geological almanack, within a few thousand years more or less; or "as near as we can learn" about such ancient matters; a very modest proviso truly. An occasion for the display of geological technics and scientific exactness blinds the writer, as usual, to the inconsistency in which they involve him. A suspension of life certainly looks very much like a " rest in nature." The Reviewer, however, shudders at the impious thought that there may be deteriorations or backward movements in the physical history. It is in the way of the favorite notion of an ever right onward, right upward, or rectilineal progress. And this might be rational, if physical development, or the perfection of nature, were the great end in the divine kingdom. This end, to be sure, is all that science can legitimately look for, as long as she confines her vision within her own field, and even this she can only guess. As she walks alone among the catacombs of geology, with her dim lamp revealing more darkness than light, with death and dissolution all around her, and the ghosts of long extinguished life starting up everywhere in the midst of former ruin and decay, what can she do, or rather what can her votary do, but to assume that there is some clue to the labyrinth, some path that amid all these windings and turnings may lead again to the upper air of heaven, thus making every seemingly backward or circular movement a progress after all. But where does science, or rather the scientific man, get this idea ? Nature does not teach it to him. She reveals broken planets, extinguished stars ; her nebulæ may be systems going out, the smoke and cinders of old wasted worlds. What has been may be again ; this is certainly fair Baconianism ; the shifting scenes may bring once more upon the stage the old catastrophies with ten-fold greater ruin. What right has science, frightened by this, to leave her old inductions, to abandon in terror her *facts*, of which, at other times she boasts so loudly, and run for shelter to a priori ideas, or to the lessons really learnt from revelation but which she pretends to read in the worn rocks of the earth and the shadowy nebulæ of the skies. In nature there is no sure evidence of progress, that may not, at any time, be destroyed by the signs of some greater catastrophe. If we believe in a progress *on the whole*, or *of* the whole, it is an a priori idea having its birth in an irrepressible longing of the soul, instead of any reliable conclusion of inductive science; but even such a progress of the whole, as a whole, may be perfectly consistent, scientifically consistent, with the relentless sacrifice and destruction of parts,—yea, of parts having an immeasurably higher rank than any that science can assure us of as belonging to us or to our world. But when we think of parts alone, the highest known parts, nothing but a revelation from God can give us assurance of exemption, or any hope of progress or even of rest that can fear no change. Let revelation go, let appearances be our only guide, and what is our position on the great wheel, that any human science should pretend to determine in what direction it is turning, or the angle of curvature as it slowly bends from the apparent tangent line, or on what side of us is that unknown centre of motion from which the upward or downward, or advancing or retrograding course of that curvature is to be reckoned?*

* When viewed in the light of science alone, there is much pertinency, and much interest, in a strange query started by Aristotle in his Book of Problems, (if it be his,) Sect. XVII, Prob. 3: "The question is, how shall we take the terms *before* and after, old and young? Or, if there can be a beginning, a middle, and an end, in a system which goes through all stages, and returns into itself, why may not we be in the beginning, as well as anywhere else? And if, moreover, there is a circle of the universe, why may not the birth and going out of things be such that they continually come again, and again perish? On which supposition of a cycle, there could neither be beginning nor end properly; nor would there be any absolute *before* and *after*, such as would come from being nearer to, or more distant from, any fixed beginning. Nor would we, in that sense, be before

But to pursue this thought, full of interest as it is, would lead us too far out of our proposed path. Professor DANA says he can not read even rests, much less decays in nature. Other men, however, of highest science, say they have discovered them, or what looks very much like them. Analogy, too, might teach that if there are decays in the lesser organisms, and this goes on as far as we can see, there may be also decays in the greater. If the flower, the fruit, the tree, the animal, the man, the nation, the race even, may decay, so also may a world; and so all nature, the universal physical kosmos, may have its growth, its maximum, its retrogradation, perhaps in time its disappearance or going back among things unseen; or it may suffer any whole or partial changes as subservient to some higher world than nature, or some higher state of being, to which all physical existence may be regarded as introductory and probationary.

Our Reviewer can not find in the rocks, or the "records of the earth," as he calls them, "any evidence of nature's rests," and, therefore, he holds to an eternal right onward physical progress.* But if he can not read it in the records of the earth, has he never read in the Book of the Lord, that even "the Heavens grow old,"

others, nor would they be before us—and this because of the continuity," τῆς συνεχείας. We have given a very free translation, but preserving the thought. It is certainly a strange idea, and yet science might be challenged for a better view of the time existence of the universe than that of this repeating cycle. An everlasting right onward progress, without rests, maxima, or *perfections* such as the Bible discloses, would be far more difficult, besides seeming to necessitate a similar past.

* This would seem to necessitate an eternal growth and progress in the past. But the natural or scientifico-religionism can not be consistent. The past eternity of nature or matter is a horrid dogma; its eternal futurity of progress is not only most scientific, but most pious!

(for this is the fair meaning of the Hebrew יבלו, Psalm cii, 27): They wear away through age; they are wasted and renewed like a garment; "like a vesture are they folded up and laid aside," when purposes in God's kingdom that the science of Newton is as incapable of fathoming as that of Thales, may require that nature should decay, go out, yea, at some period, perhaps, be wholly dispensed with in the higher economy of the olams. The Scriptures also tell us of a "*renewed* Heavens and a renewed earth," when "the former things shall have passed away," and even the old book of the Heavens, so much more glorious than the dark book of the rocks, shall be "rolled up as a scroll," to make way for the still grander volume of the grander spiritual dispensation. What shall be in the future may have been in the past. We prefer these ideas of the Bible to any guesses derived from the rocks; even though it had not been that a science equal in all respects to that which finds no deteriorations in nature had found just the contrary. There are various readings of this old book of the rocks; he is a rash critic who decides dogmatically about disputed meanings without waiting for the full variorum edition which may, perhaps, be in time expected. To read the Bible by them, at least before that time, would be something like the parallel attempt now made to confirm the dark annals of the kings of Judah from the supposed clearer records of Assyrian dynasties, or to illume the visions of Isaiah by the phosphorescent light that is dug out of the mounds of long-buried Nineveh. We would be far from disparaging the scientific interest in the one case, or the deep historical interest in the other. It is the false parallelism in which each are sometimes placed with the

Scriptures that calls out our remark. What a *terra umbrarum* would Geology be if we had no higher truths than science furnishes? How dark would be the resurrection of these long buried cities if they did not rise before us in the light which the Bible itself sheds over their mournful ruins?

Some further attention is due to the scientific theory of creation presented in the two articles in the Andover Bibliotheca Sacra. We find it almost as much a chaos as the condition of the earth on the first day. There seems to have been in the writer's mind a disproportioned combination of two schemes, one the purely scientific, as he would say, expressed in scientific language with a great display of its technical richness, the other forced into some faint resemblance to the Scriptural division. It is evident, however, that this does not come out naturally. It would never have been thought of, had it not been for the obvious propriety of having something to justify the title of the article—"Science and Revelation." It is a division that does not occur to scientific men in other countries where the boat drifts on a freer current, and the real influence from which it is derived is shown in the comparative disposition of the two authorities. The boasted harmony is all on one side. It is the swelling and jubilant song of science, with a very slender thread of Scriptural accompaniment. If it were not so serious a subject, we might say that the full and crowded notes of the one are in almost ludicrous contrast to the few thin quavers that here and there betoken the presence of the other. It is, in fact, an accompaniment more marked by its rests than by its notes; and especially may we say this of that second bar where a long semi-breve silence fills up the whole mysterious space. That there is really no heart in this harmony, is shown, moreover, by the fact of the writer's so completely shunning all difficulties. These met the interpreter directly in the face. He could not go round them, nor over them, nor keep silence about them. The critic, however, has very easy work; he may notice them or not, just as he pleases, or just so far as it suits his science to recognize them. There is, for example, the remarkable language of the second day wholly ignored. There is the still stranger language of the third and fifth,—"Let the earth bring forth"—"Let the waters bring forth." This, too, is passed over in utter silence, unless we regard as a notice of it the attempt to charge the book with naturalism in the interpretation, without, however, any effort to show how the idea of natural growth could be kept out of the fair exegesis. But it may be, that the critic admits, in some way, the natural growth of the first plants. He does not believe, perhaps, that they were all outwardly made, like waxen toys, made roots and all, and then stuck in the earth to grow or that thus the earth "might bring them forth." Was it the outward formation of an outward seed outwardly sown in the earth by the Almighty hand? That has the same difficulties; besides, we are plainly told that the first seeds grew, in some way, out of the first plants. Was it the creation of a seminal power older than both tree and seed—in other words, the creation of a law, force, or causal power, of which the outward material tree, instead of being the germinative *source*, was itself, in truth, the first *effect?* That would look like creating them before they were in the earth, before they had outward material being, whether this *before* was to be taken in the order of nature or in that of time,—a piece of Platonic mysticism, (take it in either sense,) in which the Reviewer finds "no edification." It would be the creation of ideas and laws, and these, as separate from their *products*, are things hard to be *conceived* of. Aside, then, from the philological, there are great philosophical difficulties attending every view we may take of this most mysterious process of creation,—being in fact almost equally mysterious on whatever side we may survey them. What appears very simple in one aspect, is full of obscurity when contemplated in another. The direct outward making of every new material form, and the *imitation*, each time, of some former type, without any real growth therefrom, or physical connection therewith, would appear to some minds perfectly easy and intelligible; to others it would be most unmeaning, and, therefore, most difficult of comprehension. Why could not God have made the higher creations at once without the previous imperfect stages that must come and pass away before them? There is no science that can even begin to answer this question. The lizard without toes must go before the lizard that has toes, and a most scientific zoologist entertains an audience with this as a marvellous proof of the divine wisdom and omniscience.* We must

*The lecturer expatiated on this at great length. Some lizards had toes on their right foot, some on their left, and some on both feet. Some had one toe, some two toes, some three, and some no toes at all. It was in an evangelical latitude, and so there was adapted to it a very fine peroration on the Divine plan and Divine Omniscience as displayed in this arrangement, and the glory of science in thus revealing it. It put us in mind of the impious yet frank declaration of the French atheist, that "the heavens declare the glory of the astronomer." It did look as if the glorification

admit, of course, the divine presence in every real transition from less to more ; but where is the wisdom of these repetitions, or the need of these imitations, if there be no physical connection between the stages, no connection, in some way, of a varied yet unbroken life ? There is no vaticination in it for the lower irrational race, and

of zoology or of the zoologist, was really the uppermost thought in the mind of the lecturer. Nor can this remark be deemed uncharitable, when it is borne in mind that all this rapture about the divine plan in the construction of lizards, was from one who has so vehemently opposed and denied the great central truth in the divine plan for the salvation of human souls. But in itself the whole argument is a deception and an abuse of language. There is a *plan* in these lizards, undoubtedly, and so there would be if they had been made in any other manner, with toes, or without toes. But as far as science can see, it is a plan terminating in itself, it is an adaptation terminating in itself, or in something of the same physical order. A follower of Democritus and Lucretius admits of series and order in nature, and so, in one sense, of plans. They said it was the nature of nature to work so, and so they even held to a kind of instinctive intelligence in nature, but were no less atheists still. The divine Wisdom or Omniscience, of which the lecturer speaks so confidently, is quite a different thing. It has respect not to the plan of the lizard alone, in itself considered, or as a means of showing curious arrangement, and thus the glory of science in discovering it, but to the connection of the lizard, the serpent, the animals noxious and innoxious, and of man himself, in the great plan of being. The facts, in themselves, may be very curious, very worthy of scientific exposition, they may show an admirable adaptation in the toes of the lizard to the use the lizard makes of them ; but when we talk of the divine *wisdom* in this thing there is a higher question—Why was the lizard made at all, and the rattlesnake with his fangs, and the horrid monsters whose long-lifeless remains the geologists find in the rocks,—those horrid monsters whose teeth were so admirably adapted to devour other contemporary monsters in the pre-Adamic ages. The zoologist examines those ancient teeth, he exhibits them to his staring audience, he points out how well adapted they were to their devouring purposes, he expatiates on the wisdom and omniscience of God as therein displayed, and the religious world is delighted to find that men who know so much can talk so piously. It begins to be thought that those who are so orthodox on the genus *Lacerta*, can not be so far out of the way in their doctrine of the genus *Homo* and the human pluralities. But there are some who are too irreverent, or it may be, have too little faith, for the ready reception of this naturalizing piety. As they listen to the account of these pre-Adamic monsters, na-for the higher there would seem to be other and more direct modes of conveying the lesson of the divine presence and the divine omniscience,—such as we find in the *First* of Genesis, the *Twentieth* of Exodus, and the *One Hundred and Thirty-ninth Psalm.* Of course, we are here only expressing our own difficulties, and not

ture's curious adaptations are all regarded as of inferior moment, if not utterly forgotten, in view of another suggested query that overwhelms the thinking soul. The thought will come up that every time those horrid jaws have closed, it has been on some mortal agony, some writhing, quivering flesh, some palpitating system of sensation as wonderfully harmonized, and as well adapted as the cruel teeth themselves to show the marvellous *skill* exhibited in nature's plans. Explanations of this are now and then attempted by some of our physico-moralists; but they seem less than superficial; they do not even touch the surface of the matter; if they have any effect, it is only to suggest another difficulty, ever greater than the one they attempt to solve. *Skill*, indeed! There is no doubt of the *skill*. That may be detected in abundance. But "where shall *wisdom* be found? The Sea saith it is not in me; the Deep saith it is not in me; Sheol and Abaddon, the Grave and Dissolution, say we have heard a rumor thereof with our ears: It is not found in the land of the living." And yet one who thus queries may believe in the Divine Wisdom and Omniscience as strongly as the scientific lecturer—perhaps with a stronger faith: for he goes by faith here and not by sight, whether it be ordinary or scientific vision. He can not wait until his natural knowledge connects together all those innumerable links which would make such belief an unanswerable inductive conclusion. God has given him a better guide in certain feelings and ideas of the soul, and when they have become dim or dead, grace, it may be, has renewed them, and so he believes, most *rationally* believes, where he can not see. He believes in the wisdom, where he can not see the wisdom. God is certainly wise, though nature were even still more full of enigmas. God is certainly good, he would say, though his lot were cast in some region of the physical universe where the natural adaptations for producing pain far outnumbered all that are found in our own Valley of Baca. We have no wish to underrate what is really curious and interesting in science per se, and such would we regard the lecturer's facts in relation to the lizard. We would not wish uselessly to disturb any pious sentiment, though fed merely by natural contemplations. But it does seem to us, that that higher ground of faith which every truly religious mind must admit to be necessary, is obscured, to say the least, by the modern tendency to rest in mere physical *adaptation*, and to applaud that physical religionism whose main worship is ever the laudation and glorification of science.

making our own exceedingly limited vision the measure of the divine intelligence. There may be, there must be vast wisdom where we can not see ; God has given man a priori intelligence enough to see that, and this may, perhaps, be one great difference between him and the lower animals, with whom sense and experience are the only measure of things and thought. The mode of creation is full of difficulties, philosophical as well as philological. This is our position here. But science, the science we are characterizing, passes glibly over them, or goes silently around them. At all events, it does not think of encountering them. This may be owing to modesty in "the Student of Nature," or it may be that he is so dazzled by his own light, that he does not see the difficulties that lie below his facts, and which trouble other minds of a different temperament, and a lower order of thinking.

We must, however, make the exceptional remark, in passing, that Professor DANA seems to have had some trouble in his mind about the birds. He looks into the Bible here, and finds that our old translation represents them as the product of the waters. This is rather startling, although, in itself, not a particle more mysterious than the other language, and so he resorts to Professor Bush to show that the Hebrew may be rendered "*Let the birds fly*," —thus making the language indefinite, and getting rid of the seemingly troublesome connection with the waters. We have certainly very high respect for Professor Bush, both as a man and as a scholar, but this will not do. If he will examine the passage more carefully, he must see that this rendering, which seems, at first view, rather plausible, can not stand the test.

The Hebrew construction will not admit it. It is the descriptive future with omission of the relative,(ועוף יעופף) an idiom well marked in the sacred language, especially as forming a peculiarity of its earliest state, and therefore, as we might expect, occurring so often in the Arabic. In fact, we have precisely the same expression, and in the same order, in the Koran, *Surat* vi, v. 38, טאיר יטיר, *bird that flies.* It is equivalent to a descriptive participle with the article as it occurs in Greek, and is used by the Septuagint as a translation of this very passage, πετεινὰ πετόμενα, *birds that fly,*—or to the verb with the relative, *aves quæ volant*, or *volantes*—*the flying birds.* This is the rendering of all the old versions, together with the Targum of Onkelos, עופא דפרח "*bird that flies.*" The other, or the imperative use of the future, "*Let the birds fly,*" requires a different order of the words, and this order, when that sense is demanded, is not departed from. The New Baptist Version gives the same rendering as Professor Bush, and to avoid, perhaps, the same apparent difficulty. We have all respect, too, for some of the scholars engaged in that work; but our old translation here is right. The *volatile* as well as the *reptile*, to use the words of the Vulgate, had a marine origin. Moses does teach this, whether it be naturalism or not. The expression would seem to intimate, that in some way, directly or mediately, nearly or remotely, through the types, or through the life, or through the matter, the divine creative power did bring them from the waters. Now we have heard that science finds fish types in the birds,—thereby testifying on the side of Moses. If so, it is all the better for the crédit of science. But be that as it may, such we believe to be the only fair interpretation of the strange Mosaic language, whatever difficulties it may be supposed to bring, either to the religious or the scientific side of these questions.

The Reviewer's "boat" has evidently been driven by two forces producing a sort of compound motion. There must be some appearance of accommodation to the Scriptures, and this occasionally warps its course; but the mind is ever and mainly upon something else. The Harmony of Science and the Bible! The reconciliation of Faith and Geology! In the book reviewed, there is no such unmeaning, and we may say untruthful aim proposed. It is in fact ever kept out. The Scriptures are to be interpreted, not reconciled. Science and the Bible have nothing in common. Even in respect to prime physical facts of origin and destiny, they occupy two distinct departments, one of which is far below the other. But in the Review there must, in some way, be a harmony to correspond with the title, and so in one place, there is a general enumeration of six periods. We have, 1st, Light, 2d, a mysterious blank, 3d, Division of Land and Water with commencing vegetation, 4th, Celestial Bodies or manifestations, 5th, The Long Marine Period, 6th, all that follows, though without any division Scriptural or scientific. This long marine period being a favorite notion, and there being but one period remaining, all of a later date must be thrown together, and without any of the reasons for its being a day by itself which in the Bible are so prominently presented. This scanty act of homage once rendered to the Spiritual Power, very much as the Italian Machiavelli makes his appeasing bow to the Conclave, science breathes freer and passes on. It gets into the larger field, and gives its larger view. The boat is now on its own buoyant element. It is out of the narrow perplexing currents of Moses, and here the pilot, in his freedom and his jubilancy, forgets himself again. In the outline just stated, there is some faint resemblance. In what follows, it is almost wholly obliterated,—we mean, in its principal feature, or that by which chiefly Moses would know its face. The hexameral aspect disappears. We are justified in what we have already said, that if Moses were unthought of by the reader, he would as easily find in this scheme sixty, or even six hundred days, as well as six. There is no supernatural Word dividing the one from the other,—nay, more, there are no divisions, which, for all that any inductive science can legitimately deny, nature could not have run *over* as easily as she runs *through* any of the intercluded sections. In the Mosaic account these divisions are distinctly made by the Word of the Lord, each time,* and we want no other proof. The geological account with which we are now dealing does not exhibit them in any distinct manner, and if it did so, could not, as we have before proved, ever show, by any scientific reasons, that the same nature could not have developed them all, or, which is the same thing, that they were not all contained in the first nature which God made and endowed with laws for that purpose. Science could never satisfy us that the Author of nature might not have given, and did not, in fact, give to her, the wider as well as the nar-

* "*And God said,*" etc. Let the reader observe how regularly this occurs each time. Then let him compare it with the "*goings forth of old*" of the Logos, Mich. vi, "The *outgoings*" of "Wisdom," Prov. viii, and *the Word*, Heb. xi, 3, "by which the worlds, or ages, were framed."

rower limit. And this is the point to which we are especially desirous to call the reader's attention. It is all important in determining what science may legitimately claim, and for showing, what is far more vital to our true faith, how entirely we must be dependent on a revelation for any sure knowledge of the metes and boundaries in this matter. Now the Bible has given us just this knowledge. When Moses tells us the Word went forth, or uses that transcending formula "And God said," we know that it was to do some work which nature—whether a new nature then made, or any older or previous nature—could not have done, and was not made to do, without a new divine energy. We know it from the divine teaching; we certainly know it in no other way.*

* It is, in general, more wise, as well as more reverent, to seek for the meaning of revelation, than to ask why God has given it to us as he has. And yet the latter question may be sometimes involved in the former, and, to some extent, inseparable from it. It might have been revealed to us simply that God made the world, or that he made all things, leaving the times, the manner, the order, the succession, and even the fact whether there had been a succession, an entire blank. Some think that this is, in fact, all that is meant; everything else being a mere accommodation to human notions, or a mythical adornment. We can not, however, thus regard it. There is, at least, an outline. We think we can see a reason why it was not more, and yet enough given to show us a succession, or a series of consecutive steps or natures in the divine working. It may have been to teach us that with Him there is a reserve fountain of power immensely greater than he has ever yet manifested. Had there been given to nature, *in the first place*, all the potentiality necessary to bring out the universe in time as it was intended to be, and had such, accordingly, been the revelation made to us, it would have been no less divine, but far less impressive. It would have removed the supernatural so far away, that the idea would have been dim, if not wholly lost. Had the supernatural, on the other hand, been more frequent, the depravity of fallen beings would have run into a similar, or we might say, perhaps, the same error, by confounding it with ordinary nature. There would be *resemblances* in such events, as well as in the strictly natural. Hence, science would begin to classify, talk about *laws*, and thus attempt to bring them under her jurisdiction.

It could be shown, that there are direct inconsistencies in this scheme. We have assurances from the highest scientific authority that its geological science is really no better than its philosophy; but we prefer to keep here on the higher and wider ground. In his attempt to be cosmological in the widest sense, the writer involves himself in difficulties surpassing all explanation whether of geology or of exegesis. From the wide universe in its earliest dawn of physical being, down to our little earth, there is a forced and sudden leap which is out of all scientific as well as Scriptural harmony. And so in respect to time; we come from the birth of the light in its essence, from the primordial nebulous matter that first issued forth from the invisible nonexistence, right down to the moss-breeding, grass-growing days, which, in comparison with the first, would be like the ratio of Mr. LORD'S clock measured times to the common geological epochs. The Reviewer finds fault with the interpretation given of the word beginning. He would be more orthodox here, which it was perfectly easy for him to be, since science, when it assumes this attitude, may just as well take at once the widest as any more limited ground. One costs no more than the other; and, Scripture being ignored, it is as easy to find the six days in the earliest as in the later chronology. There is, however, some attempt here at exegetical criticism. It is so striking that we can not pass it over. The writer really thinks "that Moses by the word beginning meant the beginning," and seems to fancy that such an argument is truly a settlement of the great questions whether it was the beginning of time, the beginning of God's first energizing in the universe, the first going forth of the Logos, without which we are plainly taught in the Scriptures there is no creation of any kind,—whether it was the beginning before which there was no beginning, or the beginning of a special work in time and space more directly connected with our own mundane habitation,—a beginning commencing with some existing state of the thing which is the subject of such working, and with a special act (such as the brooding of the spirit upon the waters,) that was the beginning of a subsequent and well ordered process. All these questions he would regard as answered, or, at least as silenced by the profound exegetical opinion that "Moses by the word beginning really meant the beginning"! This closes the argument, and renders any other view or remark quite superfluous.

But let us look at this soaring view, and see where it really carries us. The writer would make it the beginning of the first material, yea, of the first dynamical existence of any kind. We say the first dynamical; for although there is an attempt, very unscientific and much after the manner of the Italian priests, to excite the theological hatred against the author by the common bugbear of the eternity of matter, yet all science may be defied to show what matter is, if it is not resolvable ultimately into the idea of pure force regarded as something subsistent, and separate from a spiritual energy in which it had its origin. Life, we have before said (p. 201) was inconceivable except as an energy, a *doing* something, whether by way of outward *effect* (*out-doing*) in space, or of *resistance*, that is, maintaining itself against other forees,—as we might there have qualified and rendered unexceptionable our remark. All latent forces, as they are called, may in this way be regarded as continually acting energies,—an *inert power* being a contradiction both in terms and idea. The same may be affirmed, though in a lower sense of matter itself. Life is organizing power, acting or resisting according to an idea. But matter, in the lowest conception we can form of it, is still energy. *Rest* is not *inertia*. The latter is strictly a mere negative idea that can only be predicated of nothingness. It can have no place in a real universe. The former, as is implied in its etymology (*re-sto*, *resisto*,) is an equilibrium of powers, a quiescent balance of forces, but none the less a continual energy, an ever *doing*, as the very ground and condition of its existence. If so, then the first material creation must have been the first dynamical creation, or the beginning of any energizing in space and time below the purely spiritual or divine.

It is his determination to bring in his nebular theory that leads the writer to this. The light mentioned by Moses he would have to be the first light,—not simply the first light upon our earth, and which the plain interpretation of Genesis makes to be posterior to the waters, but the first light that ever shone in the universe, the first light ever called into being, the first light in its very essence as it came forth from the invisible, the first outbeaming of the Shekinah, the very birth of that unapproachable entity that forms the robe* of the King Im-

* We hesitate to regard such expressions in the Scripture as mere figures of speech. It would certainly seem to be taught that Deity has, somehow, and somewhere, a physical splendor which the human eye could not behold and live. Moses could only look upon its אחורים, its darker side, or rear shadow. It would seem to be the same that Peter calls μεγαλοπρεπὴς δόξα, "*the Excellent Glory*," or the *magnificent* glory, 2 Pet. i, 17, from which, or rather *under* which (ὑπὸ τῆς) came forth the

mortal. This birth of the light, then, if it is referred to by Moses, was in the work of the first day. We might say, earth's first day, if we followed Moses at all, for he makes his first mention of it in the verse wherein he begins to speak of the creation of the earth as being before that of the heavens, and this mention is immediately after what is antithetically said of the darkness on the face of the terrestrial deep. The Spirit broods upon the Waters; then comes forth the Word, and the luminous manifestation is made. But in the scientific theory, which, although, professing to be in harmony with Moses, is too ambitious to take him for a guide, we are yet far off from the earth; we have not yet come near its lower orb; we are immensely distant from it in time and space; we are not merely in the heavens, the astronomical heavens of nebular and stellar systems, but in the very remotest time and space bounds of the all but infinite universe.

The scheme requires that the light mentioned by Moses should be the first light of physical being, the first born of the cosmical creation, and this would carry us to a time before any division of the universal fluid, before the active commencement of gravitation, or of any *drawing* to separate centres of motion as the initial embryotic

voice that proclaimed the Eternal Son. The truth that God is a Spirit is not at all at war with the thought that he has made for himself such a peculiar residence in an outward glory. If, however, we regard it as a material splendor in any sense, it must be older than that light that first "shone out of the darkness" (ἐκ σκότους, 2 Cor. iv, 6,) which rested on the early Tellurian waters. For other mention of this Shekinal glory, of which the Jewish Shekinah was the earthly representative, the reader is referred to such passages as Isa. vi, 1, John xii, 41, Acts vii, 55, Luke ii, 9, Psalm civ, 1, 1 Tim. vi, 16, 1 Kings viii, 11, Ezekiel i, 26, 27, 28. Certain very strange notions of the Jewish doctors respecting it, may be found in Buxtorf's Chaldaic Lexicon, on the word שכינה.

conception of systems and worlds. We take this nebular theory as we find it presented by scientific men; but although greatly admiring it, in some of its sublime outlines, we can not be responsible for the difficulties it throws in the way of that scientific exegesis of the Mosaic creation which would make it cosmical in the widest and oldest extent of the term. The chief difficulty arises from what is said, in the books, of the motion of light. If the consideration of it draws us into a seeming digression from our main course of argument, we ask the reader's kind indulgence. Science tells us, and we are inclined to believe her, that there are worlds now visible through the most powerful telescopes, yet so inconceivably distant, that to have reached our earth within any historical period their light must have been traveling toward us for millions of years before man appeared. The ray that now terminates its long journey on the retina of a human eye, commenced that long journey when our infant earth had not yet been "robed in its garment of clouds," or "wrapped in its swaddling band of thick darkness,"* yea, had not even been born, or come forth from the nebulous womb; unless we regard it—which, scientifically, we have no right to do—as among the oldest cosmical existences that came out in distinct form and position. But we are not confined to the visible, even though it be the most remotely visible coming to us through the most far-seeing, or *tele-scopic* powers that have ever been brought to the aid of the human optics. The same scientific analogy presses us on to multiples even of such an inconceivable space and time, and to multiples of multiples so vast that all of the

* Job xxxviii, 9.

past and future that our mightiest computations can express are insufficient for the journey. Is any science so narrow, not to say trifling, as to limit the universe to the range of Lord Rosse's telescope, or to fancy that all beyond this arbitrary limit is a dreary void—a boundless space that a boundless time has never yet seen occupied, in any part, with creations? Let us test the reasonableness of this by some of its own numerical estimates. Instead of the clumsy and utterly inadequate methods sometimes employed to denote immense distances, let us take a pure mathematical expression whose inconceivable power is in direct and striking contrast with its extreme simplicity. Take at once, as its basis, the remotest celestial object from which there ever fell a ray upon the spectrum of our mightiest telescope. Call its mile distance x. Then take that transcendental power x^x, and if this be not enough, carry it up the ascending scale $x^{x^{x}}$, until the degrees of involution themselves amount to x. We are now where the mightiest distance to which the mightiest lens ever penetrated becomes a vanishing infinitesimal; and yet we have no right to stop, no analogy that does not carry us still onward, no "*sufficient reason*" to suppose that we have done anything more than make a beginning of a beginning in the estimate of God's creation. Do we shrink from calling it infinite? Certain a priori theological ideas do, indeed, forbid the supposition; but science has no resting place. The same induction that compels her to take the steps already taken, presses her onward forever and forever more. A necessary theology teaches that the universe must be finite; and yet it may be so, and still extend, most probably does extend, beyond any bounds that even such a formula could reach. We may be near the centre; we may be near the outer verge, and yet this immeasurable nearness such, that even between us and that outer verge there may be a wilderness, not merely of solar and stellar but of cosmical systems,—a wilderness of worlds compared with which the whole cosmical region through which light has ever travelled to us may be like a single leaf in the forests of the Oronoco.

Now the first light that ever shone on, or out of, these distant worlds, or in these inconceivably remote times and spaces, may have been, must have been, junior to the birth itself of that luminous essence, than which we can conceive of nothing older in time and creation. But fixing the mind upon this later cosmical radiating light, we may muse upon the question, although we can not venture to ask it—how long has even this light, this first and most distant radiation, been travelling down to us? How long before it will ever reach us, or where, perhaps, will be our world, when it arrives? We are lost. The geological epochs disappear like the fast falling autumnal leaves, or the rapid rain-drops as they vanish in the measureless waters of the ocean. All proportions fail us; all numerical ratios become incommensurable. Mr. LORD has a very easy way of getting along with this. If he takes the common scientific idea of the motion of light, which we think he does,—for he, too, would be scientific—then he has only to form the very easy hypothesis, that all these remote worlds, being all created during the solar week of our earth, were each of them made with an immense projecting horn (קרן, *κέρας κεραυνός*,) or ray of light, issuing from them, and just so long or carried so sufficiently near to us on their first creation, that their continued light would just reach our earth on the evening of the fourth day. Professor DANA would doubtless regard that as all folly, and would think, perhaps, that he wholly avoids it in his more scientific view of the Mosaic creation. He has increased the scale, to be sure, but losing sight of the principle which should govern in the management of so unwieldy an instrument, he has only increased the difficulties in the like ratio. Carry it fairly out, where it will fairly go, and the necessary elongation it demands for the Mosaic First day, and especially the disproportion it must bear to all the rest, involve us in an absurdity the more disgraceful as the scheme from which it comes is the more pretentious.

But is not revelation, too, and all religion, overwhelmed by such a view? Not at all. Faith stands unmoved and undisquieted, if we will only keep in mind the estimating principle that has before been adverted to. The greatness which science computes is quantitative; hence, too, comparative, and self-overwhelming. However far it may stretch itself, it is driven in to nothingness by conceiving still greater bounds to the physical universe.* On the other hand, Faith and Revelation connect themselves

* The same remark is applicable to that kindred system of theology that grounds itself on *utilities*, and "greatest happiness," and makes its *measure* of sin dependent on the *amount* of mischief or unhappiness produced by it, or by its example of impunity, and this, of course, on some supposed *extent* of the universe,—sin rising in moral enormity (if we may use the word moral in such a connection) as the universe is supposed to expand, and sinking as it withdraws itself into narrower spaces. Hence it must be as wholly *quantitative* as the inductive science to which it is allied. It can have no real *quality*, or absolute essence, independent of outward computation. For happiness *(well-feeling)* and utilities are ever terms of *amount* in some order or degree, and whatever is grounded upon them must partake of the same changing character. But the idea of the Good must be something constant, ever the same, be the universe small or great.

with the supernatural, where the "*least in the kingdom*" is greater than all physical existence. In a fixed relation to a Divine Centre, they present a constant value for each single world, and each individual rationality. It is the same as though that world were the only world, and that individual rationality the only rationality, except the divine, in the universe both of space and time. Hence no comparison, and no variation of quantity, can derange it. As far, at least, as any such scientific difficulty is concerned, it is a faith that might unshrinkingly accept even an infinity of natural worlds, without drawing its anchors, or parting its cables from their strong hold in God's supernatural revelation of a distinct supernatural world, or state of being.

Now, to connect this with our main argument, the scientific or nebular scheme of the Mosaic creation requires that the light mentioned Genesis i, 3, should be the first light of universal being, and so, of course, the *previously* mentioned waters must be sublimated into the all-pervading nebular *fluid*. Instead of being, in any sense, a chaotic earth, a *tehom* (תהום) of waters, it is the nebular tehom, or nebular *deep* of the universe, out of which came all worlds and all systems as well as our own. This, then, was the work of the first day; but how are we to travel from it to our own "little earth," as it is called, when such a name is thought to suit other parts of the theory? How are we to get safely down from such dizzy heights of space, and such remotenesses of time, into this "inferior satellite" which God has seen fit to make our secluded habitation, and to which is really confined all our cosmical knowledge that is not the merest mathematical estimate of masses, distances, or comparative visual angles in space. Such a rash leap might be expected from a mere blundering man of exegesis, but cautious and "exact science," as she calls herself, should have furnished a more secure ladder for so perilous an achievement. She should have made a bridge for us over this tremendous chasm. She should have shown more clearly in which one of the six days, whether in the first or second, we cross from the nebular deep of the kosmos to the dry land, or terra firma, of our own little islet of the earth.

Now, we have nothing to say against the nebular theory. Aside from any scientific knowledge on our own part, be it less or more, we could not help respecting what had been advocated by a Henry, a Peirce, and an Alexander among ourselves, to say nothing of distinguished names abroad. We must confess, too, a great admiration of the sublime physical views it presents, as well as of the genius displayed in their scientific exhibition. But, at the same time, there may be a very reasonable doubt whether it can be exegetically forced into any accommodation with the Mosaic creative history. If this nebular theory is to pursue any consistent analogy, the first works it discloses, or the first energizings in matter, can only be regarded as concerned with the rudimentary formation of immense systems of worlds instead of the later individual organic growth of single planets. This is judged on the same principle that leads us to regard the growth of a tree as a much longer and much older work than the special growth of its fruit. It is a fair comparison that would represent single worlds, and even systems, as the later quick-germinating branches, or ultimate mature products, of the great slow growing organic body, which, although only preparatory to the fruit, takes a vastly longer time for being brought to the perfection of that fruit-bearing state. Now, the product of the nebular movements are conceived to be (whether truly or falsely does not concern our argument,) immense systems of worlds emerging after inconceivable times, and countless stages, from the at first universally and equally diffused nebular ocean. This primal deep of matter, which the ambitious scientific interpreter would thus make to be the *tehom* of Moses, is regarded as condensing, cooling, separating into immense primal divisions, and thus acquiring separate centres of cohesive gravitation that divide, if they do not destroy, the allegiance to the universal power. These slowly float away; increasing condensations again part from each other the immensely distant extremities, or separate them from their central parts; new centres of gravity are formed, and thus the great mass is ever breaking up into initial and succeeding portions, dividing and subdividing themselves in degrees and stages unknown, and only conceivable in the ratio their number bears to the vastness of the finite yet immeasurable space and time they may be supposed to occupy. Next come the smaller yet still immeasurable nebular masses containing the embryo germs of unnumbered systems. The imagination,—the rational imagination, if there be any rationality in this scientific hypothesis—traces them as throwing off their rings, parting and parting again into concentric waves, surging and eddying in their abysmal vortices, whence first emerge islets of nebular worlds still greater, perhaps, than all our sight or thought includes in the visible universe. Kosmoi next appear, and, at last, stellar systems come forth from this grand march of progress. Planets are yet unborn; the sun is but an embryo, earth still lower down, an embryo of an embryo. Solar systems are among the things that next take rank and position in space—First, floating banks of still condensing nebulous ether, disturbed again, and parting into smaller rings which somehow (though science has never explained to us the strange process) break up into spheres and throw off their satellites, until, at last, we but begin to approach the confines of that time and space where geology finds the first dim letters of her real alphabet, the first rude cyphers of her vaunted "book." In fact, there may have been innumerably more stages than these. Adopt this scientific hypothesis, and there is no place in an all but infinite universe where we may scientifically stop. Ascending above satellites, planets, solar systems, stellar systems, cosmical systems regarded as a still wider and more ancient elimination, we may have many more as well—earlier in time, more extended in space. The divisions and subdivisions may be beyond any through which the almost invisible speck that floats in the deep currents of the ocean may have been parted successively from its position in the larger floating mass, the earth bank, the boulder, the rock, the mountain, up to the continent, and the globe. We may be but the detritus of the universe. A division carried, in idea, even to such an extent, would not, as we have shown, affect our true moral rank, or our true moral value; but in determining, or conjecturing, our physical place, we have as good a right to draw on the philosophic imagination for the greater as for any lesser series, and science is defied to prove the one any the less rational than the other.

All this, however, may be true or false. We care but little about it—little, we mean, in comparison with the preciousness of what God has actually revealed to us about our own secluded satellite—all the more precious, too, because so graciously revealed by Him. But we take science as we find her in her exact or inexact departments; we carry out her hypotheses as they may be legitimately carried out; and we deduce that conclusion, which, however startling, is strictly deducible from the assumption of some scientific men when they would teach us that the Mosaic creation is an expression for their nebular system of the universe.

Thus the absurdity of such assumption is shown from the utter disproportion and confusion it would introduce between the creative periods which Moses has defined so distinctly with their regular evening and morning divisions. Especially would this be the case in regard to the first and second. The commencement of the nebular movement, and the primeval light that preceded it, must be assigned to the first day. Its first evening, or darkness, with which it commences, must, in that case, have been the darkness of the old *privation*, the antithesis not of the luminous presence but of *being* itself, the darkness that rested "upon the face" of nothing,—contrary to every impression we get from the Mosaic account. Its morning was not the first morning of the now visible earth and illumined waters, when the previously created "morning stars sang together, and all the Sons of God shouted for joy," but the first gray dawn of the first nebulous undulation that faintly stirred the ocean of nonentity. Thus it lies far away from the other days. It is immensely remote from them in space ; its locality is not the earth, but the broad field of the universe ; its time is measured by no earthly change marking any terrestrial evening and morning, while its least period runs through the course of inconceivable ages before earth was born. Yet from such an unimaginable magnitude of space and time, a magnitude for which mathematical analysis finds no expression that does not start with a measuring unit transcending all that sight reveals, there is a sudden jump right down to this earth, and all the rest is occupied with earth's mosses, earth's reptiles, and the dispersion of the earthly vapor that the sun may shine upon them. What is still more absurd, the second day must be wholly overlooked, as having no work assignable to it. There are difficulties in the Scriptures, but none to be compared to this into which we get ourselves by departing from interpretation, and taking this pious talking science for our guide.

Some answer might be attempted to this, by the supposition, for it would be nothing more, that all organic bodies in the universe are of equal age, that all parts have proceeded *pari passu* from the first nebular stages, exhibiting, at every date, and at the present time, an equal advancement ; so that the same days, the same periods of gaseous fluid, water, atmosphere, land, vegetation, animal life, etc., would do for all. In other words, that the day of the week for each might be found from the same almanack, and the age of each determined from the same chronological table. But there is no evidence of this. The visible analogy of things furnishes strong evidence to the contrary. Even to the naked eye there are striking differences in the apparent states of different parts of the visible universe. "One star differeth from another star in glory." It is probable that there is a like difference in their ages. We mean their relative age; for one organism may have existed for thousands of centuries and yet be in its youth, whilst another, measured but by days or years, has already reached its decrepitude. The telescope carries the proof of this much farther. Modern discovery shows that the varieties are incalculable. They run through all degrees of infancy, of juniority, and perhaps of senile decay. Even in our near solar system, right round us we may say, great varieties present themselves in the stages of progress. There is good evidence that some of the planets are not yet as far advanced as earth in its first and second days. Jupiter, huge as he is, has not yet got off his "swaddling bands." (See Job xxxviii.) He is where the earth was when the cloud was its permanent garment. Our best astronomers have just shown that the rings of Saturn are in a fluid state. He exhibits what some, with much plausibility, think Moses may have meant of an ancient state of the earth, when there was a real sea of waters above as well as below the firmament.* Our more distant neighbor, Neptune, may be nothing but gas, or have hardly arrived at the density of liquid ether. Mars may be yet azoic, or, "as nearly as we can learn, somewhere between the coal period and the middle reptilian"; whilst Mercury may have passed that stage of condensa-

* In this way, perhaps, we might account for the flood, as has been attempted by some writers. Indeed, we know of no hypothesis that would so readily explain some of the difficulties that are involved in every other view we can take of that event. It would correspond well to certain parts of the language employed, and yet be none the less miraculous.

tion where life exists no more, and the mass, again become azoic, remains simply to preserve the balance of the system, or to show that worlds may die as well as the beings that dwell upon them,—or to serve some other among the inscrutable purposes of God. In the more distant parts of the heavens the differences become still wider. Thin nebular films flit across the field of the telescope, presenting continuous magnitudes, which, though barely visible, must occupy more space than all between our northern Pole Star and the Southern Cross, or, perhaps, than all included in the universe of stars that reach our naked eye; and yet these immense cosmical nebulæ may have not yet begun to form their initial vortices around their first centres of motion. The evidence is all in favor of diversity, immense diversity, in rank, in magnitude, and so in time and age. Some of these worlds, if we choose to call them such, may have reached their full formed organism; others have just broken their shell, or to use more scientific language, thrown off their rings; whilst, in others, the fœtal albumen out of which is to come the future ζῶον, has barely commenced its inceptive coagulation. There *may* be, there *must* be, if there is any truth in scientific analogy, (and those who would charge us with impiety should remember we are only following science here,) the same variety of age and condition in the greater as in the lesser organisms of the universe. To deny it is to go counter to all analogy and all induction. As well talk of the plant in our gardens, which comes up "the son of a night," like Jonah's gourd, having a *pari passu* germination with the oak of Etna that threw off its first *rings* centuries ago. The one would be no more unscientific than the other. And yet all this must be done to

22*

accommodate a scheme that even then has to put a still greater force upon the simple language in which Moses presents the indefinite periods in his creative history of our earth. LORD'S exact twenty-four hour times, opposed as they are to the most common observation of terrestrial phenomena, as well as to any fair interpretation of the Mosaic words, are still more rational, more consistent, than this pious science.

But how to bridge the chasm. This is the question to which we return. Prof. DANA has a most ingenious way. He leaves out the second day entirely; or, rather, disposes of it by way of apology in a modest, retiring note, thus leaving his lost reader to choose any such way of crossing this immense hiatus as his imagination might suggest. The writer was evidently pressed with some difficulty here, and with good reason; for on his theory he could make nothing of this second day. Here must be somehow found the sudden descent from the nebular heights into this "little satellite of ours." The difficulty, indeed, is great; it is evidently felt to be such; but, instead of admitting it, as students of exegesis are in the habit of doing, the writer finds ease and refuge in a note. Now we have no objection to the note per se, as our readers, perhaps, have found to their vexation. But in this case there is something quite peculiar about it. The humble appearance of this marginal remark is in curious contrast with the vaunting style of the large-print text above, where there is such a magniloquent account of what geology has brought to *light*. Alas, the mummy light of geology!—we cannot help repeating the thought —alas for us if we had no other! It cannot better be described than in the language of Milton,—

Not light, but darkness visible.

We *may*, indeed, see something when we cast among its shadows the reflection of certain a priori ideas, or carry with us amid its caverns the torch of revelation, if not as a scientific guide, at least as an assurer of the divine wisdom. But, the Bible gone—forever gone—what then would be the light of geology? It would be a revelation of horrors—of dissolving, upheaving, ruined worlds,—of progress, if it has any apparent progress, full of loops and retrogressions, without any security, even in its most rapidly advancing, or seemingly advancing stages, against catastrophies greater than any before experienced. It would reveal to us long races of mutually devouring monsters, with a human race at last "coming in with vanity and departing in darkness," born in darkness, living in darkness, dying in darkness, and, as far as all mere scientific analogy can give us any lesson, destined to furnish the exhumed fossils of another geological era, ages after they have passed off to make room for another race, it may be higher, it may be lower, according as the wheel of nature turns, or the terms *higher* and *lower* can have any meaning in her everlasting cycles of a seeming retrogradation or procession.

But we are too much tempted to digress on such a a theme. The reader is, perhaps, impatient for this lucid note. Here it is: "We have omitted"—it timidly ventures to say,—

"We have omitted any special reference to the *second day*, as neither geology nor general science, apart from astronomy and general reasoning, afford much aid in interpreting the account. The step of progress was one between that of light through universal space on the first day, and the separation of the lands and seas in the second. The event of the highest importance in that interval, that marking a grand epoch in terrestrial time, was the elimination or separation of the earth itself from the deep of waters, (admitted to mean fluid in its most extended sense.)"

This very curious production may be found at the bottom of the 116th page of the January number of the Andover Bibliotheca Sacra for 1856. We propose to make it the subject of a brief exegesis. The writer starts from the absolute beginning of all created entity, and rambles about the roomy regions of time and space, though seemingly without chart or compass, until he finds himself brought up in the "dry land of Labrador," and among the azoic rocks of this Western continent. He takes an observation, and finds it must be somewhere about the beginning or middle of the third day. But what has become of the second? The question seems to have startled him. It is too important a period to be passed wholly over; some account must be taken of it, and as "neither geology nor general science apart from general reasoning afford much aid," the only resource was this guessing note, which, after all, affords no explanation, or even hint at explanation, of the mighty difficulty. And this is all the light "Geology," though aided by "general science and general reasoning," can throw upon the grand epoch which Moses sets forth in such graphic and lucid images. The author of the note, however, means to have room enough. "The *step* of progress was *somewhere* between that of light *through universal space*, on the first day, and the lands and seas." *Somewhere*, then, between these two bounds of "universal space" and the "dry land of Labrador," and at *some time* between these two dates, the absolute beginning of all things, and the azoic period of this Western Continent, our mother earth was born. The author of the Book of Job was not so ambitious to determine the exact natal chronology. He takes the infant Tellus in her swaddling robes, and this poetical description corresponds well to the birth-day as written by Moses in the old Family Bible, when thick darkness rested upon the waters. "These waters," says the note, "are admitted to mean fluid in its most extended sense." The writer means, in the sense of his nebular æther, or whatever might be that first matter of the universe that just rose above nonentity. But by whom is this admitted? There would be no objection to it if other things in the account favored such an interpretation; for the two ideas of the liquid and the aeriform fluidity run into each other, and terms to express the one, in any language, may very easily and naturally flow into the other sense. If, therefore, it could be shown that such a blending was in harmony, or might have been in harmony, with the thinking of the Mosaic age, (in such a way as has been abundantly proved in respect to the indefinite extension of the word day) there might, in that case, be constructed a very respectable argument in favor of such a view. But we do not think that this can be shown. No hermeneutical evidence could be brought from any word or passage in the Bible for its support.* There is,

*Something might be conceded to this view, if there could be found a single instance, in the Old Testament, of the Hebrew מַיִם being used in this extended sense. It is employed sometimes to denote other *liquids* than water, but never anything in a gaseous or aeriform state, even if we may suppose the Hebrews to have had that idea at all. The air or wind they hardly regarded as material substance. The Greeks had the notion, but they never employ ὕδωρ for it. The plural form of the Hebrew word comes from the idea of *abundance* as suggested by the image of the vast waters of the sea or ocean, and from this comes its metaphorical sense of overwhelming sorrow or affliction. But throughout, there is the thought of the element water instead of the general idea of fluidity as opposed to solidity. The term fluid savors of science. It denotes a *state* rather than any particular substance, and we look in vain for anything like it in the use of the Hebrew word.

moreover, no need of it to elevate our view of the passage, or to give it any additional grandeur. For, unless we make greatness consist alone in space, the conception of a world of waters with darkness resting upon them, and the Divine Spirit brooding over them, and the Divine Word commanding the light to shine out of them, is a much grander conception than that of thin gaseous nebulæ, or universal æthers, having aside from their vastness hardly anything for the imaging faculty, and furnishing even still less material for the constructive views of the scientific reason.

There are a few remarks more to be made on this very remarkable note. "We have omitted," it says, "any *special* reference to the second day." Why is the word *special* used here, except from a sense of difficulty, and a consciousness on the part of the writer that he was not using the Mosaic Record fairly? It would seem to imply that there has been a *general* mention of this important period,—something which, though not carried out in scientific detail, would, in some other way, be worthy of its rank and value in the creative calendar. But there is no mention of it whatever, either general or special, except in this apologizing note. It remains a dreary vacuity, an ominous blank in a scheme that is ushered in with so much parade as the grand diapason harmony of the creative revelation. Again—it says, with still more modesty—"we have omitted any special reference to the second day, as neither geology nor general science, apart from astronomy and general reasoning, afford much aid." There is certainly a great deal of generalizing here, and no little effort, it would seem, to keep clear of any distinct meaning. Not but that Professor DANA can write distinctly enough when he chooses, but the absence of all meaning was the very thing wanted in this emergency. To seem, therefore, to say something on this second day, and yet, in reality to say nothing, or next to nothing, about it, would appear to have been the purpose of the note, and this purpose, it may be said, has been quite successfully accomplished. It is hinted, that some help, in this distress, might be got "from astronomy and general reasoning." We can hardly imagine what that help could be; but why did not the writer avail himself of it, be it scanty or not. It was certainly a matter of importance that this blank in the days should, in some way, be filled up. As it stands, it is really a deformity in Professor DANA'S geological hexapla; it is a sad discord in his "harmony." But if "astronomy and general reasoning" failed as well as geology, why could he not have paid Moses here the compliment of consulting him about a matter on which he professes to give very distinct knowledge, and that, too, as the Professor firmly believes, coming from the inspiration and revelation of the Creator himself. But whatever view may be entertained of Moses in his general claim of authority, or of the Scriptural account as being unnecessary when geology speaks, still, in such a case as this, it ought to have been treated with at least the respect certain sceptical ethnologists pay to the Bible when they can fill up a gap in their profane history in no other way. When the hieroglyphics and the Sphynxes fail, they come to Genesis. Now Moses says distinctly that on the second day God made the rakia or sky, which he named "*heavens*," as something built over the earth, in which sky, or firmament, or "heavens," the heavenly bodies afterwards *ap-*

peared,—the very sky, we think he meant, in which they appear now,—the same "old *rolling* heavens" on which so many generations have gazed, and of which the most scientific mind can form no grander conception than to image them just as they are, and as they ever have appeared. In Professor DANA'S theory, the sky, or rakia, if it have any meaning at all, or is anything but a blank waste in cosmology, is the universal nebulous fluid throwing off its rings, cosmical, stellar, solar, planetary, satellital,—thus parting into immense divisions and subdivisions, among which our solar system (for all analogy is against any attempt to set bounds here) may have been the millionth, and our earth the millionillionth in the order, not only of space, but of time descents.

There was something, however, which made this ambitious view of the Mosaic language too much for scientific consistency. The difficulty is felt to be pressing. Still, when once assumed, the theory could not be easily abandoned, or laid aside, although the writer must in some way get down to the earth. To do this at once would be too great a venture. The third day is evidently terrestrial, and can be nothing else. The second day, is therefore, wholly omitted in the scientific text, and the bewildered reader, not knowing where he is or how he got there, is left to cross the gulph, as well as he can, on the trembling suspension bridge that is so hastily constructed in the note.

We learn something from this. Science, too, when hard pressed, even "exact science," or "positive science," as it may be called in more senses than one, has to talk about mysteries, and call in "the aid of general reasoning," and even then to confess that she knows nothing of matters she had set out so vauntingly and confidently to explain. Is it uncharitable to say that such science is allied, at least, to the gnosis of which Paul speaks, 1 Cor. viii, 1? It is a knowledge *physiacous*,* rather than physical, a knowledge that "blows," or "puffeth up," instead of "edifying," that is, building reverently on the only safe foundation for human thought. But it is enough for us to be certain that Moses knew nothing about nebulous fluids and nebular rings. Of great times and olams, and olams of olams, he and the men of his day were fond of thinking. The xcth Psalm, which has been so often quoted, shows how familiar was the conception to his solemn musings. Elsewhere we have given a reason for this, derived from the very laws of thinking. Time belonging solely to the inner sense, as the measure of successive thoughts rather than outward distances, its mental extension is easier and earlier than that of the corresponding space conception. Hence it required no outward science, either for the birth or the rapid nurture of the thought. It has given rise, too, to a very ancient and wide spread use of language which other and more modern conceptions never would have originated. Such an idea, then, of great times lay harmoniously in the mind of Moses, and, in perfect consistency with the genius of his own and the other earliest Shemitic languages, he called them *days* with their wondrous nights and mornings; but this had nothing to do with any science. He knew no more of Professor DANA's rings than of Mr. LORD's "ecliptic axes"; and although he may be of little account in their scientific or unscien-

* Not from φύσις, but from, φυσάω, or φυσιάω, to *blow, puff, blow up*. Hence, φυσήματα, *blowings, bubbles*, etc.

tific schemes, yet the forcing upon him of so much geological or astronomical knowledge really over-does the business. It is too much for the credulity, either of the sciolist or the religionist.

This extreme nebular view of the Mosaic account may be met by the same answer that we have given to Mr. LORD's narrow hypothesis. They are both, although in different ways, opposed to what may be called the archæological and eschatological analogy of Scripture. First, — to compare it with the narrower view,— the creative days are no more common solar days than the great days of prophecy are such. The darkness on the waters, the Brooding Spirit, the sky appearing, land appearing, vegetation, animation, man — these are no more confined within the clock-measured limits of twenty-four hours each, than the great "Latter Day" of the world, the "Day of Judgment," the "Day of Christ's Reign," or the Ημέϱα Αιῶνος of St. Peter. And so — to run the second parallel — these creative epochs of our own planet have no more connection with universal nebular condensations, and the origin of galaxies, stellar, and solar systems, than the corresponding predicted periods of earth's eschatology have to do with the destinies of Sirius and Orion. There is grandeur enough in Moses as he is. Science can never elevate his thought, or mend his language. "And darkness was upon the face of the Deep, and the Spirit of God was brooding o'er the waters,"— the same waters that afterwards in obedience to this life-giving power "brought forth the living thing" each after its type, idea, or kind. How remarkable the conception! We have become familiar with it; we have marred it by our science and our philosophy. But throwing these aside, and going back to the early day when this was written, we can never exhaust our wonder in the contemplation. Whence came it to these primitive writers of Job and Genesis? The difficulty is certainly not met by saying that they took it from others, even if there were any proof of such a mere assertion. Whence came it to the early human thought at all? Viewed even as an imagination, a picture of the mind, it is hard to account for it without the aid of the supernatural, or to resist the belief that it came from a knowledge higher than any to which science can ever hope to attain. There is grandeur enough in Moses as he is, we say again. It is the only greatness that can truly and religiously affect us. The nebular view of the universe may be physically right in itself. It strongly challenges our admiration. But, after all, it has mainly guesses for our science, whilst it presents but a cold waste for the imagination. It connects itself but little with any devout feeling, and has really no basis in any fair interpretation of Scripture.

CHAPTER IX.

SCIENTIFIC SIX DAYS AT WAR WITH EXEGESIS.

The Word Bara.—The Beginning—The Shemitic Mind—Words for Creation.—The Hebrew—The New Testament Terms—The Philosophical Greek—The Arabic Words for Creation—Emotional Aim of the Bible.—Did Moses think of an Absolute Principium?—Six Arguments: 1*st. From the First Verse generally—*2*d. The Words Heaven and Earth; Do they denote Universality?—*3*d. The Earth the Locus of the First Energizing mentioned by Moses—*4*th. The Light after the Waters—*5*th. Heavens Built over the Earth—*6*th. The First Verse, if severed from the rest, must be Extra Dies.—Parallelism of the Mosaic Account with the First of John,—Patristic View of its* 3*d and* 4*th Verses.*

SUCH is a fair statement of the scientific difficulties in the way of this nebular accommodation of the Mosaic account. There may be errors in detail. There may be some things the sciolist may call blunders, and for which we should not be much concerned, even should he prove them to be such. For the general view the author holds himself responsible, and the foundation that has been laid for it, he thinks, can not be shaken. But now, turn we to another proof, to the more sure ground of rational exegesis. Connected with these questions is the meaning of the word ברא, rendered *create*, the meaning of the word ראשית, or beginning, the meaning of the expression used to denote the origination of the earthly light, and the discussion of the order in which the first creative events — we mean those recorded by Moses — actually took place. We will touch upon these in the briefest manner consistent with their importance, avoiding, as much as possible, what has been elesewhere and previously said.

The author has been asked, "what Hebrew word he would substitute for the one used, that would convey the precise idea of creation out of nothing,"— (*Bibliotheca Sacra for Jan.* 1856, *p.* 103). He answers very briefly, — there is no such Hebrew word; there is none such in the old Shemitic languages, and the only reason that can be given for it is that there was no such idea in the Shemitic mind,— we mean no such idea objectively contemplated, or that had made itself outward in their actual thinking. The root ברא is sometimes used to denote the "making of a new *thing* in the earth," as in Jeremiah xxxi, 22, or a *prodigy*, something before unknown, or that had not appeared, as in Numbers xvi, 30; but how different this is from that most difficult of all metaphysical conceptions, the bringing into substance from absolute nihility, every candid, intelligent reader must at once perceive. In one sense, and a very intelligible sense, the production of any new *thing*, or of any *new state of things*, is a making of what *was not* before, and so a coming forth from *not being*. In this view the human artist creates what before was not. The rags are not the paper that is made from them, nor the paper the rags. Neither are the paper, the ink, the cloth, in a true sense, the book, even regarded in its mechanical or artistic execution, much less the words, and still less the thoughts contained. The extraordinary nature of the act makes no difference in the case. The opening of the earth, Numbers xvi, 30, was not the elimination of any new substance, nor of any new force, but only the bringing out of a new effect from causes natural or supernatural. In other words, trace it as far as we will, it is ever, in such cases, to be regarded as a new *thing*, not new *matter*. And yet it does not follow, but that if the question had been distinctly put to an ancient Hebrew or Arab, Do you believe the world, or even matter (making him understand the distinction) to be as old as God? he would not have said No as distinctly as the profoundest theologian or metaphysician among us; as intelligently, too, we might say, since, in respect to this primal idea, all minds are on a par—it being rather a necessary logical negation we are compelled to utter, than any thing we can reduce to a conception, or any form of rational thought. So we believe that the descendant, whether of Isaac or of Ishmael, would have promptly answered, had the query been presented to him; but it was not a speculation of that Hebrew mind, nor a form of that Hebrew mode of conceiving, nor, consequently, a phrase of that Hebrew mode of language which God in his wisdom selected as the human medium of his oldest revelation. We venture, therefore, to say, that creation out of nothing is neither affirmed nor denied in the Old Testament,* although the divine *building* (κτίσις) of this present world of ours, and of the *heavens*, or sky, immediately around it, and the *ap-*

* We mean, by any use of this word; although there are passages where the idea may seem to be expressed in some other way, as Isaiah, xlviii, 13.

pearances of the heavenly bodies therein, are most sublimely set forth,—far more sublimely and impressively than could have been done by any metaphysical language that would have been required for the abstract idea. Such speculations about the eternity or non-eternity of matter, were on each side of the Children of Shem—beyond the Indus and beyond the Halys. They entered into the early Greek and Hindoo philosophy; but the Shemitic mind, that lay between, was too simply practical in its worship to think much about them, and too pure in its theism to feel much alarm about them. Paradoxical as it may appear, we may even venture the opinion, that this pure theism was saved from a philosophical deterioration, by that very thing which some would object to as the anthropopathism of the Old Testament. It is pantheism with its philosophical dialect and its irreverent attempts to explain the inexplicable archæology of the universe, that has bred the wildest theological monsters. It is the scientific theism that runs into a dry nature worship, whether disguised in the mythological forms under which the crude yet ambitious knowledge of the early times sought to conceal itself from the vulgar, or the talk of laws, and forces, and principia, which now serves as the medium of a like spirit, and a cover to a like false yet vaunting religionism. The anthropopathic images of the Jewish Scriptures preserved that all-important idea of personality,—an idea of so much more religious value than any abstract notions of causation or originating power, and which is ever tending to perish from the minds of those who claim to themselves what they would call a higher style of thought and language. We believe that every one must feel this who enters deeply into the spirit of the Old Scriptures; neither can such a one fail to have observed the remarkable fact, how intimately connected, sometimes, is this anthropopathic language with other declarations that startle us by a spirituality of conception surpassing the highest human utterance.

And thus do these Scriptures speak of creation. We recognize this combination of the unutterably sublime with the simplest forms of speech expressive of architectural or constructive ideas. The same mode of thinking and speaking comes down, too, to the writers of the New Testament. *They*, certainly, were not compelled to employ language merely adapted, as some would say, to the infancy of the world, and only used in the early days because nothing better and higher could then be obtained. Philosophy, in the meantime, had grown to swelling dimensions. The language in which they wrote abounded in her choicest, most carefully compounded diction. There was certainly no lack of metaphysical terms in the Greek, as is shown by the fact, that, in this respect, it has become the store-house of the modern philosophical speech. Especially was this the case in regard to the language of generation or origin. Plato's Parmenides and Timæus furnished enough of this lingo of the *being* and *not being*, and the οντα, and the μὴ οντα, and the γιγνόμενα, and the οὐδέποτε γιγνόμενα, to have enabled Paul to express any metaphysical ideas of origin he might have deemed true or inspired. Even if he had not read them, he must have heard much of them in the jangling schools of Tarsus, the third great seat of Greek philosophy, but he adopts the same Old Testament style, and talks just like Moses, and uses the same class of simple constructive words. Of the Hebrew *bara* what better exegesis can we give than the New Testament κτίζω, κτισις? No Greek philosopher ever used these for creation, and Evangelists and Apostles need not have employed them had they not supposed them the best representatives of the idea expressed by the Hebrew word. The author of the Epistle to the Hebrews had to express one of the sublimest acts of faith, and the sublimest of physical ideas, even the origin of the worlds or ages by the Eternal Word, and yet, in giving us this ineffable process, he employs one of the most purely artistic, constructive, architectural, words in the Greek language, καταρτίζω, *to put together, to frame, to arrange in order, to refit, to repair, to restore*, etc., all of which imply existing entities. It is the same word that is used Mark i, 19, of mending fish nets, that is applied here, Heb. xi, 3, to the building and framing of the worlds. We have reason to be very thankful for this style of speech. The man who stumbles at it shows himself as deficient in taste as he is low in his theology. The other mode is conceptionless, and therefore false,—false, because it assumes to convey an idea, and yet presents no images through which that idea can gain a habitation in the mind. The apparently simpler language is the more sublime, and therefore the more truthful,—if the higher object of revelation be really an emotional or *living* idea, rather than barren scientific or philosophical knowledge. We have a more lively thought, and so a higher and *truer* thought, of God's power and glory, when he is represented to us as acting on what is,—dividing waters, sending light into chaoses, separating lands and seas, fashioning, arranging, organizing worlds,—than could ever come from any abstract language attempting with ill success to set forth a conceptionless origination from a blank nonentity. And so in regard to the idea of nature, we have a more vivid, and therefore a more truthful impression of the Divine imperial majesty, when we centemplate Deity as ruling over nature and matter, controlling them, subduing them, commanding them like strong subjects, or, it may be at times like rebellious foes, than when we think of him under the bare notion of origination, or as a power diffused through nature, and thus to the mind's conception hardly distinguishable from it. The abstract ideas are doubtless true. We are forced by reason to acknowledge them, but it is as a necessity of our intellectual or logical thinking, rather than as connected with our true spiritual life. And on this account, may we reverently suppose, has Scripture kept the latter in the back ground, or barely given us the premises from which to infer their truth, whilst the other ideas are made so prominent both in the older and the later revelation. Such is the method of the divine writers. When we have more of the same spirit, we shall be better prepared to interpret the language in which they convey truths transcending all human philosophy, and leaving infinitely below them all human science.

As having a direct bearing upon this question, we have taken pains to examine carefully the Arabic words for creation, as they occur in the Koran. This is the more pertinent, as the Koran is not only the oldest style of Arabic well known to us, but evidently imitates the thought and speech of an antiquity greater than its own. Mohammed, it is clear, tries to be more philosophical than Moses; but these old Arabic verbs carry us back to the same simple yet grand ideas we find in the Hebrew. We give them in Hebrew letters, for the want of Arabic type. The most common is

Cha-la-qa, (חלק), the primary sense of which is that of *smoothing*, *polishing*, like the Latin *polio*, and the Greek ξέω with its compounds and derivatives so often found in Homer. There is the same primary image in the root as it occurs in the Hebrew, although, in that language, it is never used for creation. The creative idea, as given by it, is that of *finish*, or *perfection*,—the bringing of a thing from a rude or unwrought to a finished state. In this, as well as in the primary sense of *smoothing*, polishing, *shaving*, it resembles the Hebrew ברא. Accompanying it we have

Ba-da-a', (בדא), the primary sense of which is *manifestation*, or *revealing*, bringing from an invisible state; hence that of *beginning*, and *creation*, as though it were a bringing out of darkness or invisibility.

Ba-ra-a' (ברא), the Hebrew word itself with the radical idea of *separation*, and hence of *setting free*.

Ju-bu-lu (גבל), a purely formative word, like the Hebrew יצר. It signifies to *shape*, or *fashion*. It has the same plastic sense in the Syriac; of which the reader may be referred to a proof in Romans ix, 20, where the Peschito, or old Syriac version, employs it, and its noun derivative, for the Greek πλάσμα—πλάσαντι—"*Shall the thing formed say to him who formed it*," etc. Hebrew, *Gabal*, *Galab*; Greek, Γλύφω; Latin, *Sculpo*, *Scalpo*; Ang., *Sculpture*.

Fa-ta-ra (פטר), primary sense that of *opening*, *bursting*, *coming forth*—*fidit aperuit*. Hence it is a word of *birth*, or generation. It has the same sense in the

Hebrew, although, in that language, never used of creation.

A-sa-ra (אשר), (Hebrew, אסר), sense of *binding.* Hence it denotes creation from the opposite aspect of *constructing*, or *putting together*, instead of *separating* from a previous mass, which is the predominant image in other words.

Da-ra-a' (דרא), to *send forth — sparsit.* Connected with the Hebrew זרח, and Latin *Sero.* The creative idea is involved in that of semination and growth.

Qā-na (קנא), to *get — acquire — possess.* We have elsewhere remarked upon this word as having in Hebrew the sense of *generation*, and so of *creation*, examples of which may be found Genesis iv, 1, xiv, 19, 22, Psalm cxxxix, 13, Proverbs viii, 22. Compare the order of ideas in our Saxon *get — be-get — be-gotten.*

Tū-na (*Ta-ya-na*), (טאן), the plastic sense — *to form*, or *fashion* (of earth.)

Lā-ha (*La-wa-ha*), לאח, or לוח, the sense of *shining — shining vapor.* A noun from it is used to denote the *mirage*, or the appearance of seas or lakes in the desert, — thus giving us the idea of order and beauty standing forth from waste and desolation.

Should any one say that such sensible images are all that could be expected in the early age of the world, or that language is thus necessarily sensuous, we can admit the view without the least hesitation. Language traced to its roots is ever sensuous, and must be so, not because it is addressed to the early men, but to all men, as men, who can never do without sensuous images in their thoughts. It was so, doubtless, in the early speech, but let it be remembered that when the writers of the Bible came to use a language which philosophy had vastly improved, (if it was an improvement,) and carried as far as possible out of the sensuous into the abstract, or seemingly abstract, they still adhered to the old style, representing creation as a *building*, a *putting together*, a *framing* of *worlds or ages*, and, in the most supersensual (or rather least sensuous) conception they ventured to employ, a bringing forth of the phenomenal, not from absolute *not being* (μὴ οντων) but from the non appearing (μὴ φαινομένων) — the *non apparentibus*,* as Calvin truly renders it. We admit the necessity of language, and we only ask those who make the objection to give it all its force. We understand, notionally and logically, the proposition, *what is, once was not.* We can carry it thus notionally and logically to the extreme negation of all sense conception, but what have we left but a blank in thought, unless the sense reacts, and images a dark nihility, as, in some way, the material *ex quo*, out of which all things in some way came? We may, at any time, if we please, have this blank thought as a refuge against that apprehension of matter's eternity which some would regard as the sum of all heresy, and which the author himself holds to be atheistical. But when we

* We have already referred to one of Professor DANA's exegetical criticisms on the word beginning. There is another on which he ventures in respect to the view taken of Hebrews xi, 3. He calls the reading, and the version, which would be in accordance with this sense, "a liberty taken with the sacred text." Mr. LORD does the same thing, but as he puts it on the ground of sheer falsifying, and without the least shadow of refutation, we can not regard him or his charge as worthy of any notice. When any man of any real weight as a Biblical scholar makes the objection, our brief defence would be, that a view sanctioned by the two oldest versions, the Latin and the Syriac, brought out by Calvin, and sustained by the best modern German authorities, is so far from being a "liberty taken with the sacred text," that it has the best of all critical arguments in its support.

have reached such an extremely rarefied, or rather nihilified negative, what is it, for strength and vividness, and power of religious emotion, as compared with the conceptions aroused by the radical images of these Arabic and Hebrew words? If God has made the revelation in this manner by way of "accommodation" to us, why should we not be accommodated by it? We may seek to get above them; we may, in so doing, involve ourselves in any amount of darkness under the name of the profound; and it will not do us much hurt, perhaps, unless it obscures the impression of those accommodating images with which He who made the human soul as well as the physical worlds has so graciously furnished us. When this is the case, it may be found that we have gained dimness for brightness, vacuity for fullness, a dead gnosticism for living thought,—that *living thought* of the Living God which Revelation aims to give us, as something vastly more glorious than any mere knowledge whether it take to itself the ancient form of a philosophical pantheism, or the more modern guise of an arid scientific theism.

Should the question be put in this form—What Hebrew word would Moses have probably employed, had he actually wished to convey this idea of an absolute creation of matter from previous nonentity, or of force, activity, and motion* from a previous negation of all these ideas? We may answer, that it would most likely have been this word *bara*. This, however, would not be on the ground that such is the radical idea of the word, but because it would come as near to it as any others of the

* We have no words that are strictly the negations of these. *Immobility* and *rest* are not the *negation* but the *opposition*, or resistance, of *activity* and *motion*.

formative class, and its use for something new and before unseen (although without any recognition of the metaphysical idea) would make it yet more suitable. Still, the whole decision of this depends on the context. It is purely a question of interpretation, with which science has nothing to do, even had she any means of answering it. It is, moreover, altogether distinct from that other view of the absolute beginning, at some time, of material existence, as matter of fact. To deny that is atheism. But whether Moses meant such absolute beginning of all undivine existence, is a question that has been entertained by the best men in the Christian church. It affects no man's orthodoxy, or reputation for orthodoxy. It may be that Moses took in all of material being as far as he knew it, or that he meant to teach, and was inspired to teach, the general truth that all things came from God. But this may have been in various ways, and for various purposes. The aim may have been an impression of the Divine power and greatness, rather than a lesson of curious knowledge. The accomplishment of this aim might have been attempted in the use of general terms universal in extent, so as to satisfy the philosophical state of mind, but comparatively feeble in respect to strength and vividness of emotion; or it might have been effected, perhaps better effected, by presenting, for such a purpose, a picture partial and temporal, yet most graphic, of the Divine power in the building of the visible heavens and earth, with all that is visible in them, regarded rather as they *appear* than in their essence or essential causality. It may even be conceded that if Moses had been interrogated, as one has supposed, he would have said that he meant all things, in space at least; and yet, the question returns, What is the fair import of his language, and how does it authorize us to fix any metaphysical notions upon his pictorial words?

We have elsewhere remarked, that it could not have been the beginning of all spiritual being below the Divine; for angels, "Sons of God," "Sons of the Morning," or *Luciferi*, are recognized as being in existence when God laid the foundations of the earth. Angelic existence implies some kind of dynamical occupancy of space, which it is very hard for us to separate from some idea of the material, unless we ascribe to such beings attributes we have been accustomed to think of as specially Divine. But be that as it may, we come back to the first verse in Genesis, and we ask,—What does it fairly mean according to the conceptions it creates in our minds? "*In the beginning God created the Heavens and the Earth.*" Does it refer to something antecedent to all that is mentioned in the subsequent verses, or is it, in fact, a *title* or caption to the whole account? so that the *Heavens and Earth* there mentioned are the same Heavens and Earth described immediately afterwards in the second and eighth verses. We would confess that the main arguments inclining us to the latter view, arise from the great difficulties (not scientific, but hermeneutical,) connected with the other. In the first place, there is no intrinsic evidence that the first verse is thus severed from the others, or that it stands by itself denoting a period of distinct and antecedent working,—much less a period so remotely antecedent as would be required for a scientific hypothesis commencing with the absolute elimination of light. This would be our *first* argument. It is negative, we admit, and not conclusive. The opposite view has most respectable advocates, and was held by some of the Fathers. It would not be at war with any other conclusions we have deduced respecting the indefinite length of the days. That interpretation is entirely independent of it, and may be maintained, with equal force and fairness, without denying that Moses meant the absolute principium, or expressing any opinion about it. He may have meant some ineffable antecedent act; but if so, then it might be very fairly argued, that to such act he also meant that the word *bara* should be specially, if not exclusively, applied. That was creation, then; all else was a mere arrangement of what had been created in the beginning. But other uses of the word, not only throughout the Bible, but in this very account, are at war with such a supposition. There were creations after the primordial act,—creations, beyond all doubt, the fashioning or organizing existing materials both into outward form and internal constitution. But without dwelling farther on this, we proceed to our argument—

2d. If the First verse means a creating act antecedent to all organization, then its words *Heaven and Earth* can not be taken in their definite, visible, or local sense, as they are afterward employed, but must be regarded as general terms for the first matter as yet undivided and unformed. Some have supposed that this was actually expressed by the particle אֵת, which was understood to denote the *matter*, the *substance*, of the Heavens and the Earth. The best Hebrew sholars, however, reject any such notion, regarding this little word as simply a sign of the accusative case, or rather as having very much the same force with the Greek and Latin reflexive pronouns; so that את השמים and את הארץ would be the Heaven *itself*, or the *very Heavens*, and the *very Earth.* We would not attach much importance either way to any argument drawn from the use of this particle, but, thus regarded, it would favor the interpretation which makes the Earth and Heavens of the first verse the same with the Earth of the second, and the Heavens mentioned in the eighth below. But if Moses meant the origination of matter per se, "why could he not have said so"? We use the language of an objector, which is applied to another purpose, but is more applicable here. If it be said that the Hebrew language furnished no such word as *matter* in its elementary or philosophical sense, or *first matter* distinct from any particular forms it might assume, this would only show how foreign all such metaphysical or elementary conceptions were from their clear practical modes of thinking.* When something like the idea of

* The Hebrew had roots from which such words could be formed, whenever the progress of speculative thinking might make them necessary for those who used the language. We have already referred to the plural of עפר, the word for *dust* as thus employed, Prov. viii, 26, (*Six Days of Creation*, p. 323,) and we might cite another that would seem to come the nearest to such an idea of any terms in the Hebrew Bible. It is the word עֶצֶם, much employed by the Rabbinical writers to denote *substance*, and having something of the same thought in a few places of the Old Testament, as Genesis ii, 23, where Adam says of Eve, according to the common rendering, "*This is bone of my bone*," but it may be translated, *substance* of my *substance*. We might suppose this idea of substance to come from the sense *bone*, so frequent elsewhere, were it not that such a view would be out of harmony with the spirit of the remarkable expression, Exod. xxiv, 10, where it is used to denote the very substance, or *supposed* substance, of the Heavens themselves, (עצם השמים,) "*the very substance of the Heaven in its purity.*" This would rather lead us to refer such use of the word to the primary idea of *power* or *strength*, which belongs to the root as a verb. It would take us directly and naturally to

first existence from nonentity is to be expressed, which we think is intended, Isaiah xlviii, 13, then we have the bold personifications of poetry, so much more effective than any prose statement that would have required the other kind of language. "*I call to them, they stand up together.*"

No doubt Moses was as orthodox here as any of us, but did he think of primal matter per se? That is the question. Did it come within the plan of his sublime description? It is said, with some apparent force, that if not taught here, this great truth of first origin is wanting in the Bible. That we think is an error. There are other places where it would appear to be expressed, such as the one just referred to in Isaiah, and still more *clearly* in John i, 3, which seems to go farther back in time, and to be more universal both in space and height, than the account given by Moses. And yet if it were not taught in the Scriptures, it would detract nothing from the evidence of their inspiration or their dignity. The being of a God is not taught, as a direct lesson, in the Bible. It is everywhere assumed, not as something which might be deduced from any scientific search into nature, but as a thought which the human soul has no right to be without, even for a moment. It can not be innocently destitute of it, that is, innocently atheistical,

that notion of *force*, *resistance*, and so, of *hardness*, which is the ultimate of all our thinking about matter. The same word seems to be used of the primal matter, or primal causal energy (whatever that may be) of the human organism, in the passage before quoted from Psalm cxxxix, 14, "My *substance* was not hid from Thee when I was made in secret and curiously wrought in the lowest parts of the earth." The thought is, that this primal matter, or primal force, is "naked and laid bare to Him with whom no creation is invisible," (κτίσις ἀφανής, Heb. iv, 13,)—thereby implying how obscure it is, and difficult of conception, to the finite human mind.

during the time that would be necessary for drawing a conclusion from physical facts, or outward testimony of any kind. The same may be said of the dependence of the universe on God, whether that universe be great or small; for the amount of space and time here makes no difference. It was, therefore, a sufficient design in Genesis to give us that which must ever be to us the most glorious example of God's working, namely, the *ktisis*, or building of our own earth and the near visible heavens above it. That all things else, known or unknown, came from the same hand, and this in respect to time as well as space, would be, not so much an inference, as a thought inseparably connected with it, and so, we might say, revealed in it. He who made us, made all things; "and without him was there nothing made that was made."

But let us look at the objection in another form. It regards it as a derogation from the dignity of revelation, if Moses, in his graphic picture, is not supposed to begin with the absolute principium before which time was not. But there would seem to be a ready answer to this by putting a precisely similar question. If all things in time, why not all things in space? Why not all worlds as well as all ages,—that is, all *aeons* or *olams* in one sense as well as in the other. If it be said that the one is to be inferred from the words *Heaven and Earth*, however partial the space knowledge or conception with which these words were connected in the mind of Moses, then we also say that by a like inference we mount up above the particular times presented in his creative picture; although, whether we shall gain anything by so doing, either in clearness of thought, or vividness of emotion, may be a very serious question.

It may be said that the world had not then science enough to have understood the language necessary for such a space revelation, in the attempt to convey anything like an adequate conception. That may be. But are we sure that the world had science enough then, or has science enough now, or ever will have science enough to apprehend adequately the ineffable mystery of primordial formation? The *fact* may be inferred from an account necessarily partial so far as we can make it matter of conception; but did such primordial birth of entities, as entities, form a designed part of Moses' vivid picture? This is the question, and this brings us to another view of the subject. We say, then—

3dly. The beginning, of which the writer of Genesis I speaks in the first verse, must have been a beginning on this earth, the very earth we now inhabit; and this is maintained because the earth, or the waters of the earth, was the place of the first distinct act mentioned in the account. "The earth was without form and void,* (or waste and desolate) and darkness was on the face of the deep." Here we have the opening of this grand drama with its six sublime acts. It is the date and the locus of the first special energy—we mean the first special energy *recorded*. "And the Spirit of God brooded on the waters." Now, if by the word create, in the first verse, Moses had meant an act, or acts, prior to this, we think he would have used the same language; for we may regard it as an established Bible truth, that all creative acts, and creative agency, are through the Spirit

* These expressions do not refer to the "earth's *outline*," as Professor DANA takes it, (Bib. Sac. Jan. 1856, p. 115.) The formlessness, or *wasteness*, was the absence of all internal division, of all diversity of appearance. It was a wild waste of waters.

and the Word. (Vide John i, 2, Coloss. i, 16.) But for such antecedent act, if Moses meant to set it forth, there is no mention of any such agency of the Spirit; there is no such going forth of the Word. Would the formula, so emphatic and constant afterward, have been omitted in the great primordial scene, if the writer really meant to make it part of his description? This "brooding on the waters," then, is the first creative act, if not of the universal origination, at least among the acts pictured, and meant to be pictured, by Moses. If so, then this was the *beginning*, not of all things absolutely, but of the Mosaic account.

4th. In the universal creation, it is not easy for us to conceive, and still less easy to believe, that the absolute origination of light was later than the constitution of the water. It is not an objection of science, but of our common thinking. Light, in itself, must have been before the grosser fluid. But we would not depend upon this alone. Scripture confirms the thought that it must have been the oldest of material manifestations, if it is material at all. We refer to passages already quoted, which represent it as the raiment and dwelling place of Deity,—language which, for reasons already given, we can not regard as simply figurative. Again—the *Luciferi*,* or light bearing "Sons of the Morning," or "Morning Stars," must have been light, or must have had light,

* In these *Luciferi* there is a reference, doubtless, to Angelic or superhuman beings. But the old belief did also connect them with the stars as their abode, or as their luminous representatives. We have alluded to this in the other volume, *Six Days of Creation*, pp. 349, 350, to which the reader is referred. Whether this old belief, in the days of Job, be fanciful or not, it shows the idea that stars really existed before the creation of the earth, and that is a just argument in the interpretation of the Mosaic account.

when they "shouted for joy and sang together," at the laying of earth's corner stone. The language may be poetical, but it is very significant. It is inconsistent with the idea of a universe shrouded in "primeval darkness," to use our critic's language. Such darkness, did, indeed, rest on the earth when this ancient music of the spheres was heard, but there must have been morning somewhere ἐν τοῖς ἐπουρανίοις, "in the Heavenly Places," or, rather, as the word means, the Super-celestial Places. When we come, however, to consider the particular chronology of the Mosaic creation, and the picture of events as they took place on our earth, nothing can be more clear than that, if it observes any order of ideas, the waters, and an earth covered with waters, were before the light there mentioned. It could not, therefore, have been the primordial light of the universe, but only its first shining on that dark, and undivided, and therefore *formless* waste of waters. We see not how the conclusion can be avoided. If light is earlier than water, then the argument deduced from it respecting the absolute principium being intended in the Mosaic account utterly fails; and this would equally be the case whether light is regarded as a substance or an effect.*

* The primordial light must have been before the waters. Such is the argument of Professor DANA, p. 114, January number of Andover Bibliotheca Sacra. To be sure, he denies that light is an "independent entity." "It is a result," he says, "of chemical change," or "produced by molecular disturbance." Here he thinks he has actually seized the mystery. Light is "molecular action." Hence, he argues very sagely, light being molecular action, matter without such molecular action would not be light—that is, it would be dark; and so, also, having no heat, it would be cold and dead. "Let it be endowed, then, with *intense* attraction (moderate attraction it seems would not do) and it would produce light as the first effect of the mutual action begun." "Thus science, in its latest developments, declares as distinctly as the Bible, on the first day light was."

5th. In the Mosaic narrative the Earth is created before the Heaven. Such, also, is the representation in other

Here we have again the curious parallelism; only science, as usual, holds the most prominent place. It is not behind Moses in anything. It talks "as distinctly" as the Divine revelation which would have been wholly unnecessary had it been delayed until these "latest developments."

Such a scientific display may wonderfully strengthen the faith of certain religionists who know as little of science as they do of the Bible; but need the intelligent reader be told that there is really no light in it? The "latest developments" are yet at a vast distance from the real mystery. They do not tell us "where light dwelleth;" they can not "show us the path to its house." Boast as they may, the challenge in Job is yet unanswered. The philosophy of a Humboldt frankly admits this; the science of other men resents the assertion, as though it were an insulting derogation from the claims of the second "revelation."

Light, then, is an effect—an effect of some condition of material substance. This is all that the Professor's fine words amount to. We would ask, in the first place, does he mean the sensation to which there is frequently given this name, or with which it is so often confounded? Light, in that sense, is a mixed product, an outward material working in some kind of combination with an inward sensorium, or sensorial action. But no one ever expressed that more clearly than Aristotle did two thousand years ago in his treatise Περι Ψυχης. "The latest developments" have ceatainly done nothing in that direction, unless something should result from the clairvoyant experiments of Dr. Hare and the Mesmerisers. But light is an *effect*. What then? An *effect* is an *out-working;* and this out-working is all that science can see. It is an out-working conditioned on a certain state of matter, and this state of matter is another out-working conditioned on another state, and so on up to the primal material entity. So, also, is water an effect. It is conditioned on a certain combination of oxygen and hydrogen. These, too, may be effects—each of them—and their conditioning forces may be effects, and so on, effects of effects, as far as science can trace, should she rub her glasses to the utmost. She has for some time been engaged in splitting up matter into any number of "independent entities," though all along suspecting that she is in the wrong direction. She may be near the other leg of the hyperbola of progress, where it curves round again to the ideas of simplicity and unity. She may, perhaps, in time, discover the first matter. But as far as we can see it is ever an ef-fect. It is, all along, a *doing*, an *activity*, (for that is all that science has ever seen and therefore all she can infer) until we get up to this first matter, and what that is but a *doing*, an *activity* still, we can not tell. Nothing, then, is gained by this. We might as well take light for an entity, as any of the material states in which it is said to be condi-

parts of the Bible—"Who formed the Earth and stretched out the Heavens over them." "To the Lord belong

tioned, even if science knew far more than she does know, or ever will know, about these conditioning causalities. Instead of knowing "where light dwelleth," either as an entity, or an effect, our scientific Professor can tell us nothing about the material condition even of its secondary modifications, or the molecular state on which depend varieties of color. He may use as much technical language as he pleases, but it all comes out in this bald, barren proposition,—a certain atomic or molecular condition is the ground for the reflection of a certain color in distinction from any other. Very likely. We could almost have told that a priori. The Professor may be safely defied to tell what that molecular condition is which makes the paper on which he writes of one color, and the ink he uses, of another. He can no more tell us how one hair is black or white, than he can make one hair black or white.

Again, he says, the light is conditioned on the chemical affinities of the molecules; but who knows if it may not be the other way, the affinities of the molecules conditioned on the light? Chemical affinity may be conditioned on the presence of a substance which is the ground both of the affinity and the ultimate visibility; and this conditioning substance we may call light, although it is invisible to science, which can only see results, *effects*,—out-workings, even of light itself. On such a view, it would be very much a question of naming. We may stop at any one manifestation, or we may call everything an *effect*, and deny it the name of an entity, until we mount up, actually or in thought, to the first matter, or the first *activity*, the one universal material substance of the universe. Is everything else a manifestation of this primal matter or primal activity? For we must say for ourselves, we find it very difficult to conceive of it in any other way. To such a question no science can say Yes or No. Are there one, or two, or more first material principles? The discussion of this question commenced in the first Ionic Scientific Convention of which Thales was first President; and we must say that the meeting of 1856, which lately took place in the city of Albany, had not yet arrived in sight of a decision. The modern gathering, had, doubtless, a vastly greater array of facts, and those facts, too, arranged and classified in a vastly more scientific order. They, therefore, had a perfect right, which right they fully exercised, to talk much more of progress, and blow a louder trumpet; but in regard to these *first facts* they were pretty much on a par with their brethren of the olden time. And so it is even now. Our scientific Professor, with all his talk of molecules, can tell us no more about these primal harmonies of matter and the universe, than the blind player on the street organ; he knows no more than the child "where light dwelleth, or what is the way to its house"—we mean in the sense of this Bible query. He is as ignorant here

the foundations (the columns of the earth) and he hath set the *tebel* (the visible round mundus or sky,) over them."—1 Sam. ii, 8. This might be called poetical imagery; but there can be no doubt of its having its origin in the prose description of Moses. After the general title, the first work is the earth, and on the earth. Then we have the making of the firmament above the waters. This firmament is called the Heaven. That is its name, and this naming is followed throughout the Old Testament. It is conclusive as to what is meant in these poetical expressions. What is of still more importance, it determines the manner in which other Hebrew writers, whether historical, didactic, or poetical, interpreted the Mosaic language. The order is most significant and unmistakable, if we will only view it from the right stand point—The Earth—The Firmament, or Sky,—The

as on the questions, whether what he calls gravitation is the finality of physical action, or the terms employed in respect to it are the finality of scientific language any more than vortices and epicycles;—although he was so absurdly indignant against "the mind" that would place them in any sense, and for any purpose, in the same category.

We are not derogating at all from the true dignity of science, when we thus call to account those who would injure her by unmeaning claims. This swelling talk has too long been addressed to the easy popular thinking, and its correction is demanded, not only in deference to higher ideas, but as a service to science itself. But to return to our starting point—the *nature* of light has really nothing to do with this discussion. Be it an *effect*, an *out-working*, a conditioned state of matter, an activity, an entity, an independent substance, or anything else about which a logomachy may be started, still the real question remains the same. Was the light mentioned by Moses the beginning of light, the first manifestation of light, if you choose, before which light never had been during an endless ante-past eternity, or was it the first light, making the first morning, on earth's dark waters? This is the question. Whichever way decided, it is one solely of interpretation. Science has nothing to do with it. No "revelation" she can make can herein contradict Moses. No gabble of any of her votaries about "affinities and molecules," can ever confirm him.

Heavenly bodies appearing therein. Whatever changes this disturbs the whole harmony of the narrative. It makes the picture full of distortions. Now such an order of events is inconsistent with the supposition that Moses meant to set forth, in the first verse, an antecedent working in which the Heaven (in that case necessarily the astronomical heaven with all its hosts) was before the Earth. It will still less agree with the scientific representation that expands the Mosaic sky into nebular rings. It is, however, in admirable harmony with the view that regards the work of the Fourth day, not as the absolute *making* (from nonentity) of the then new matter of the Heavenly *luminaries*, but the making* them to be luminaries (מאורות) in that clear firmament, sky, or heaven, which now, through some causality unknown to us, and not revealed to us, is prepared for their visibility, or as the locus in which they *appear*. How the idea of the astronomical Heavens afterwards came in, or the Heaven of Heavens, has been elsewhere shown.

This Jewish idea, or, as we may rather call it, the ancient idea, of the Earth and Heavens, or sky around it, as forming the Tellurian mundus, is found in various parts of the Bible, and almost always presented in the same way. The Earth is the main thing in the picture. It is the foundation, and the Heaven is built around it. The latter, is, in fact, a part of the Earth, having its origin from it, and its existence dependent upon it. When the Earth departs, the Heavens depart, or are

*If the name *making* can be given to any organization short of the first matter of which they are composed, or its absolute orignation, then it may be given to such light-producing arrangement, or constitution, as well as to any other. Every study we can give the language and the context confirms this view.

"rolled together as a scroll." So St. Peter speaks of the Heavens and Earth of old, which arose from the water and had their consistence through and from the water,* and the Earth and Heaven that are now reserved for the judgment of the fire. In that great physical catastrophe "the heavens shall pass away," the atmosphere be destroyed "by fervent heat," the sky dissolved, the *luminaries* therein put out, and darkness come again over whatever may be left of the charred and blackened earth. We are not prepared to interpret Scripture on these points till we come back to this old conception. And it was a true conception. This sky above our heads, and the luminous points that appear in it, are truly Tellurian.† The glorious sight would not exist for a world wrapped in rings and belts of darkness. It is the stars as they appear in our firmament, as they are pictured in our *rakia*. They come from the far off "depths of space," these luminous points—

ἐξ αἰθέρος βάθους.

However unequal their respective journies, with equal radii do they appear through Earth's revealing sky-light dome. They fall upon the blue Tellurian eye-ball very much as the Tellurian images themselves strike upon the aqueous firmament of the human eye, whence they are

* 2 Peter iii, 5. The best rendering of this verse is that which regards ἐξ ὕδατος as implied in the first clause, or as belonging as much to the first clause at to the second; so that it would read "the Heavens of old and the Earth were of water," or *from water*, which was the old doctrine of Thales, derived probably from Moses.

† We use this word here from necessity. *Tellus*, in distinction from Terra, denotes the *world earth*, or the earth as a world, or the centre of a world. It is, therefore, the only word that will take in what Moses means by the "Earth and the Heaven"—the latter being included in the idea of the same world.

represented on that still more central *retina*, in which, and through which, each secluded soul sees all it ever sees of outward mundane things. What lies beyond in the distant regions whence these appearances come, is another question, which we answer more or less perfectly, or rather, more or less imperfectly, according to our science. The ancients may have known much or little about them, but it would not change the reality, the *real appearance*, or the language. They could speculate as well as we. Our science has given us no advantage in this respect. They had theories, some of them, even about an "infinity of worlds." There was nothing to prevent the Jewish mind taking the same direction. David, musing on the Heavens, may have had, and we sometimes think he did have, some such thought of immense existences, or immense fields of being, lying behind those luminous points, or that luminous picture which he describes as the embroidered work of God's fingers. Something arose in his mind which sunk man into insignificance, and from which the Seer does not recover himself until he comes back to the earth, and finds relief in the contemplation of man as lord of all below the skies, placed in dominion over all terrestrial animation. But science has changed all that, it may be said. All our theological views, says one, must be modified in consequence of the modern discoveries in astronomy. Not at all — we reply. Our earth is still the same secluded place in the universe that it was in the time of David. God meant it should be thus shut out. He has, perhaps, secluded all other parts of the universe in like manner. To us, and to every other world, if there are such other worlds, it is the same as if no other than itself existed.

He is the God of *our* world, the same as if this single planet were the only theatre of his creative and providential power. And science has not, can not, change this in its essence and reality. It may give rise to a different view of the universe, but it is only in forced conceptions, having their ground in intellectual or mathematical estimates that can not be retained permanently by that imaging faculty which, after all, must ever rule our emotions. We come back again to the old picture,—yes, we will say it, *to us* the old reality,—that places us precisely on a par with the men of the olden, yea, of the oldest time. We talk much of our scientific views of the universe, but there is certainly a deception about it. For the most part, we have simply made definite, to some extent, what the old mind contemplated as indefinite. We have obtained something like satisfactory estimates of nearest distances. We have increased the conceptions of space extent. Where the ancients rested in hundreds and thousands, we have gone on to tens of thousands; where they had tens of thousands, we talk of millions. And yet we are deceived in the real value of this by making estimates of space magnitude the real test of greatness. Our scientific calculations look vast, indeed, when viewed from our stand point; but examine them carefully, keep out the swelling pride of mere space discovery, and let reason, pure reason, have fair play. On such a view, how do these splendid constructions of mathematical genius wither up into the merest skeletons and ghosts of knowledge? It is a knowledge of spaces, forces, masses, and that, not in their ideas, but as represented by points, lines, curves, angles, sines, cosines, and tangents. That is all. And that is much, says the mathematician. It is so in the scientific aspect; we have no wish to underrate it on its own field; and yet what does it tell us more than the unshaded outline map of some unknown and unknowable continent? We see in such map points and distances; we see waving lines of various lengths crossed by rectilineal parallels; but in all higher and truer knowledge connected with our human interests and human sympathies, it is as void as the waste ocean that surges around its unknown shores, or the blank space that rises immeasurably above its formless surface. There are beings of a higher rank than human, many orders of them probably, whether the inhabitants of stars, or of worlds of a different kind too ætherial to be seen by our grosser vision; but for this knowledge we are indebted to the Bible. Science here is as silent as the Pyramids. She would rather regard the human race as the highest to which the physical or creative progress has yet arrived. But Scripture has revealed it to us; for the knowledge has a nearer bearing on our spiritual destiny, than any science we may possess of the visible worlds of astronomy. Nothing *there* is known which can in any way affect our Scriptural theology. Whatever of life there may be in those conceived or estimated spaces, whatever rank of being, whatever goodness, happiness, beauty, or their opposites,—whatever political or social condition, whatever moral state, confirmed or fallen, redeemed or lost,—all this is no less matter for the imagination, and no more a knowledge which is to change our theological belief, than it was in the days of Abraham and Pythagoras. But we are rambling again. To resume the order of discussion, we have—

6th. An argument from the Mosaic division of the creative times. It is clear, on the face of the account, that the whole creative process *there set forth*, whether universal or partial, or whatever it might embrace, was meant to be included in six days or divisions of time. "In six days God made the Heaven, the Earth, the Sea, and all that in them is." Whatever, therefore, was *extra dies*, does not belong to this account. It may have place in some other or greater chronology, but does not come into the Geology or Ouranology of Moses. But if the first verse denotes a separate antecedent work, whether nearly or remotely antecedent, it would be thus *extra dies;* for nothing is more clearly impressed upon the account, than the fact that the hexameron commences with the night. It is as clear, too, that the light is the first morning. It is equally evident that this is the antithesis of the darkness resting on the terrestrial waters. Put them together, and we have the two limits of this First day. Can the great primordial act be assigned to the night? If so, it was the beginning of the night, for the light was its termination. But if the beginning of a night, what was before it? We get into strange positions here; and the reason is, that every man's soul must feel that there is neither consistency, nor harmony, nor rationality in such a view. If we make the Mosaic light, or the command for its outshining, the primordial act, then the darkness before it was the darkness of nothingness. This might seem consistent in itself; but no one can read the account, and reconcile such a view with the language of Moses. If the darkness was the darkness of nothingness, the waters were the waters of nothingness, or, to adopt the scientific term, the "fluid" of nonentity. Here is chaos certainly; but it is in the mind of the one who attempts to form such a conception. All is confusion, waste and void, a mental tohu and bohu instead of one of the most vivid pictures language was ever employed to express. The reader will see, of course, that the remarks do not apply to the fact of such origination, but to the supposed representation of it by Moses. The primordial act, through which matter is supposed to have come into being, is no where in the diorama of this first day; it is therefore not set forth in the *Mosaic Creation*, whether Moses thought of it or not. No rational mind, we say, could think of calling it in question as a fact; but that does not make it any the less extra dies. The creation recorded by Moses was all in six days. To find what lies fairly within these limits, be it partial or universal, belongs to the truthful interpreter. Whatever lies without, and can by no consistent effort be brought within, may be left to the vaunting theories of an ambitious science, and the speculations of a bigoted unbiblical theology.

We can not close this excursus without adverting to the obvious parallel to this Mosaic account which is presented in the beginning of the Gospel by John. We have a *beginning* mentioned there. We have also a *light*, and a *darkness* in which (not out of which, as in the Mosaic account, 2 Cor. iv, 6,) the light shone. This Light was a much older light than the one revealed Genesis i, 3; even as the *beginning* here is a far more ancient beginning. It was the Εἰκών, Colos. i, 15, the Απαύγασμα τῆς δόξης, Heb. i, 3, or first *out beaming* of the Divine Glory, the light which "the darkness apprehendeth not," that is, which no darkness overtakes (κατέλαβεν, Jo. i, 5,) or succeeds*, as it does the physical light. Here, too, we have a parallel mention of an older and more universal creation. The Apostles' knowledge of the universe was, perhaps, not much, if any, greater than that of Moses, but he is directed to the use of language, not only wider in itself, but exceeding, by its manner of expression, the very idea of any partial work. "*All things were made by Him, and without Him was there nothing made which was made.*" Could not Moses have used similar language, had he thought of taking into his picture any thing more ancient than the waters and the darkness that rested upon them. The contrast, as well as the parallel, would seem unmistakeable. The one begins with light, the other with darkness; in the one the light is followed by an evening, in the other the darkness never overtakes or comprehends it; the one embraces all things, the other the Earth with the Heaven immediately above it and that is made after it. To this corresponds the language of Paul, Colos. i, 16, where he, too, evidently goes beyond the Mosaic account both in language and idea—" Who is the Image of the invisible God, the First Born before all creation. For in Him were *all things* created, all things in the Heavens and all things upon the Earth, *the visible and the invisible*, whether they be Thrones, or Lordships, or Principalities, or Powers, *all*

* The arguments for the common rendering of this passage are strong, especially as favored by the context in the 11th and 12th verses. Still, in the Greek verb itself there is much to support the other view, which makes a strongly marked parallel, or rather contrast, with Genesis. The sense of *understanding, taking by the mind,* belongs to the word, but it is quite unusual; the other sense is almost universal. Where this light shines, there is no night or evening there.

things by Him, and *for* Him were created." Whatever these invisible things may mean, (a question we have argued elsewhere,) they are clearly something beyond, above, and distinct from, the visible or phenomenal (τα φαινόμενα, "*the things that are seen*,") to which the account of Moses seems wholly confined. Here, too, we have the Life as well as the Light. "In Him was life, and the life was the light of men." In Genesis, the going forth of the Word, or Logos, is ever the origin of physical life, but here is something higher. It is the identification of the Light and Life—the Life was the Light of men. *The Logos in nature*, is certainly a prominent, though much neglected doctrine of the Bible; but here is something that we must receive as a still greater mystery. It passeth understanding, and yet it is not on that account to be denied, or lowered to something clearly within our comprehension. The Ζωή must be more than a moral influence, or moral teaching, however high the truths thus taught. Writers called evangelical have maintained this moral-suasion ground; but if they take no other, we see not how they are to defend themselves against the more consistent Socinian argument, or deny the interpretation which would make the Logos here but another name for the impersonal Reason.

"*Without Him there was nothing made which was made.*" There is a different division of this third verse, adopted by some of the Fathers, and having support in some of the old versions. If it can be philologically justified, it is entitled to respectful attention for the meaning which it would seem to bring out. They took the ὃ γέγονεν of the third verse, as the beginning of the next clause—"That which was made, in Him was life."

The proposition, then, would seem to be, not simply that life was in the Logos, but that the natural creation had its life in Him who was also, in a spiritual sense, both the light and the life of men.

Between the First of Genesis and the First of John there is not only a parallel but a contrast. One is wholly pictorial, yet none the less real. It is true as a picture. Its truthfulness is according to the vividness with which the ineffable causalities are represented, as they *appear*, and in the order in which they appear, on the canvas of the mind's conception. The other, transcending all conceptions, gives us only the most general names for primary ideas,—the Word, the Life, the Light, the Universal Origination. Its truthfulness is according to its universality. The aim of science, in distinction from both these, would be to give us the *particular* and linked causalities. It has been shown that, however correct in itself, or for the very short distance it goes, it must ever fail in respect to primal powers. The falsehood of its ambitious attempt consists in its unmeasurably short-falling; paradox as it may seem, its *inadequacy* here is in the ratio of the accuracy and minuteness of its details. From such a view one reflection presents itself strongly to the mind. There *is* an ineffable truth in creation, even in the physical creation. At some period of our existence that ineffable truth may be brought nearer to our minds. Who will then be found, though far below, to have had his eye in the right direction? The man who has taken the simple pictorial Bible account, or he who has sought for something better in the ambitious path of science? If infinite wisdom is, indeed, the author of the Scriptures, there can be but one answer to the question.

CHAPTER X.

ANTIQUITY OF THE EARTH.

Geology claims the Sole Credit of the Idea—What may be fairly Conceded to her—One who is not a Geologist may Reason about Geology—The Geologist himself may be unfitted for Cosmical Questions—A little Science wakes up Thought in Thoughtful Minds—The Idea once aroused is seen every where—Antiquity of the Earth seen in the most Common Phenomena—Nature, in general, Honest and Truthful—Geological Changes referred to in Job xiv—*The Ancient Philosophy—The World-Problem—The Schoolmen and the Galileos—The "Students of Nature"—The Epicureans the Ancient Scientific Boasters—Natural Theology.*

ASIDE from the supernatural fact, the hexameral division, as has been already remarked, is the principal feature in the Mosaic account. The length of the days is a subordinate question. A thoughtful mind would, indeed, feel that there was something extraordinary about them in the manner of their division, in their mysterious mornings and evenings made without a sun or any astronomical changes, and their strange commencement in each case by the intervention of a supernatural Word. Such thoughtful mind would carry this sense of the extraordinary into the duration. As long, however, as there was nothing outward, that is, no outward knowledge associating itself with the length or shortness of the times, the idea of such extraordinary duration might remain undeveloped; especially since in itself it is entirely indefinite,—a long or a short time satisfying the philological conception, although the general mysteriousness that pervades the whole remarkable history favors the wider notion. Still, the ante-solar day might be of any length*; and there was little to disturb the view that had become in a great measure constant in modern times, until Geology began to proclaim its discoveries. This is its merit, and it is willingly conceded to it. It waked up the common mind to a thought, which, although slumbering in the masses, had been entertained by meditative souls as perfectly consistent with the language,—a thought that when fully aroused is found to be in beautiful harmony with the greater analogies of Scripture, as they direct our minds to the prophetic destinies of this world and God's apparently slow working therein.

This credit, then, may be cheerfully conceded to Geology. It has made common this idea of the antiquity of the earth. And yet nothing can be more false than the notion that any great amount of natural science, or geological science, is necessary for the satisfactory apprehension and holding of such an idea. There may be given to the remark a wider application. In nothing, perhaps, do our more boasting class of scientific men show a more unphilosophical blindness, than in the evident conceit, they so often manifest, that the man who does

*There is something striking in the view of Professor Pierce, thnt this hexameral division denotes an order rather than any particular times long or short. It is well worthy of attention, and we should prefer it to either the twenty-four hour, or the nebular scheme. Still we can not divest ourselves of the idea of a chronology.

not profess to understand conchology, and mineralogy, or even geology, in their scientific order, is, therefore, unqualified to reason about them, or any of the great physical questions connected with creation and origin. Now this is narrow — very narrow. There is, indeed, required some knowledge of these sciences, as sciences, that a man may estimate correctly their true position; but such knowledge need not be extensive nor minute. He may make blunders occasionally; and he can afford to do so, without mortification, if the higher result of his argument is unaffected by them. There are beyond these, and above these, other departments of knowledge, of higher interest, and demanding severer thought. There are students of God's Word who can well afford to be ignorant of many things esteemed highest by these " Students of Nature." But even in geology, it requires no great amount of technical geological science to reason, and reason correctly,— not on the numerous questions of fact and inference disputed among professional geologists themselves,— but upon the bearing of the science and its discoveries on the great fields, both of inductive and revealed truth. There is some reason to think, that the man who looks at the universe as represented in his scientific cabinet, is, in fact, thereby less qualified for such an argument. He is too fond of showing off his science in its partial aspects; there are certain cherished views, or scientific hobbies, we might call them, certain narrow niches and corners of truth, which have become special favorites; these are hostile even to the wider cosmical survey in its physical aspect, and much more so as such survey connects itself with the spiritual mundane destiny.

Science, as we have said, wakes up thought,—thought beyond her own discoveries, or the strictly scientific domain. And this is the main use of her. But she does so only in thoughtful souls; and such is far from being the character of all scientific men. To many she imparts only *dry knowledge*, very scientific it may be, but of very inferior value. The thinking of men had not been much turned to the antiquity of the earth,—we say again, in comparatively modern times, for it has been shown that it was an ancient speculation, philosophical as well as traditional and poetical,—but in modern times, for certain reasons, the thought had slumbered, until Geology again awoke it; just as in other cases, that might be mentioned, we are sometimes startled by the fact of modern research calling out an old, sometimes a very old, idea. Now give Geology all credit for this, and yet it requires no great amount of exact geological knowledge to reach out to the great conclusion. In fact, a man's common every day observations, if he be at all what we have called a thoughtful man, are sufficient for this. Let the mind be once upon the track, and he need not, for this purpose, study Buckland or Lyell. The ideas of great times, great spaces,—those old native ideas that had been haunting the soul's dreams—start up and carry him through without the aid of diagrams or fossil drawings. Let something fairly arouse the thought within him, and he sees it represented every where. He can not ride through the Hudson Highlands, even in the rapid flight of the rail road car, without seeing how the earth shows growth—that is, the evidence of *gradual*,* or

* It may seem hardly necessary to remind the intelligent reader, that this word is here used in its etymological strictness, of a proceeding *per*

serial succession. He sees this just as clearly as he sees a similar though shorter growth in his woods and gardens. The appearance of time, succession, dependence, of one step waiting for another, is as significantly and as suggestively marked in the one as in the other. He must, also, regard them as equally truthful—that is, as much indicating what they appear to indicate—unless he is forbidden thus to think by a clear, positive revelation. Such a reserve proviso he must ever have; for Scripture has intimated that there may be, sometimes, a false face on nature. She is a σχῆμα, a *show*, or outside *figure*, ever passing away; and this may be in fact very rapid as measured on one scale when it may seem to be slow, very slow, as graduated on another. She works irregularly, too, in a fallen world, where it is part of her mission to make the physical, in some measure, a picture of the moral deformity. Hence, nature may be more full of paradoxes here than in other spheres, whether her irregular workings, her deformities, her catastrophes, her noxious births, are to be viewed as current retributions, or ancient adaptations to a world foreordained to be the birth place, and the long abode of fallible and actually fallen beings. But, in general, she is to be regarded as honest, so that her *appearances*,* so far as they seem to

gradum, which we can not separate from some corresponding duration having as many distinct times as there are appearances of distinct steps. Growth, also, is taken in the general sense of successive addition.

*Throughout the two long articles of Professor DANA in the Andover Bibliotheca, there is nothing more absurd than the misapprehension he has everywhere manifested in respect to the author's use of this word *appearance*. In the Six Days of Creation, it is employed uniformly, and with studied consistency, as representative of a high reality—that real, substantial, powerful, though in itself unseen, thing *that appears in* it, or through it. The author makes just the distinction that the most perfect of languages so easily suggests between the *thing that appears* (that is, makes

indicate her modes and steps of working, are not vain lying shows, but truly represent the unseen powers that lately, or long ago, have left their marks upon her face. She does not show *apparent* effects that had no causes, nor steps that had no succession, nor succession that had no corresponding times. Whether God ever makes immediately products apparently organic, having the appearances of succession, and yet no succession in reality, no movement per gradus,—it is hard for us to say. We can not affirm it or deny it. It is so difficult for us to know how time and space, succession and motion, enter into the *essence* of his working in distinction from its *manifestation* to finite beings, that, in such cases, our only safety consists in clinging close to the language of Scripture and its fair exegesis. In the record of such facts as the creation of the first human body, and the formation of the female organism therefrom, we have a special

the appearance) in the active or middle sense, and that which appears, or the *appearance*, in the passive. This one remark is a sufficient answer to all the places in which Professor Dana has used the word as a bugbear, in his charge of Platonism, or otherwise. He has ever confounded φάσμα, or φάντασμα, a subjective *apparition*, with φαινόμενον, a real appearance of a real thing. No other philosophy, we may remark, makes so *real* a world as the Platonic, or is farther removed from that subjectivism whose ghosts are the ghosts of nothing, whose φάσματα are the *fantasies* of nothing, and which is, therefore, a system of nothingness from beginning to end, as unsubstantial on the one side, as dead materialism on the other. Mr. Lord makes the same charge, but we would only say of him, as civilly as we can, that his utter want of knowledge of the philosophy he so ferociously assails, makes it unworthy of notice. He has something which he calls mind, or spiritual entity; all other reality, to his thinking, is found in *hard matter*. An immaterial entity which is not mind, he holds to be nonsense. Of course, whether he sees it or not, there being between this *mind* and this *hard matter*, no intermediate reality of any kind, the latter is the direct pantheistic image of the former, or it is the veriest ghost of nothing, or else, however unintelligible and irrational the thought, it is eternal and self-subsistent.

revelation to which "we do well to take heed," and study it deeply, without being overwise, either in our literalism, or our symbolism, or our philosophy. And yet it would be not a proud, but a reverent thought to be humbly entertained, that the best and most honest interpretation we can put upon it, may, after all, have much remaining still of the ineffable and the unknown. In such cases, however, we are fairly warned of the exception, and have a caution not to go by appearances, or, at least, not to draw from them the same conclusions that we derive from the common or ordinary manifestations. The human body of Adam, when first made, may have presented the same appearances in the bone, the flesh, the blood, that exist in the present adult healthful human organism, and which indicate growth, and maturity as the result of growth. It may have presented such an appearance, it probably did present such an appearance—we can hardly conceive of it otherwise whilst thinking of it as a human body at all, or as representative of other human bodies—and yet in the peculiar circumstances of that extraordinary case, we would have no right to adopt either of the two conclusions that would present themselves to some minds as the only ones. It would be very rash in us to hold, either that the appearances, in such case, must be the appearances of nothing, in other words, mere φάσματα, or that they necessarily indicate the same outward astronomical time, and the same mode of generative working, as is now required for such an organic result. If there were appearances of growth, succession, maturity, then would there be a reverent warrant for concluding that even in this extraordinary creation, there were realities in the working corresponding to them, in other words, a growth, a succession, a maturity, but in their time, and their modal causality, ineffable, that is, altogether transcending, and not to be measured on the scale to which the present appearances are to be brought as their only intelligible standard.

These remarks apply to what may be called the extraordinary creations among creations,—for such there are on the very face of Scripture—but in other cases, and especially where the inspired writer uses the very language of natural causality, the appearances of nature may fairly enter in our reasoning as determinative of the great facts of succession, if not of their precise chronology.

We may say, then, that in general, and when we have no positive revelation to the contrary, nature is to be trusted, with all allowance for our exceeding ignorance of her immensely varied laws, and for what, for all we know to the contrary, may have been their immensely varied, and frequently varied, rates of energising. In thus trusting nature, the meditative man who has but the rudiments of exact science may be on a par with the most boasting savan. Nay, for reasons to which we have elsewhere alluded, he may even have the advantage of him. In his broader thinking, there is less disturbance arising from any cherished partial views; in the absence of a blinding scientific interest, there is less in the way of those great conclusions, which the broad face of nature suggests as promptly and as strongly as the more minute discoveries. Such a meditative spirit can not, for example, walk on the lake beach, and see the smooth, round stones as they are worn into ovals by the long action of the waters, and then their exact resemblances on the distant hills, without feeling that the appearance of time in the one case is just as truthful as that in the other. Nature renders the same verdict of facts in both, and if there be no arrest of judgment on the higher written evidence, superseding such parol testimony, as we may call it, he takes her verdict as she honestly gives it in. He draws from it the most natural and obvious inferences. If it took ages to form these smooth ovals in one spot, it took ages to form them in the other. And yet, on other good and satisfying evidence, he knows that ages, historical ages at least, have intervened since the causality that there once energized has been quiescent. Troy has been taken, yea, the Pyramids have been built, since any important geographical change took place in those regions. The most ancient of known historical events have passed away since there "*the water washed those stones*,"—to use the clear language of Job (xiv) describing the same phenomenon. To a thinking man how full of thought this very ancient allusion, together with similar accompanying words in the same remarkable chapter of inspiration! "*The crumbling mountain falleth into ruin; the rock is removed from its place; the dust of the earth covereth over the things that grow out of it.* The sea (the lake) faileth and drieth up; yet man lies still;*† *he waketh not from his sleep until the Heavens grow old.*" All the verses we have gathered from this ejaculating, sigh-

* Its long buried fossil plants, as the Geologist would style them.

† The Hebrew שכב, here employed, is the word used so frequently for lying down to sleep. This is its main sense, too, in the old Phœnician, as is evident from its frequent use in the inscriptions that have been discovered in that earliest form of the Hebrew. Especially is it the case with the very remarkable one lately discovered near old Sidon, and which has been so carefully studied by the scholars of Germany and the United States.

ing chapter, express, in their connection, the same sombre thought, so mournful, yet so full of interest in respect to our physical as well as spiritual destiny. Throughout the passage the contrast is between the transitoriness of man, and the long, slow changes of nature, so steadily yet irresistibly going on while he is sleeping in the bosom of his mother earth, awaiting his own great supernatural change that shall surely come in the latter day.*

* The Arabians have a formula highly suggestive when considered in connection with that idea of reviviscence which we think is found in this chapter—"*To God is the return*," or *to God belongs the return* (אל־מציר *al-ma-si-ru*). It is one of the solemn cadences of the Koran, so often employed at the close of verses, and has every appearance, like others of those cadences, of being a very ancient form of speech. There are other expressions in the Koran of a similar kind, and used in connection with it as exegetical of its meaning,—such as "*God killeth and He maketh alive again*," "*He bringeth to death, and He bringeth back from death*." The manner in which these are employed leave no doubt of their reference to the resurrection, and thus considered, they may greatly aid us in getting a right stand-point for interpreting very similar language in the Old Testament. Compare Deut. xxxii, 39, and especially 1 Sam. ii, 8. "*The Lord killeth and He maketh alive; He bringeth down to Sheol, and He bringeth up again*"—*Dominus mortificat et vivificat, deducit ad inferos et reducit.* It is easy to give this another sense; and yet there is a view which greatly favors the more impressive thought, and makes it seem not only possible, but probable and easy as coming in connection with such ejaculatory language, and even along with expressions referring to the present state. We refer to the undoubted Oriental belief in what may be called the human cycle, or the doctrine that the human life would come over again on this earth. Carry this along, and we have a stand-point for the interpretation of some of the most striking passages in Job and the Psalms. It was not exactly the Christian idea of the resurrection, but it was the germ of the doctrine as held by the Pharisees, and Jews generally, in our Savior's time, as well as by the Arabian tribes before the days of Mohammed.

In connection with this, we may refer to the rendering of Psalm xc, 3, as given in the Prayer Book Psalter—"*Come again, ye Sons of Adam*"—and Luther's touching translation—Kommt wieder Menschen-Kinder, *Come back, ye children of men*—which are also countenanced, to some extent, in the ancient versions. The common rendering is strongly supported by the seeming reference to Gen. iii, 19; but it is certain that the word שוב freely and equally admits both senses, a *turning*, a *returning* to, or a *returning*

In this true view of the passage, how suggestive is it of our leading thought—an early credited antiquity of

from. So it is applied to the Children of Israel, both in their backsliding and their repentance, or *conversion*. Compare Jeremiah iii, 1, where it is so affectingly addressed to the adulterous wife—*tamen revertere ad me*, and Luther again, *doch komm wieder zu mir—yet* still *come back to me*. The use of the same word in both clauses of Psalm xc, 3, would also seem to show that there was intended a special significance in the contrast of its double, yet equally easy and equally prominent senses. It may be said, too, that the other view which makes them both refer to the same event, weakens the parallelism by making the command come after the act.

There is a confirmation of the reviviscent sense in the fact that it seems to explain the train of thought which otherwise might appear abrupt, or without clear transition. The first thought is, that God is "our dwelling place," or his peoples' dwelling place, "in all generations." He is *yet* the God of the dead, as well as of the living. Then we have the Divine Eternity. With this connects most naturally the mention of "the thousand years," as a "watch in the *night*," suggestive of the long sleep in the grave,—so long to our conception, so short to Him. "*Thou* overwhelmest, or *buriest* them; they are as a sleep, or they sleep." The Syriac here has a paraphrastic rendering in some way suggested by the Hebrew זרמתם. "Their generations are asleep," or they sleep through generations. Next we have mention of the *morning*, when there shall bloom again that which in the evening was cut down and withered. Is the greater morning meant here, the morning and evening of the cycle? It would not do for us to say rashly or confidently that this is the most obvious meaning, although we may feel strong in the thought that it is suggestive, and may have been so intended, of the wider sense,—the longer sleep, the greater reviving, or *springing again*, such as is almost ever denoted by the Hebrew חלף. We would not rashly affirm this, but let the reader compare Psalm xlix, 15,—"The upright shall have dominion in *the morning*,"—the same word, and in connections remarkably similar, yet leaving no doubt of the reference being to the *great day* and the greater *morning* of the world, when, as is so clearly expressed in the next verse, God shall "redeem the soul from the power of Sheol."

"Unto Him shall be the return." Slow, immensely slow, are the changes of nature while man is sleeping in the dust; long is she preparing for the catastrophies that attend or precede the greater cycle, but "the morning cometh as well as the night." Whether primarily intended in this passage, or only suggested by it, still the doctrine of the great human change, or חליפה, may be supported, even from the older Scripture, if we seek to study it in the spirit of the Great Interpreter, rather than that of the old Sadducceism he so triumphantly refuted.

the earth as something immensely older than the human race, who are said to be "but of yesterday" in comparison with its longer duration. Especially is this language remarkable as we remember its place in that most ancient Idumean Drama. How old the earth as compared with man! What marks of age, as shown by slow physical changes, does it exhibit in contrast with the brief human cycle, whether regarded as of the individual or of the race! No other or less thought would have had the force or interest demanded by the comparison. "*The waters wear smooth the stones.*" The Hebrew verb, שחק, as we have remarked elsewhere, means to *attenuate*, (Greek of the LXX, λεαίνω,) to reduce to fine dust. Had the Hebrews or Arabians been scientific geologists, they would have made from it their scientific word corresponding to the modern term *detritus*. It is the same phenomenon now so frequently witnessed, and which presented the same old look in the early age of Job. "*The waters wear smooth the stones.*" The flood could not have done this work of shaping and detrition. We know exactly how that fearful event took place. It is presented to us in a picture which in grandeur and vividness is second only to that of creation. We know from the same source, how brief the time it occupied. We know the very days of the month on which it began, in which it reached its hight, and when it terminated. The changes it wrought were mighty, doubtless; but very different they must have been from the appearances we are now contemplating. Effects must correspond to causes. The effects as seen in these smooth ovals, so undisturbed in their regularity and in their exact likeness of each other, and their exact correspondence to the contiguous, or once contiguous, working power, must have been very slow and gradual effects, unless nature lies to us, and lies, too, without a reason, that is, any apparent reason. They are gradual and regular effects, and, therefore, whether natural or supernatural, they could not have come, we venture cautiously to assert, from a sudden, abrupt and violent cause.

But our unscientific man whose meditations we have been endeavoring to follow, need not travel to the lake shore or the mountain top. He need not climb the Chimborazo with Humboldt, or trace the wilds of Superior with our equally adventurous American Geologists. In the evening quiet of his parlor fire-side, he may muse on the lump of coal with its suggestive layers, or the marble mantle-piece with each point and shade significant of *effects*, as these of causes or activities now resting but once at work, and these again of times or intervals of duration, which, however regarded absolutely or in themselves, must be pronounced long if measured by the countless stepping places presented to the eye in these dead yet still speaking tablets of a causation that has passed away. Yes — even these common objects commune with us of the mysterious past. They tell the same story. It is change, if we may not call it growth, slow change as measured by its visible lines and points. It is time, succession,— long succession, apparently,— just as truthfully indicating what it seems to indicate as the worn channels of the streams or the century-formed rings of the oak.

Aside from the nearer or more obvious deductions, there is also another class of questions — yes, questions in nature,— that lie beyond the track of inductive science, and yet belong to the common thinking if it be vigorous, if it be truthful even, though wholly unscientific. They are beyond science; but the road to them does not lie through her province. They were discussed by the ancient mind with a keenness that modern philosophy fails to equal. No modern school ever entered more profoundly into the questions of origin, first matter, first motion, first form, first unity, first diversity, first organism, first laws, ideas, types, and which was first respectively, *things*, outward things themselves, or the *principles* of things,—that without which they could not be things or have in any sense a self-hood or ipseity—no modern school, we say, ever entered more profoundly into questions like these than some of the earliest thinkers. Bacon and Leibnitz may be ransacked for anything on these subjects more acute, and we may confidently say, more satisfactory than the reasonings of Aristotle in his *Physica* and *Metaphysica*. We might extend the remark to other thinkers of that remarkable period in the world's intellectual history. We might safely go farther up the stream of time, or we might come nearer to our own age, and still find evidence of the position, that what is called science is not the only, not even the best preparation of the soul for the examination of the higher cosmological questions,—if we *will* discuss them aside from revelation. All the Galileos of later times never went so deeply into these world-problems, as the Schoolmen who have been so foolishly contemned in the common comparison. It requires no great amount of faithful reading for an intelligent mind to be convinced that there are truly wonders in some of those forgotten tomes. It requires no great erudition to read Anselm, or to study occasionally a chapter of Aquinas, but no thoughtful man can do so without feeling that the modern world, the very modern world, we mean, does not, and perhaps can not, supply their places. As one contemplates with astonishment the profound speculations of these men of the cell, the thought fairly arises whether the exact and exacting detail of certain forms of modern physical or experimental science, and the piece-meal views they give us of the universe, may not have actually narrowed the minds of some of its votaries,—so that, strange as it may seem, there may have been actually more true *freedom of soul* in the cloister, than among many of these boasting "students of nature" who roam the sea shore in search of shells, or penetrate the depths of the mine to find, if possible, the age of the earth. We would not speak sweepingly, or even generally. The tendency to which we allude is most evident in certain quarters, and in certain aspects of this "scientific age," but there *are* those who unite the character of the scientific man and the philosopher. These may be known, however, not more by the deep value of their studies, than by the entire absence of that absurd boasting which is becoming so offensive in the lectures and inaugural speeches of the times.

History is ever giving us cycles. They may present a wider spiral, (as they do sometimes a narrower,) but however magnified in some aspects, and diminished in others, they hold similarities of feature that the observing student can hardly fail to recognize. How strikingly is this truth confirmed when we call to mind that the shallow Epicureans were the scientific boasters of their day. There is no trace of such a spirit in the humble and reverent Socrates; Plato ever lived in a region of thought too lofty to allow its utterance; Aristotle's "stream of flowing gold," as Cicero styles it, was too gravely solid for such froth to rise and float upon its majestically moving surface. It is only as we approach a somewhat later time, that we begin to hear a sound reminding us of our own most modern age. It comes from "the herd of Epicurus," magnifying their master as the "Father of the then modern philosophy," and filling the age with their clamor about physical knowledge, and the wonders it was achieving, and the still greater wonders it was going to achieve. Styx and Acheron, with all their ghosts, were paling in its presence, as the myths of Christianity flee before some of our modern savans who live and write under other influences than those of our New-Haven and Andover orthodoxy. There was the same proud talk, too, about what mind had done and what it would do:

> Omne immensum peragrans—
> Unde refert nobis Victor, *quid possit oriri*,
> Quid nequeat; finita potestas denique quoique
> Qua nam sit ratione, atque alte terminus haerens.

It would roam through all space; it would tell us of origin, of all that could be, and of all that could not be; it would go to the very bottom of nature; it would give the reason of all things; it would make immovable landmarks, and fix the deep, permanent bound of an unchanging causality. Such wonders had it begun to perform; such still greater wonders would it yet perform. We could almost translate it in the deep irony of the Scriptures—"It would put an end to the darkness and search out all perfection; its eye would see every precious thing and that which was hidden would it bring to light; it would enter the gates of Hades," and heal the terrors of "the valley of the shadow of death;" it would solve the problem of life; "it would find the place of WISDOM and assay the value thereof."

> Vitæ ipsam *rationem*, eam quæ
> Nunc adpellatur SAPIENTIA; quæque per artem
> Fluctibus e tantis vitam, tantisque tenebris,
> In tam *tranquilla*, et tam *clara luce*, locabit.

It would discover the long sought means by which the human race would be at last rescued from "the mighty billows of darkness," and brought to repose "in clear and tranquil light." It had much to say, too, of its *utilities*, its boasted

> Commoda vitæ.

But alas for ancient or modern science! What a contrast does all this present to that view the Bible gives us of the mysteries that surround our existence, and of the evils, the physically incurable evils, in which it is so deeply sunk. Even in the merely natural aspect, how poor a thing it really is! But compare with this empty prating the true profound of the Scriptures—even the true physical profound—compare with it those solemn, searching interrogatories in the xxviiith and xxxviiith chapters of Job, consider, moreover, the age of the world, keep in mind all of literature, science, or philosophy, that was outside of this "enclosed garden, this fountain sealed" of Jewish wisdom, and we have an evidence for the superhuman character of the Scriptures which it would seem almost impossible for any sane mind to resist. It is indeed the true profound, revealed to us not in attempted explanations, but in the awful disclosure of its unfathomable depths.

But what of those ancient pretensions, some one may say! What comparison between the science of those times and the splendid structure that has been reared since Bacon showed the right way! Be the difference, in other respects, what it may, the boasting is certainly very much the same in both cases. What is there—it is a question that may well be asked—what is there in this kind of knowledge, be it great or small, that ever tends to the exhibition of such a spirit? The language, too, is so very similar. In this respect, at least, the warp and woof of many a modern lecture, or modern inaugural, might be taken, almost verbatim, from Lucretius and the Fragments of Epicurus. The very cant was the same. Atoms, molecules, *declinationes*—it comes near enough to *affinities*—were their favorite words; *ideas* were bugbears (τερατώδη,) as they are even now to the sciolist. Contemptible, too, as may seem this ancient science, the positions, we say it boldly, were the same; we mean the relative positions which render the boasting in both cases equally trifling and inane. It was not the small amount which gave it this aspect—for it looked to the future, and drew upon the future, even as we do now—but it was the vain assumption that it, or any amount of experimental science, so called, could ever solve the deep problem of humanity,—we might say, even the deep physical problem of our world and race. But in the presence of the still higher questions, how contemptible its boasting figure! its inane prattling about Styx and Tartarus, and the *lux clara, et tranquilla*, the "serene and tranquil light,"

fluctibus a tantis oriens tantisque tenebris—

and the *finita potestas*, and the *alte terminus haerens*,

and the *commoda vitæ*, and all the other great things it had begun to do, and would still more perfectly do for our poor priest-ridden, religion-haunted world!—in all of which, by the way, we can not help remarking how the terrors of Hades ever revealed themselves in the so frequent mention of the victories that science was going to achieve over them. How much profounder the truth involved in those fables of Styx and Acheron, than in all their physical discovery! how much deeper the mine of thought, even in Homer and the Greek dramatic poetry, than was laid open in all their science had taught or would ever teach! and yet how pitiably unconscious do these old braggarts seem to be of it! Now this is the thought that renders true and just the parallel we have drawn between the ancient and the modern science,—we mean, as we need hardly tell our readers, the boasting aspect of it, and the schools by which such aspect is mainly represented. It is not a question of quantity, but of a relation. The science of Epicurus was certainly a very small affair; though of considerable value when compared with the lack of it. It was not, however, its quantity, we say again, which gave it this appearance, but the fearful problem with which it stood confronted, and which, in its empty insolence, it had dared to face. Now, modern science has vastly grown, and therefore, it may be said, has some right to use this vaunting language that sounds so preposterous in the mouth of its elder brother. It has vastly grown, indeed, and yet it may be in fact, a very small affair in its relation to the darkness that still rests as dense as ever, even on the great ultimate, or more interior, truths of nature herself. The physical deep, or the deeper physical, is no nearer being sounded than in the days of Job. There are questions, near questions, in relation to the most common states of matter, and suggesting themselves to our most obvious thinking, which science can no more answer now than then. *Molecules*, *fluids*, *affinities*, give no more help in the case, than *atoms*, *declinationes*, or *homœomeric parts*. Science is yet upon the surface of things, or, at the utmost, but a few inches below. The most candid and philosophical among her votaries have admitted this with humility, though without humiliation. The noisier "students of nature" fancy that they have sailed many a league, when they are yet upon the banks of the Ebro. Like Don Quixotte and Sancho Panza in their strange colloquy, they talk of having "passed the equinoctial," when they have "only dropped a few fathoms below their point of departure"; they boast of "the parallels they have crossed, the constellations they are leaving behind," the immense cosmical progress they are making, when they are yet upon the earth, and the most common questions of earth right round them stare them in the face, and reprove them, or ought to reprove them, for their ignorance as well as their presumption.

But conceding to science all she claims, there is another view of the matter which becomes still more serious from the very concession. Modern science has vastly grown. Let us admit it without limitation or disparagement. But here comes the thought we are most anxious to press upon the reader's mind, because we are certain of its presenting a truth whose importance no comparison can effect, no admission can in the least diminish. It is the truth which places our natural knowledge, great as it may be, in the same scale, and measures it by the same standard we applied to the ancient pretensions. Modern science has grown, vastly grown ; admit it freely ; but so, also, has grown, be it ever remembered, fearfully grown, the mighty problem with which such science is yet confronted. It is this thought that renders its pretentious attitude, its Baconian clamor, above all its claim to be a second revelation, even still more absurd, still more irreverent, than the noisy Epicurean boasting. Science has grown in the multitude of its facts; but in a still higher ratio has grown the problem of human life, grown in depth and height, in grandeur and intensity, in awe and mystery. Even the physical has a more tremendous aspect than it ever could have in the days of Epicurus. The darkness here has increased faster than the light. History has added her testimony to something in our race and world with which science can not grapple, and can never hope to grapple. The disease, the woe, the natural woe, is deeper than her ken. Even physical sorrows multiply faster than her remedies. The cure, or seeming cure, not unfrequently creates a new disease, or makes the old one start up in still more hideous forms. Her utilities, her much lauded inventions, of which she sometimes boasts as though she could really make a rail road to the celestial city, her arts refined and useful, her commoda vitæ, what do they but engender an all-governing secularity, or diseased civilization, prolific of a new brood of monsters worse than any of which she had boasted of having delivered the world. Such is the incapacity of science even to answer the lower question, Who will show us any true, permanent, earthly good? But when we consider how this problem of life has grown upon us in its unearthly aspects as revealed in the Scriptures, when we think of the still deeper mysteries that have come out of such revelation, the increased evidence of the inconceivable human wickedness which no art softens and no science subdues, the immense disproportion yet existing between earth's scanty wheat and its wild overspreading tares,—when we take into our minds all that is expressed in those exhaustless words of Scripture, "the world lieth in wickedness," "the creation groaneth and travaileth in pain,"—in view, we say, of a problem presenting such aspects as these, and which revelation, history, and experience, have brought to such tremendous dimensions, what trifling, like the trifling of some scientific men! what folly can be greater than the claim we sometimes hear that physical science is to remedy all this, or (to take the seemingly more pious asssuption,) that she is even to assist the cure of our humanity in the character either of a concurrent or subordinate revelation! The old boasting was rational when compared with this. Science then was in its infancy, we say; "it spake as a child." But if the race has grown to manhood—and surely under the pupilage of revelation it should have taken some steps toward it—then "should we put away childish things." We know much more about the cave in which we dwell; we have studied much more carefully the shadows that come and go upon its dusky walls; we have discovered some order of succession among them to which we give the name of laws; we are even able, in many cases, to vaticinate, or tell how they will come and come again, or make their circuits whilst the panorama lasts, or the scene remains unchanged; as the eye grows keener, too, and the pupil enlarges in the twilight, we see continually more and more that had escaped our previous ken. And we are very much amused with all this. Some get wonderfully elated, and talk of "annihilating space," and "subduing the elements," and "taking all the gloom and terror out of nature." So we boast. But alas! in presence of the greater question that ever keeps up with the march of natural knowledge, and goes before it, and ever confronts it with a yet sterner aspect, the modern is still more trifling, still more absurd, than the ancient gasconade. In the light of the Scripture, we are compelled to say, it is not only irrational, but profane; in presence, too, of the deeper woes of humanity, the remedy it so boastingly holds out is as heartless, as unfeeling, as it is wholly inadequate. In its own field, as pure science, it demands our respect like other things that are honest and of good report; but when it assumes to be religion, or theology, or to patronize revelation, it demands rebuke for its self-ignorance and presumption. This is for the present age, and especially for our own country, its most harmful aspect, more harmful,—it is one of our deepest convictions—than any direct opposition its avowedly infidel votaries have made to the Bible, or to any particular portions of the Bible.

When we think how the Church is yielding to it, how much it is doing to *secularize* our Christianity and give false views of its mission, how it is making popular unscriptural ideas of reform having their ground in the *commoda vitæ* rather than the spiritual health, how it is ever marring our better philosophy by the rejection of everything that can not be thrown into the crucible of experiment and induction, how it produces now, as of old, and as though it were inseparable from this kind of knowledge, a vain-glorious spirit so opposed to what should ever be the humble and healthful position of our humanity,—how, in short, it is ever putting the earthly before the spiritual, thus breeding a wordliness which even its most sincere professions of piety can not counteract—in view of all this, we can not help feeling that one of the most unbiblical, and we might say, anti-christian, aspects of the present time, is to be found in the extravagant claims and undue popular estimate of physical science. The age is most one-sided in this respect, and needs righting. We say this with the more frankness and sincerity, because we are equally sincere in the admission, the glad and hopeful admission, that some of our noblest minds and truest Christians are occupied with this department of human knowledge. May their appreciation of higher truths prevent the evils that might come from the disproportional popular tendency, especially as that undue tendency is stimulated by the loud-talking in their own ranks, or by timid religionists who are so easily flattered or awed by their pretensions.

A similar train of thought is applicable to much that we are so fond of praising in modern times under the name of natural theology. And here, to prevent misapprehension of our meaning, we would make a distinction which must come home to the common understanding of every sound and unsophisticated mind. Nature is ever praising God. The Scriptures abound in the thought. She is ever telling of his glory, his kingdom, his providence, his invisible power and Godhead. But it is the fair, round, honest, open face of nature that does this, that *face* that we all perceive and understand at once,—that we see by the naked eye and without the aid of scientific glasses. It is the broad earth, and sounding sea, the mountains towering high, the heaven serene above, the sun in his burning strength, the moon walking in brightness, each knowing its place in the firmament, its glorious rising and its majestic going down,—the seasons as they roll, the countless hosts of heaven whom He calleth all by name even as a shepherd knoweth his sheep. It is the erect up-gazing form of man, his dominion over all the lower tribes of animation, his wondrous outward frame in its *visible* beauty, the still more wondrous soul that shines through it even as the invisible Spirit of God makes itself seen in the material creation. It is this broad fair face of nature, that is ever "telling the glory of God." So, again, on the other hand, could we get down to the bottom of nature, clean through it, we may say, where it joins on to the supernatural, or lies open before the supernatural; could we get down to the first causalities, the deep primal springs where the touch of the Divine hand vibrates through all her immense machinery, conveying his general or special commands, yet without any breach of her vast length of serial law, to us so immeasurably long, to Deity quicker than the lightning's flash? could we do this; could we ever hope to do this; then, perhaps, we might hear another voice of nature, mightier than all and more glorious than all that had ever sounded from her upper surface, or the side that God has turned to us. It may be, that we shall some day know this; at some remote period in our existence we may be permitted to hear, and hear directly, without links or inductions, this deep bass in the universal chorus. But we can not hear it now; we have no organs strong enough to bear it, or even to receive it; we have no intellectual strength that can do anything more than take a few feeble steps in an immeasurable journey towards it; it is hid from our sight, far away from our thought; we can not even approach it either by the steady march of the understanding, or the swiftest flight of the swiftest imagination.

We have presented the two extremes. There is a middle region which is "neither day nor night," or rather where there is just light enough to see the terrific darkness. It is the region of natural theology, to use the name without admitting its propriety; it is the dark labyrinth of physical *adaptations*, as distinguished from *ends*, or true ultimate designs. As we descend into this region the pure upper air grows dim. As we get down among the wheels of the vast machinery we lose the light of heaven above, and yet find no sure standing place for our groping feet below. It is like the insect who has gone down into the interior of the great Haarlem organ. He is crawling among pipes, and keys, and springs, and pedals; if an intelligent insect—a supposition that may be rationally entertained—he may be deep in acoustics, estimating the times of aerial pulsations, or measuring with his microscopic eye the chords that subtend vibrating arcs; but the glorious anthem that is rolling above is all unheard, or comes to him only in dull and discordant tones. The comparison is not extravagant. Its justice has been verified in men who have seen nothing but mathematics in the heavens, and chemical affinities upon the earth. This interior anatomy of causation, where there is nought before the eye but passing links, joined letters of which we can not spell the words, with double readings, too, and oft times double interpretations, may be all very curious as matter of inductive science, but it is certainly *unnecessary*, if not unfavorable, to faith. Especially is this true of that favorite department of natural theology which is now so much occupied with the old animal and vegetable remains. If men will not believe without it, they will certainly not be led to believe by it. If they heed not that fair outspeaking face, if they hear not that mighty voice of the universal *living* nature, neither will they be persuaded though one should lay open the realm of the dead, and bring before them the fossil ghosts of departed ages. The mathematical *ideas* of the heavens are more religious than these, more nearly allied to faith; but who does not know that the most acute astronomers have been not only practical but avowed atheists? Such has been the melancholy result where revelation has been unacknowledged and the Church despised,—a pretty sure indication of what may be expected when "the science of theology or the theology of science," to use a play of language which lately called down plaudits on the religious hustings, has become preeminently the light of the age.

In all this, however, there is no detraction from its real, honest value. When the study of this mid region of natural adaptations is pursued as science only, it may have an interest making it worthy of our most earnest effort. We are looking for links, and we are rewarded and rejoice in finding that for which we are looking. When thus regarded, as science, we may say of it, too, that it is safe; it will not cheat the soul with idola. But make it a part of theology, call it religion, and it is a contiuual breeder of darkness, producing delusions, spectra, phasmata, cheating appearances of ends that are never ends but links, of seeming designs that are only endless adaptations, such as the pantheist, the man who holds to nothing higher than νοῦς, or *intelligence*, in the universe, or even certain forms of self-acknowledged atheism would be ready to admit. Make it a part of religion, we say, and doubt is its natural product. We are in the deep waters, and the only safety against overwhelming scepticism is in not thinking at all, or at least beyond the present links, the particular sequences that present themselves to our observation. The eye must never be turned from the immediate passing adaptations. One must be satisfied with this; like the man in the labyrinth, who is contented with taking angles and feeling the width of passages, or the zoologist who has caught a curious fish without any ventral fins, and is in raptures at the discovery of the means by which the poor animal contrives to move itself along, and make the best of its want. But our man of science is too ambitious to be thus content. He has discovered mere adaptation, and he admires it as that very wisdom which inspiration declares can not be "found in the deep," whether it be of the earth or the waters. The old philosopher would say it was nature accommodating itself to circumstances; but neither of them can answer, or begin to answer, the higher question involved, not in the structure, but in the end for which the animal himself was made, or tell us why animals were made at all,—especially why made to suffer pain and dying agony. The old follower of Democritus was called an atheist, but what of the name? As far as any piety is concerned, or devout religious feeling, or any true faith in a true divine wisdom, believed though unseen, both are on a par. Both have equal need of revelation here, and without it we have little reason to regard the naturalizing theism of the one as any better than the atheistic naturalism of the other. Such is one and a true aspect of what is called natural theology. Even Bacon, the great modern authority, warned his disciples against it. He saw the danger of turning the mind from the study of the true "*final causes*," when this transcending name should be given, as it is now given, to mere links in nature. And experience is here with the Father of the modern philosophy. Without great care, the exclusive search for physical adaptations breeds instead of curing scepticism. When the argument is confined to those leading facts that are common to all minds, it has its highest power; it is conclusive. The moment we begin to dive into nature, to bring up from the abyss that truth which is all *around* and should be ever *in* us, that moment the argument begins to lose its strength; its light begins to fade. Hence the minute pains-taking of Paley, going into the very arcana of the human system, is so much less convincing than the unsurpassed argument of Socrates in the Memorabilia, or the admirable imitation of it by Cicero in his treatise De Natura Deorum. Above all, how does everything of the kind pale before the short Bible argument of the Ninety-fourth Psalm — "*He that formed the eye shall he not see? He that formed the ear shall he not hear? He that teacheth man knowledge*" — *shall he not know?* as is so distinctly answered, not in words, but in the expressive aposiopesis, or silence, of the Hebrew. But even this inimitable argument, it will be seen from the context, is not for the existence of a God, but rather as a proof of his sure providential justice. How shall we account for the striking fact, that the mode of reasoning now so popular under the name of natural theology, is so rare, so almost wholly unknown, we might rather say, in the Holy Scriptures? How comes it that Christ never employs it, that Apostles and Prophets, in all they have to say of the divine wisdom, and in all their calls to the adoration of the divine providence, never resort to proof from this adaptation of natural causalities, although they so frequently appeal to natural objects as illustrations, or personified witnesses, of the divine glory?

In Jeremiah viii, 7, there is mention of the instincts and habits of animals. But look at the real thought, and we find in it no attempt at proof of the divine existence, nor any argument for the divine designs in nature. The lesson taught is the insensibility and rebellion of man—"*Yea, the stork in the heavens knoweth her appointed times, and the turtle, and the crane, and the swallow watch the time of their coming; but my people know not the judgment of the Lord.*" A similar remark is applicable to the striking examples in the latter chapters of Job. All that is said of Behemoth, and Leviathan, and the wild goats of the rock, is grandly descriptive, brought forth in illustration of the divine glory—as we have before remarked about nature in general—and especially of the absolute divine sovereignty—that sublime doctrine to which the naturalist or the mere rationalist is ever so averse. It is the assertion of God's power and right to do and make things as it pleases him, which is there so strongly set forth, even to the stumbling of many who can see neither moral nor philosophy in it. It is to overwhelm us with this thought. Instead of being a lesson of adaptive design, or of instruction in the mysteries of the divine ways in nature, it would seem rather to teach the great truth, elsewhere so strikingly conveyed, that "it is the glory of God to conceal a matter," and that thus, paradoxical as it may appear, there may be a most impressive revelation even in what he hides from our view. The whole passage would seem intended to silence rather than explain,— to silence those "who would darken counsel by words without knowledge," and who will not believe in the divine wisdom unless they can see it with their eyes. It is to produce the very effect it did produce on the mind of Job—"*I know that Thou canst do everything, and that no thought can be withholden from Thee; I have uttered that which I understood not, things too wonderful for me which I know not: Wherefore I abhor myself and repent in dust and ashes.*" Does natural science, or zoology, or that which is called natural theology, thus humble a man, or does all experience of the world show that it is a kind of knowledge that, as far as it is not counteracted by other influences, has just the contrary effect? What the naturalist would call evidence of adaptive skill, as proof of the divine existence, is far remote from all these examples. In reading them we hardly think of it, the soul is so occupied with other and more majestic ideas. Still farther removed from every feeling which these chapters inspire, is the modern talk about *utilities*, or contrivances to produce happiness, or greatest quantity of *well-feeling* (for it all comes to that) in the greatest amount of animated or sensational matter. God is good—God is merciful. The Bible *teaches* that abundantly; but how different its illustrations and proofs of it from those which naturalism would present as its best evidence, although, to a thinking mind, there is hardly one among these supposed physical utilities, or apparatus for enjoyment, that is not in itself, and aside from higher considerations, suggestive of a greater doubt and a greater difficulty than it removes? Alas, for us, if we had to prove the preponderance and predominance of good from no better evidence than is furnished by nature and the world—especially our world—aside from any implanted a priori ideas of the soul, or any express revelation from the sphere above!

"*Great are the works of the Lord, sought out of all who have pleasure therein.*" Naturalism has sometimes usurped the text, although it is entitled to only the smallest part of it. It is taken as the motto of a lecture, occasionally of a scientific book. This is pardonable, and perhaps commendable. Another use does not strike us as being quite so proper. It is sometimes found at the head of a sermon, so called, which does the Scriptures the honor of selecting from them a text, whilst its substance, if substance there be, is made up from geology, and telegraphs, and the wonderful discoveries and inventions of the age. But what are these "works of the Lord"? The context will show us. They are his works of empire and of providence, his dealings in history, above all, his *works of grace*, to use an old fashioned term which progress is beginning to render obsolete. They are his glorious deeds as recorded in the annals of the chosen people, his mindfulness of his covenant, the redemption of his elect, the final triumph of that Church for which the world was made, and for whose sake alone its physical as well as its social and political order are preserved. These are the "works of the Lord" which a naturalizing theology is so inclined to ignore, especially as they appear in their Scriptural aspect. And hence comes it that where this naturalizing spirit prevails, or this naturalizing faith, as we might call it by way of accommodation, there the pure Scriptural faith declines. If the latter does not go wholly out, it becomes a weak and inefficient power, a mere light make-weight to something else, which, although not consciously avowed as the controlling influence, is yet predominant in the secular creed and secularizing spirit of the times,—in short, a system of theology so purely and wholly natural, so mixed up with *science*, and progress, and everything else, that the old student of Baxter or Pascal would hardly know its face as taught in some of our seminaries, and held forth in not a few of our pulpits. The Baconian is a man of facts, and we appeal to him to solve the problem, and to answer the question that so naturally suggests itself. Faith in the Scriptures as the highest authority for the soul in all things wherein it speaks, love for the Scriptures, deep study of the Scriptures,—do these increase with the naturalism of an age, whether it take to itself the name of science, or of natural theology, or of natural religion? But we do not need the Baconian with his array of inductive and crucial experiments. Every intelligently serious man knows that but one answer can be given to such question, and what that answer is. What makes it worse, is the fact, that in proportion as the real revelation falls into a collateral and even subordinate position of authority, there is growing up this cant about the other, or as it has been styled, " the Elder Scripture," the Bible of Nature, the " Book of the Rocks." The lamentably perverted use of the word *inspiration*, in certain transcendental quarters, is bad enough, but it is more defensible, and less mischievous, than that corresponding abuse of the term *revelation* which is such a favorite with a certain kind of naturalizing orthodoxy. We say more defensible, inasmuch as poetry and philosophy are above science, more divine than science, even as the spiritual transcends the physical, and emotional, or *living ideas*, are higher things than any inductive *knowledge*.

For "the restoration of belief," the age must return to the study of the Bible. Recourse, too, must be had to the same inexhaustible fountain, not only for the strengthening of faith, but to elevate the general mind and general thinking. The holiness of the Scriptures even the infidel is compelled to acknowledge. Their heavenly beauty touches the devout spirit now, even as it affected the soul of the Psalmist when he said, "*Thy word, O Lord, is very pure, therefore thy servant loveth it.*" But it has another, we will not say a higher, mission. Even in the mere intellectual aspect, the Bible is before all other means of spiritual culture. As a continual suggester of new ideas, or as shedding a new glory on old and common thoughts, there is nothing to be compared with it in the whole range of outward knowledge. "*The entrance of Thy word giveth light, it giveth understanding.*" It is that by which we see the light of other things. Let the head be bowed upon the sacred page, let the mind be brought into docile yet intense communion with it, and there will flow forth from the study of one Epistle of Paul, or even of one Psalm of David, a power of thought, of ever-widening, ever-rising thought, of thought begetting thought, transcending any intellectual effect that might be expected from any department of natural science, or any chapter in natural theology. There would be this growth, this invigoration of mind, in the proper study, of our noble Anglo Saxon version; still richer and stronger would it be, could the soul feed directly on those roots of heavenly marrow that are furnished by the noble tongues the divine wisdom has chosen as the first media of its revelation.

Could we make our readers feel that there is some truth in these views, some valuable truth that ought to be proclaimed and strongly urged — could we convince any of them heartily that this Bible study, with such a feeling in it, is the great want of our age, and that it would be the most effectual means for the restoration of faith when outward aids from nature and from science had all failed,— we should feel that we had rendered them an important service, however one-sided might appear the writer's own zeal in the substance or manner of his argument.

CHAPTER XI.

WHAT IS NATURE?

Can there be a True Nature?—The two Great Questions—How can there be Evil without God?—How can there be a Nature that is not God?—Can God make a Nature to go by itself?—Laws of Thinking, higher than Laws of Nature—Deteriorations in Nature—Was there Death before Adam's fall?—Nature as well as Spirit left to itself—In what Sense?—Motion by Impulse—The Axiom, "A Body once set in Motion will forever continue in Motion"—The Mystery of the Rolling Ball—Force—Is it an Entity?—Science finds Formulas—Philosophy Wonders—Faith Adores—Ideas, as well as Laws, in Nature.

CAN there be a true nature? What is a nature? Has nature, or what we call by that name, in any sense a *proprium*, or self-hood? Is it an entity, a power by itself, made to be by itself, or is it ever, and in all its parts and manifestations, an *effect* of an immediate, immanent divine working never leaving, never intermitting, never varying as to its immanent presence, in space, time, or degree? Thus stated—and we can not state it more precisely—it may be called the second great problem for the world's thinking. For next to the question, How can there be evil, real and not merely relational or apparent evil, without God being, in some way, the author of it? is this other question, How can there be a nature, a true in distinction from an apparent nature, in other words, a nature or a world coming from God, which is yet not God,—or how can it possess any entity of itself, or be anything distinct from the divine power regarded as energizing as immanently, and as immediately, in its continuance, as in its birth and primal activity? Some men, in discussing the first of these two questions, annihilate evil. The mysterious problem dwindles down into an easy formula of optimism. The profound analytical expression involves simply an identical proposition, as the mathematicians call it. After all its evolutions and eliminations, it runs out $x = x$. Evil is only apparent. So, too, do some deal with the other great enquiry. The result is, nature is only apparent,—apparent in the most unreal or pantheistical sense, as representing nothing between the appearance and God. They make it simply the common instead of the uncommon divine manifestation. The natural and the supernatural have no *real* difference. God's *immediate* power carries on every part of the process. All the apparently intermediate steps are as directly his as the beginning; he is as much, and in the same sense, the immediate pervading agent, as he is the originating cause, and sustaining ground. In other words, there is no real nature, no real *birth* of one thing from another, no true natural or intermediate causality. It is only an appearance, a false appearance, too; for it seems to represent some *mediate* power, when there is really no such mediation between the appearance and Deity;—all the apparent links being as much immediate, and, in one sense, outward to each other, (that is, without real connection,) as the one chronologically first;—every movement of every wheel and cog being direct from the touching hand of the machine-maker, although, for the purpose of confounding and deceiving the beholder, he brings out these immediate tactual effects in an order of sequence suggestive of real, inward, connective causality. Reduced to its logical positions, this is the view presented in the Andover articles entitled "Science and the Bible." In his attempt to talk piously about God in nature, and to make others appear atheistical, the writer, without seeming to be aware of it, runs down into sheer, undiluted pantheism.

On this view, too, matter would be only an appearance, —not a φαινόμενον representing a real power, but a φάντασμα, in other words, a lying appearance, or *apparition*, suggesting the thought of an inward energizing entity that has no real existence. So, also, the world is just such an appearance, or phantasm. Far from having the rank or religious dignity of Plato's *idea*, of which some are so much afraid, it is only an *idolon*, an umbra, or shadow without any object, a lying appearance, we say again, without anything that appears. What is worse than all, as far as this argument is concerned, creation *disappears*. If there is not a nature made, and then in some way "left to itself," (the expression which is so much objected to,) then is there no difference conceivable between the starting and the on-going. Then, also, of course, creation is as much going on now and everywhere, both in time and space, as it was in the beginning,—whether the great or any other beginning.

But this annihilation of nature, causality, creation, and the world, can not stop even here. It must push on until it takes the position that God *can not* make a nature, a causality, a world objective and real. He can not make them in any sense self-existent, or possessing anything that may be called a self-hood, or that may in any way be said to be left to itself, by any withdrawal, *in any degree*, of the prime originating power. We say, *in any degree;* for the same difficulty attends a less or a greater withdrawal. If in any of the passing phenomena of nature, there is, in any way, *less* of the divine power and presence than in the creative start, then something, or some part, or some degree of the subsequent on-going is "left to itself," as truly, though not to the same extent, as though there had been a greater withdrawal. It comes, then, to this — God could not make a nature; He could not give a power and a law that could, in any sense, go by themselves; for we can just as easily conceive and believe, that God is matter, as that he is an immanent *force*, or that the one is any the less a created, on-going, *ex-isting* entity, than the other. In other words, he could not so make this power and law as to work out an idea without his own immediate finger touching, like an engraver's tool, at every point and particle of the picture. We must come to this, or stop in the position that a pious science has called naturalism.

Now should any one turn upon us and ask, Can you show how this can be done,—how God can make a real nature that is not himself? The answer would be promptly, No. Our thoughts do not reach an infinitesimal distance towards the solution of the mystery. *How* it is we can not know, can not even conceive; but the *fact* we are compelled to admit,—the *fact* that God could make such a nature, or world, or system of forces, as something *in time* self-existent, having a temporal self-hood, a spatial being, a life or motion exhibiting succession of *e-vent* or *out-coming*, or, in some true way, "going by itself," after He had thus made it to go by itself. And why, then, do we believe it? It is in obedience, we answer, to higher laws than the laws of nature, even the laws of the soul's thinking, the laws of our rational thinking, which God also made, but did not make them to deceive us. We are compelled to admit it, because we can not think God, and think a world, without it. In no other way can we keep both ideas. We are compelled to admit it, or lose something else which we can not part with without losing that which gives all truth its only moral, and, we might also say, philosophical value. Above all this—above all the laws of sense induction, above even the higher laws of our thinking—by faith do we hold to these "unseen" and never to be seen entities which are neither God nor matter, though coming from God, and from which "unseen things are made the things that do appear."*

* It has been held that these "unseen things," from which the worlds *in time* (τοὺς αἰῶνας) were made, or generated (γεγονέναι), are simply an expression for the divine power generally. But does it look like it? Would it be an easy and natural phraseology for that idea? Take the passage in Hebrews either way, it comes to very much the same thing. Whether we read "*Were not made of things that do appear*," or "*Were made of things not-appearing*," it would give us the same idea. When, too, we bear in mind the mode of employing the negative particles in Hebrew, and its influence on the New Testament Greek, we may regard the old Versions, and especially the Syriac, as having made the right translation, whether they read ἐκ μὴ, or μὴ ἐκ. Now this, in either aspect, is not the natural mode of saying that things *seen* were made of *nothing*, for which the proper words would be μὴ ὄντος, or μὴ ὄντων. Again—why the plural form, whether we take it, "*things unseen*," or read, "*not from things seen*." If it means the divine power generally, which is an unique or undivided idea, how do we account for this mode of speech, which would

But no finite mind can any more solve the problem than it can solve the similar problem of evil. It precisely resembles that great question in this, that whoever chooses to take the very easy position, and the very easy task, of assailant, can drive, or seem to drive, his antagonist to the wall by asking questions he can not answer, or by deducing *conclusions* which no definitions drawn from what we see and know by sense, or sense induction, can fully *exclude*. This is very easy work; it is also very foolish work. Its folly appears in the fact, that the assailed party, who would hold the real existence, either of evil or of nature, may turn right round and drive his antagonist to the wall by a like series of unanswerable questions, involving logical difficulties precisely similar, until he is compelled to give up the idea of any nature at all, or of a world as anything different from the originating, sustaining Deity.

It may be remarked, here, that this fine rhetoric about "God in nature," which is such a favorite with many of our sentimentalists, scientific and religious, is not in the Bible style. God is omnipresent; but there is every where recognized in the Scriptures a real nature with its tremendous self-acting forces "fulfilling His Word." It is this which imparts their inexpressible sublimity to so many passages in the Old Testament. These declara-

seem to intimate *a variety and a multiplicity in the proximate unseen source, or media, corresponding, generically if not individually, to the seen things that come from them.* No doubt the *exertions, outworkings*, of the Divine power are as various as the things it makes, but the plurality in the *unseen things* is contemplated as existing previously, per se, whether in time, or before time. If we say that the *unseen things* denote the Divine mind, as well as Divine power, still the language is far fetched. The contrast, (between two classes of *things*, the seen and unseen,) the multiplicity, the conception of media, or means *ex quibus*, are all unaccounted for.

tions are not all poetry, and if any of them are poetry, they are the poetry of Heaven and mean something. "*The Lord was not in the wind* which rent the mountains and brake the rock in pieces" before the Prophet's vision; "*He was not in the earthquake; he was not in the fire.*" And yet most sublime it is, most true it is, and no figure, that "*He maketh the winds his messengers, his servant the flaming fire.*" God is not electricity, nor immediately energizing in every movement of electricity, and yet most sublime it is, and truer than any figure,—"*He calleth for his thunders, and they come forth and say — Behold us — Here we are.*"

The other doctrine of nature is one we are compelled to admit from the necessary laws of our thinking. It ceases to be nature when conceived of in any other way. Though condemned by the Andover authority, it has been maintained by the wisest of the ancient and modern thinkers. Bacon and Cudworth both teach it, although, in other respects, they represented two such different schools. We must, in some way, have a self-subsistence in nature, as something given to nature, and which God could give to nature, whether we can explain the method and the rationale of it or not. There may be this self-hood, and yet God the supporting ground, as he is the supporting ground even of spirit. We may not be able to explain the difference between this supporting ground and a constant immediate energizing in every act of nature, but such difference there must be, whether we can see it, and understand it, or not. The proof is in the higher laws of our thinking, we say again. There must be a nature, or we fall into a pantheism where the moral and the physical both perish. But a nature, as such, can be thought in no other way. Therefore, there *is* a nature having a life of its own, a subsistence of its own, imparted to it,—a nature in some true sense going of itself,—and, therefore, having both growth and deterioration.

In the other volume, such a doctrine of nature was presented to show, not only the fact, but, in some sense, the need of periods in the creative work,—that is, if God chooses to work by the method of natures or growths as it appears from the Scriptures he has done. Thus viewed, the constant tendency of nature, or a nature, general or partial, to degenerate from the primal force, (or, in other words, when thus left to itself to manifest its necessary *finiteness*)—this, taken in connection with God's from time to time renewing it, and even supernaturally raising it to a higher law than before, may be regarded as constituting those periods of torpor and reviviscence which are so appropriately styled *evenings* and *mornings*. This attempt at explanation may be a failure; but certainly the theism of the argument is unimpeachable. If such an interpretation of Scripture is wrong, it should be shown to be wrong both philosophically and exegetically. That was the true, as well as the manly way of refuting it, instead of frightening good Christian people with such an unscientific outcry of "naturalism," and "Platonism," and the "eternity of matter," and other horrid spectres of a similar kind.

From this, too, comes the position that in all natures, thus left to themselves, the result, if unchecked, is, at some time or other, death or disorganization. God makes a nature to go by itself, but not forever by itself. Every exception by which a natural thing, or a spiritual thing connected with a nature, is exempted from this law of finiteness, and hence of decay, is by special covenant. And this is applied to show the absurdity, the unscriptural as well as logical absurdity, of views like that of Mr. LORD, which maintains that there could have been no death in the animal races before the fall of Adam. Geology is charged with impiety for pretending to find evidence of any such thing; but he might just as well have maintained it of the vegetable world. The Bible gives no sanction to such a view. Mr. LORD, with all his determination to be orthodox, has departed from the doctrine ever maintained in the Church, that the immortality of Adam, if secured, was to be by special sustaining power in pursuance of a special covenant made with him, and for him and all his posterity. If he obeyed, he was to be raised out of nature, and secured in a higher condition. It was "a covenant of life on condition of obedience." To say, then, that death could not have taken place, or would not have taken place, either in the animal or vegetable kinds, before the fall, or without the fall, is to deny the very grounds on which was covenanted to Adam, and is now again covenanted through Christ, eternal life.

Thus, too, if we carry out the view into which some would run in their fear of detracting from the divine power (should a self-hood in any sense be ascribed to nature) God must not only be in the same nature at every moment alike, without any variation in presence or degree, but he must be equally and alike in all natures, the decaying and the dying, as well as the reviving. These would be only different signs of one and the same presence. He is in all natures, and equally in all natures,—not only the good, but the bad; although we are aware that there are some who deny that there can be any such thing as a bad nature. They do not believe in the φρόνημα σαρκὸς regarded as "the fault and corruption of the *nature* of every man, that *naturally* is engendered of the offspring of Adam." But call it what we may, it is something in God's universe in some way and in some sense "left to itself." God can make a *spirit* to go by itself,—a *will* to *will* what *He* has not willed, or which, in a certain sense, and a true sense, can even will contrary to what He wills. This is indeed a mystery; but how much easier than this, though both are incomprehensible, to make a nature to do, *of itself*, just what it was made to do! The want of a true will makes the difference between a *personality*, strictly, and that lower thing we have called a *self-hood*, or self-subsistence; but this want makes no difference as to the other question, whether nature is the exercise of a foreign power ever immediately energising from without, or a power *imparted*, that is, *parted* in some sense, and in some mode, from the original starting source?

Some might fancy all difficulties obviated by conceiving of nature as a chain of impulses, each one operating in a manner outward to the other,—the whole series being set in motion by the Divine hand, and kept in motion by a continual impact, or a continual transmission of the original divine power through every successive ictus. As a mere conception, this need not be objected to, although it is so wholly outward and mechanical. It may do as a figure, but it lacks the radical idea of a nature. It has no real inward *nexus*. As a comparison—the way in which we have several times employed it—it may illustrate the scientific ignorance; but nothing is gained by it towards removing the real mystery. The reason of this is, that motion by impulse,— especially the continuance of it when parted in time and space from what would be called the impelling cause or force,—is just as inexplicable as gravity, or magnetism, or any other unknown causality. We can just as easily conceive of any other power being given to nature, and exercised by it, as this which to the unthinking seems to present so little difficulty. Take the common axiom which is presented, and then so naively passed over by some of our scientific men in their books of Natural Philosophy, as though it involved no mystery—"A body put in motion will continue in motion indefinitely." It would *never* stop, they sometimes venture to affirm, unless outwardly resisted. How they, in their brief existence, have learned this, as matter of fact, it would be hard to tell; certainly they do not pretend to hold it by virtue of any a priori ideas. That would be very unscientific. But the reasons they sometimes give for this assumed fact of never stopping has some strange features. Every body, it is said, will continue in that *state* in which it is, if there is no cause or power producing a change. In a state of rest, therefore, it needs a moving power, in a *state of motion*, a resisting power, to make a change. But what is meant by a *state* of motion? Motion is continual *change*, and that is the only idea we can have of it; μεταβάλλει γὰρ ἀεὶ τὸ μεταβάλλον, as it is so well expressed by Aristotle, *Physic. Ausc.* III, I, 4. It is the only way we can think the phenomenon. It is continuous causality with continuous effect, the active and passive ever combined,—ever μεταβάλλον, and ever μεταβαλλόμενον. We can not conceive why it should not require the same power to carry it through one space as through another. But *what* is that power, and *where* is it? Is it the divine hand carrying it directly through every point of space, the same as though that divine hand took it up at one point, carried it through every intermediate point, and had ever precisely the same hold of it as in the first start—whether that start was made by a new fact of divine energizing, or was the universal divine force carried all along through all the long chain of motions from the beginning of nature and of time? That would involve all the consequences before pointed out. It would utterly confound God and nature, or rather wholly absorb nature into God. We select this simple and common example, because it contains the essence, the condensed quintessence, we may say, of the great question. Some would see no difficulty in it, and might, perhaps, wonder what there could be in so simple an affair to cause difficulty to others. What can be more clear than the scientific fact, and the scientific statement, of impulsive motion? And yet there is, indeed, a mystery in this rolling ball. It carries with it, in fact, the *great physical secret* of the universe — the separation of God from the world. It is a force left to itself, as matter is left to itself. Why is it not as much an entity? Is the existence of matter, or its subsistence, but the continuation of the creative force?

If it be thought that we are making too much of a marvel of this, let us look steadily at the thing, and see what we really know about it. The ball is at rest at A, then in motion at M, then in motion at N. Take it at the latter point. It is apparently the same matter, the same internal arrangement of particles, with the same chemical affinities existing between them. Something, certainly, has been added, but it is nothing that *appears*. Again; it is parted, both in space and time, from the visible, starting, motive cause, and that can exercise no power over it, and produce no effect in it, or upon it, unless it can be supposed that a thing may act *when* and *where* it is not—a supposition that would violate one of those higher laws of our thinking, of which we have already spoken, and without which, in fact, we can not think of physical causation at all. And yet there is certainly something here more than the matter in its state of rest. There has been imparted a something, yes, an *entity*, which is truly present with the ball, and goes along with it,—as truly present as the particles of matter of which it is composed,—being in every proper sense of the word as *real* as the matter, and having just as much of a real self-hood, or self-subsistence. There is, in short, an immaterial, invisible something here that makes the wondrous difference; and this, with all reverence would we say it, is not God. Now science—we mean a certain kind of science that is inclined to talk pompously —says she knows all about it; she knows just what this thing is. It is *force*, she declares, neither more nor less; it is *force* that carries it on according to that famous *law* —"a body once set in motion," etc. This satisfies the man of positive science eschewing all metaphysical nonsense. Such a "student of nature" sees no mystery in the thing whatever; he has got a word, and that contents him. Now the contemned word-hunters would tell him that the conception of force (φορά) runs down radically into that of sustained motion; it is a *carrying along*. So that his word, after all, is only the scientific expression of the outward phenomenal fact. It does not bring him a particle nearer this unseen entity of which we are in search. What is there *in*, *on*, *with* or *about* the ball at N which was not with it at A, or was quiescent at A? His *force* is simply a mathematical expression for an effect. There is a certain *time;* he calls it t; a certain space has been passed over in that time; he calls it s. He puts v for velocity, m for mass, etc., and makes a formula. And now the mystery is revealed. To be sure, his *time* is only the expression of a visible motion; it is a comparison of an earthly with a celestial motion, one of which is no more absolute than the other; but he has a formula, and that satisfies him. We may fairly ask, however, What has he done more than express an outward appearance? Surely, he will not venture to say that this outward appearance is the whole of it. There is certainly something in the ball at N which was not with it at A. It is something that goes with it, and belongs to it, until it (that is the dynamical entity we call the force) finally stops from any cause,—changes, we should rather say, for it only seems to stop, when, in fact, it merely disappears, becomes latent, or goes off, by action or reaction, into something else, where it is either carried on in some other isolated wave, or else empties itself, suddenly or gradually, into the great sea of *force*, with its mighty currents ever swaying, surging, eddying throughout the universe. It has disappeared, not perished; when it rises again it is a new birth, not a new creation. Here steps in philosophy; but what can she do? She wonders. To some that may seem but little; still it is a great step in advance of science,—at least the kind of science we have been speaking of. Such science wonders, too; but it is at her own marvelous achievements in having invented these formulas; and so the real wonder in nature goes unheeded. Philosophy wonders at the mystery. All philosophy, says Plato, begins and ends in wonder. But Faith adores. Both have their gaze upon a higher region than science, though neither Philosophy nor Faith would undertake to solve the problem,—to tell *how* it can be, or *why* it should be. But Faith believes that "by the Word of the Lord," as something more than a sublime figure,—by the veritable going forth of the Eternal Logos,—"were the *ages* made, so that from things unseen came forth the things that do appear," and that these unseen things themselves are not God, but true entities that God has created. Thus it believes in God, and at the same time in a real nature, a real world, a real force in nature, and a real law in distinction from any mere generalization of outward phenomenal sequences having a false appearance of causation, or presenting only the aspect of *signs* with nothing after all of which such signs are really *significant.*

And thus, too, the true idea of law becomes complete, both in its divisions and its rounded outline. To this three things are necessary. The scientific theist charges upon the atheist, or sheer naturalist, that he has the absurdity of a *law* without a *law-giver.* It may be retorted upon the former,—when he attempts to talk piously, in the style of the Andover articles, about "God in nature" immediately energizing in every effect,—that he has the equal absurdity of a *law* without a *subject.* We must hold, then, one of these three views. It is either—

All God, which is pantheism—or,

All Nature, which is atheism—or it is

God, Law, and Nature,*—*Lawgiver, Law, Subject*,—the two last proceeding from the first, yet each by itself a subsistent reality,—the second, or middle term being that by which alone we can truly *think* the others, without severing the dependence, or confounding the distinctions. We say, *think* them as *fact*, for it hath not entered, and can not enter into any human mind, yea, we may venture to say, into any angelic mind, to comprehend or even think the deep mystery in which they are essentially united.

There is another topic connected with this, and one, too, of no light interest. There is a *force*, or, rather, there are *forces*, in nature in some way left to themselves to act *out* the power which God has put *within*. But there is no easy stopping place here, and so we go farther. If we would avoid that annihilation of nature and the world to which the false fear of naturalism leads us, then we must hold that there are in nature, created in nature, given to nature, remaining in nature, belonging to nature as part of her self-hood and her reality,—without which she could not be nature,—not only *forces*, but *ideas*; and if *forces* and *ideas*, then *laws*, which are forces acting according to *ideas*. The laws of which science sometimes speaks, are a very different thing. They are but dead classifications, such as might be conceived of as existing in a universe without intelligence; for in any supposed state of the world there might be classifications of *things* in space, and of *events* in time,—that is, something which, when discovered, might in this sense

* These as they stand in the outward or created world. In the ante-creative or hyper-creative state, they would be *God*, *Truth*, *Power*,—ever united, yet distinct.

be called an *order* and a *law*. But there is, moreover, an intelligence; although we do not venture to define the fact or mode of its passivity or activity. It is here that modern physical speculation ignores that old doctrine of the Logos in Nature, that is made so much of in the Bible. It has become almost obsolete, very much as some modern theology almost ignores the mystery of the incarnation, or gives it little place in the redemptive system, although retaining it in its creeds and symbols.

But the proper treatment of such a subject, with its Scriptural proofs, demands a treatise by itself. There is need here of but one remark in relation to it. Until this doctrine, now hardly recognised even in theology, is made a fundamental and all-pervading axiom, science must be atheistical. Without it, it can never be truly religious in itself, whatever may be its pretensions, or however sincere and genuine the piety of many most excellent and most religious scientific men.

www.ingramcontent.com/pod-product-compliance
Lightning Source LLC
LaVergne TN
LVHW010204110826
845151LV00002B/601

* 9 7 8 1 4 2 5 5 3 5 4 9 0 *